SIX PLAYS

SIX PLAYS
Romulus Linney

THEATRE
COMMUNICATIONS
GROUP

Six Plays is published by Theatre Communications Group, Inc.,
355 Lexington Ave., New York, NY 10017.

Linney, Romulus, 1930–
Six plays / Romulus Linney.
Contents: Childe Byron—2—Tennessee—Heathen Valley—F.M.—April snow.
ISBN 1-55936-053-4 (pbk.)
1. Byron, George Gordon Byron, Baron, 1788–1824—Drama.
2. Göring, Hermann, 1893–1946—Drama. I. Title. II. Title: 6 plays.
PS3562.I55A6 1992
812'.54—dc20   92-15893
CIP

Cover photo copyright © 1992 by Sandra-Lee Phipps
Book design and composition by The Sarabande Press

First Edition, September 1993

PREFACE

The plays published here by Theatre Communications Group reflect the three kinds of plays I have written.

There is historical theatre, which I hope is about the present as well as the past, like *2* and *Childe Byron*. There are plays from the Appalachia of my youth, like *Tennessee* and *Heathen Valley*. Finally, there are more modern plays about American life, often about artists, like *F.M.* and *April Snow*. Within these categories I seem to have what I need, and when I am not functioning well with one, I turn to another.

Most, however, are not urban in content, and while I have had very satisfying productions in New York, especially by the Ensemble Studio Theatre and the Signature Theatre Company, and in some other large cities like Los Angeles, London and Vienna, it has often been in theatres across my country, some large, some modest, that these plays have had the most appeal, and have been artistically best understood.

I am therefore very thankful for the resident theatres of the United States, who do my work often and well, and to them I express my gratitude.

Romulus Linney

CONTENTS

F.M.

For Charles Parness

Characters

CONSTANCE LINDELL
MAY FORD
SUZANNE LACHETTE
BUFORD BULLOUGH

Time

Fall, 1981.

Place

A small Southern college, near Birmingham, Alabama.

A dreary classroom in a small Southern college. A long seminar table. Chairs sitting about at random. Enter Constance Lindell, a woman in her thirties, attractive and intelligent. She stares at the room bleakly.

CONSTANCE: Wonderful. (*She shrugs, smiles, drops her briefcase onto the seminar table, opens it, takes out a class list*) One, two, three. And me.

She smiles again, and sets up chairs, one at each end of the table and two in the middle. Enter May Ford. She is a nervous woman in her forties, wearing a flower-print dress.

MAY: Creative Fiction?
CONSTANCE: That's right.
MAY: Are you Constance Lindell?
CONSTANCE: I am. How do you do?
MAY: Oh, my goodness. What a pleasure. I'm May Ford. I'm taking the class.
CONSTANCE: Good. Come in.

She smiles at May, takes her briefcase to one end of the table. She opens it, takes out a notepad and a pen and the class list.

MAY: It is such a privilege to have you here. With your wonderful books. Everybody here is just—well, truly excited. Really we are.

CONSTANCE (*With a smile*): All three of you.

MAY: Three?

CONSTANCE: That's the class.

MAY: My goodness. And here you are, so distinguished. Oh, this college. They just don't get the word out the way they should. They really don't. Could I sit here?

CONSTANCE: Please do.

May takes one of the chairs in the middle of the table. She removes a small manuscript from a tote bag, whose side is decorated with prints of flowers. The manuscript is neatly clipped into a colored binder, which is also decorated with flower prints. Next May pulls out a small thin vase and sets it by the manuscript. She then takes from her bag tissue paper in which is wrapped a rose. She puts the rose into the vase, and smiles at Constance.

MAY: Isn't this silly? But you know, when I work, I need some small part of God's beautiful natural world to look at. I mean, when writers write, they have to face reality, don't they? I mean, they certainly need escape, don't they?

CONSTANCE: They certainly do.

MAY: I use flowers. What do you use?

CONSTANCE: Oh, this and that.

Enter, precisely on time, Suzanne Lachette, a very attractive-looking young woman, neatly dressed, and smiling a very pleasant smile.

SUZANNE: Good evening.
CONSTANCE: Good evening.
MAY: Good evening.

Suzanne takes the other chair in the middle of the table. She puts down a manuscript in a black spring binder, and sits.

CONSTANCE: Suzanne Lachette?
SUZANNE: That's right.
CONSTANCE: May Ford, Suzanne Lachette, and according to this class list, a Buford B— (*Pause*) Buford Bulla. (*Pause*) I suppose that's the way you say that. Not here yet.
SUZANNE: It is time, isn't it?
CONSTANCE: Yes, but let's give him a minute. Since there are only three of you.
SUZANNE (*Pleasantly*): Only three? Well, good. We can work in depth. Dig in. But I do think people ought to be on time. (*To May*) Don't you?
MAY: Well, I think, yes, of course, any class should begin when it should begin. It is a mark of respect for the subject and for the other pupils enrolled, but, on the other hand, perhaps Mr. Buford Bulla hasn't found the right room, or maybe some car trouble? I'm sure he'll be here soon, and we can all get right off to a wonderful start.

She bends over quickly to smell her flower. Suzanne looks at her pleasantly, smiling.

SUZANNE: I bet you wouldn't say that if his name was Betty instead of Buford.

MAY: I beg your pardon?

SUZANNE: Never mind.

CONSTANCE: Women are used to making excuses for men? Is that what you mean, Suzanne?

SUZANNE: Well, aren't they?

CONSTANCE: I suppose, some.

SUZANNE: More than some, I think. And I think we ought to start the class.

CONSTANCE: All right, if you wish. This is an extension-program course in writing fiction. One semester. Wednesdays, six to nine-thirty. My name is Constance Lindell.

May applauds. Suzanne stares at her.

SUZANNE: Is there something I don't know about?

MAY: Her wonderful books! Haven't you read them?

SUZANNE: No. (*To Constance*) Should I have?

CONSTANCE: Not at all.

SUZANNE: How many wonderful books are there?

CONSTANCE: Two.

SUZANNE: Both novels?

CONSTANCE: One collection of short stories.

MAY: And they're just wonderful! Every last story! Simply wonderful and—marvelous! Really fine!

SUZANNE: I'm sure they are. I look forward to working with you, Constance.

CONSTANCE: And I with you, Suzanne. The course will be conducted as a workshop, without lectures. I work more like an editor than a professor, which, I must warn you, can mean slow, painstaking and unglamorous labor. You both have manuscripts in progress?

SUZANNE: I certainly do.

MAY: So do I.

CONSTANCE: Good. I usually try to begin without any grand statements or aesthetic pronouncements about writing, except maybe it's a way of life more than anything else.

SUZANNE (*Politely*): Excuse me. But what does that mean?

CONSTANCE: Not very much, forget it. In any case, neither I nor anyone else can teach you how to write. What I can do, perhaps, is help you to teach yourself. What I can do certainly is encourage you to pay close attention to each other's work. To each other's struggle to write well. A class can often have insights deeper than its teacher, and within writing that seems awkward and even preposterous, real talent is sometimes buried. Our criticism must be candid, but I hope, always supportive. We are here to help each other.

MAY: That is simply inspiring! I am ready!

SUZANNE (*Smiling*): *Help* each other? *Writers?*

CONSTANCE: Why not?

SUZANNE: Because two writers in one room is like two scorpions in one bottle. And teacher makes three.

CONSTANCE: You've taken a writing class before.

SUZANNE: I sure have, in this room. With the dummy they got last year, from God knows where. After that fool, you're lucky anybody showed up.

CONSTANCE: I see. So, to begin, what we need is a bit of background on each of us, including me. Let me ask you who you are, where you are from, what you are working on, and why you write. May?

MAY: My name is May Ford. I'm from Fontana, ten miles away. My husband is in the furniture business. I have three children, eleven, thirteen, and fourteen, and my hobbies are roses and needlepoint.

SUZANNE (*Quietly*): And writing.

MAY: Yes, I suppose you can call it a hobby. The book I am working on is a novel. It is called Hollyhock Road. It's about a woman who finds herself in middle age, and at the end of all pleasure, and who is redeemed by the beauty of the natural world she discovers around her. I *am* having a little trouble with it.

SUZANNE (*Quietly*): I bet you are.

MAY: Why do I write? Well. (*Pause. She thinks about it carefully*) Because I need to. I need to believe that in spite of everything, there is the same purpose and goodness in human beings that there is in God's wonderful natural world, and if we seek, we will find.

CONSTANCE: Thank you. Suzanne?

SUZANNE: My name is Suzanne Lachette. I live here in town. I work at the University Medical Center, as a lab technician. Divorced, at last. One child, a female, thank God. I am also writing a novel. It is about a woman ending her marriage, and facing life as it is. The title is Scaulded Dogs. It's coming along fine. Why do I write? That's easy. Writing is the only way I can say something and keep it the way I said it. How's that?

CONSTANCE: Just fine. I'm Constance Lindell, from Chapel Hill, North Carolina. Also divorced, remarried, my husband teaching this term in another school. No children. I am working on a novel, too, no title yet, and at the moment anyway, I think I became a writer because I couldn't do anything else. Henry Miller said somewhere, if you just get desperate enough, you'll write, and I think that is what happened to me.

SUZANNE: You read Henry Miller?

CONSTANCE: With pleasure.

SUZANNE: Yuck.

CONSTANCE (*Smiling*): What's wrong with Henry Miller?

SUZANNE (*Smiling*): He wrote with his penis.

MAY: Oh! I mean, well, people will write for all kinds of reasons, won't they?

SUZANNE: Henry Miller was the worst example of male arrogance in all literature. He thought women were bathrooms. I'm surprised you enjoy him.

CONSTANCE: Well, I do. The procedure of this workshop is simple. A chapter, or a section ten to twenty pages long, is read aloud, then discussed.

MAY: Read aloud? But isn't that vulgar?

CONSTANCE: Vulgar, May?

MAY: Maybe not vulgar, exactly, but common, surely. I mean, the whole purpose of writing is to say beautiful things in silent print, instead of just blabbing about it like everybody else, isn't it? So to read what's written aloud, is to make it back into what you didn't want it to be in the first place. Isn't it?

CONSTANCE (*Slowly*): I think I see what you mean. But reading manuscripts aloud in class is the only practical way we can focus on it together, at the same time.

SUZANNE: Excuse me. We could read them before we came in.

CONSTANCE: That means copies have to be made, for one thing, and manuscripts don't get read, for another. I prefer we read them together, here. It takes up the slack.

SUZANNE: And lots of class time. But all right. I see your point. Fine with me.

CONSTANCE: One more thing. When a manuscript is read, before we jump in with critical judgments, I ask for a period where only questions are asked. Logistical matters. Who was where when what happened, and so on. To clear things up, so that what is not clear gets all sorted out, and

9

we know what the writer was trying to do, even if he didn't always succeed.

SUZANNE: Or she.

CONSTANCE: Or she.

SUZANNE: I have a question now.

CONSTANCE: All right.

SUZANNE: How many other courses have they got you teaching?

Pause. Constance stares at Suzanne a second, takes a deep breath.

CONSTANCE: Three.

SUZANNE: Freshman comp?

CONSTANCE: Two. One survey of world lit. For sophomores.

SUZANNE: That must be difficult. Plus office hours, I would think, and plenty of advising.

CONSTANCE: Add it up, Suzanne.

SUZANNE: Certainly. You're not exactly an artist in residence here, are you?

CONSTANCE: I think I said before that writing is a way of life more than anything else. Plenty of good writers, like me thank you, are in exactly the same boat. But that isn't the point. The point is, am I going to conduct this course, or are you?

SUZANNE: You, if you can. Frankly, I'm doubtful.

MAY: Do we get to have coffee breaks, or anything like that? I sure could use one.

CONSTANCE: We break after something is read. And I suppose Mr. Bullough isn't coming after all, so let's start. Who would like to go first?

SUZANNE: I defer to any novel as much about plants as people. Go ahead, May.

MAY: Oh, no! Scaulded Dogs is such a brilliant title. I know it will be just overwhelming. I'd be scared to death to go before that. You first, please.

SUZANNE: No, you first. I insist.

MAY: I don't think I can. We *know* you can. So, please do.

SUZANNE: I wouldn't think of it. Gridlock. (*She smiles at Constance.*) Constance?

Ready for her, Constance flips a coin.

CONSTANCE: Heads, May. Tails, Suzanne. (*She catches the coin, slaps it onto the table, looks at it*) It's tails. Suzanne.

MAY: Thank God.

SUZANNE: Let me see that, please. (*She gets up and peers over at the coin*) Very well.

Suzanne goes back to her seat and prepares to read her manuscript. She checks her chair, and gets set in her position at the table. She centers her spring binder in front of her. She thinks a minute. She clears her throat, and begins to read aloud.

Scaulded Dogs. Chapter One.

Frank came in the door without ringing the bell, of course. The familiar lurch showed Laurinda that he had already been drinking, although her mother's clock on their fireplace mantelpiece pointed to only four in the afternoon.

"I wasn't expecting you," she said gently.

"It's still my house," he said sneering. "Even with you in it."

Melinda felt like the head of a big kitchen match, rasped across a hot stove, struck into sulphur and fire. But she bowed her head, and said nothing.

11

F.M.

*Constance puts one hand briefly over her face, and sum-
mons up powers of endurance. May radiates a look of
serious appreciation.*

MAY: Oh, that's wonderful. Powerful. That match thing. What
a metaphor.
SUZANNE: It's a simile, not a metaphor. (*To Constance*) I beg
your pardon, but we *do* get to read uninterrupted, don't we?
MAY: Oh, I'm sorry! (*She claps her hands over her mouth*)
CONSTANCE: Yes, you do.
MAY: I won't say another word!
CONSTANCE: It's all right, May. Sometimes it is useful to take
notes while someone is reading, so you can remember
what to ask about. Go ahead, Suzanne.

*May takes her notepad and pen and is quickly poised to
take her notes.*

SUZANNE (*Reading aloud*):
Frank looked at the open ledger book into which Laurinda had just listed their common possessions.
"What you get and what I get, eh?" he said, squinting
at her hard work with contempt. "Bet I know how that
works out."
Since Laurinda had been scrupulous in her fair division
of their property, this stung her bitterly, but she put it
behind her, to face as bravely as she could a more vital
issue.
"You didn't come for the children yesterday, when you
said you would. They were expecting you."
He dismissed her words with one wave of his hand.
"Well, something came up," he said, minimizing the
wounds he had inflicted on his own children. "I have to

12

make money, after all. To keep you in ease and comfort, not to mention your lawyer. Ha ha."

Constance stares into space, determined to keep listening. May makes industrious notes.

That was his idea of a joke. Laurinda stared at him. To think she had once given him her love, and thought him capable of its return. What treachery. There he stood, a smug, self-satisfied, domineering drunk. An intolerant, arbitrary bully. A superficial, narrow-minded, short-sighted, besotted provincial bigot. A self-indulgent, flatulent, gruesome eyesore of a man, odious and repellent, a repulsive buffoon!

Enter Buford Bullough, with a lurch and a stagger. He carries a cardboard box and a battered portable phonograph. Buford is a wreck. He sweats. His eyes bulge, stare wildly ahead of him, as if seeing, somewhere in space, something astounding. He wears a worn hunting shirt, jeans and jacket, heavy boots and a baseball cap. His hair is all unkempt. He puts the box down at one end of the table and sits quickly. In one hand he carries a can of jumbo-size soda, open. He drinks from it deeply, pulls a kerchief from his pocket and wipes his face. The three women stare at him, speechless.

BUFORD: Sorry ah'm late. Just pay me no mind.
CONSTANCE: Mr. Bulla?
BUFORD: Bull-loo. Bewford Bull-loo.
CONSTANCE: Mr. Bullough, then. May Ford. Suzanne La-chette.
BUFORD: Hidy.

13

SUZANNE: Good evening.

MAY: Hello theah.

CONSTANCE: Go ahead, Suzanne. (*To Buford*) First chapter of a
novel.

BUFORD: Ah see. (*He puts his chin on his hand, elbow on the
table, and stares at Suzanne with fierce concentration*)

SUZANNE (*Reading aloud*):
So once again Laurinda saw there was no possible way
to communicate with Frank. None at all.
"Frank," Laurinda said. "I had hoped you would think
of the children if not of me. Some tincture of grace I had
hoped for, to color this bitter medicine we must take."

*Buford's attention span snaps. He reaches down and with
one hand opens the top of the cardboard box. He sees
Suzanne glaring at him, and pays attention again.*

"Correction," said Frank. "You must take. I am still a
healthy human being."
It was hopeless. "Very well," she sighed. "What do you
want, Frank?"
"I want what's mine," said Frank. "And a lot of it is in
this room right now."

Buford looks at the cardboard box.

"All right, Frank," said Laurinda, patiently. "I have
done my best. You look and see what you think should be
yours instead of mine. I'll consider any changes you may
suggest."

Buford reaches into the cardboard box.

"You'd better," said Frank. "I just might take it all. Or
smash it all, every stick. How would you like that, lady?"

Buford takes out a bottle of bourbon. Turning slightly, and holding the bottle below the table, he pours bourbon into his soda can.

Oh, Laurinda thought, the brute. The coarse, insensitive, sadistic brute. Why had she married him?

Buford puts the bottle back in the box, and takes from it a huge manuscript, tied by a rope. It is composed of many sections, each novel length, held by a rubber band. He puts the manuscript on the table and stares at it.

There he stood, his whiskey breath plain as the scent of a skunk, still weaving in front of her, a slack-jawed, leering, childish, smart aleck of a man, a swine absolute and unmitigated, a boorish, filthy-minded—

Suzanne stops reading and slams her spring binder shut.

Since it is blatantly obvious that Mr. Bullough does not care to listen to my work, I will not continue to read it!
MAY: Oh, Suzanne! Don't stop! That was all just wonderful!
SUZANNE: May, you try it. It's a bit difficult to read aloud the deepest meditations of your heart and soul, with a man unpacking a suitcase, like somebody going fishing. Not to mention slipping whiskey into a soda can. What is it, Bullough? Corn whiskey?
BUFORD: Bourbon. Ah need it.
SUZANNE: I'm sure you do.
BUFORD: Lady, ah certainly am sorry if ah bothered you.
SUZANNE: My name is not Lady. It is Suzanne Lachette. La— chette!
BUFORD: Miz Lachette, ah certainly didn't mean to. Ah was listening.

15

SUZANNE: Oh, please!

BUFORD: It's just that well, you see, ah'm here to do it, and ah, well, it's just inside me all the time like a drum going boom-boom-boom all the time. It don't never stop, so ah have to get ready, you see. I mean, boom-boom-boom! Hit's awful. You will understand.

SUZANNE: If your writing, Mr. Bullough, is no more illuminating than your speech, that is not very likely.

CONSTANCE (*To Suzanne*): You're sure you won't continue?

SUZANNE: Positive.

CONSTANCE: Would you like us to discuss what you've read?

SUZANNE: Hardly. I cannot at this moment allow my work to be pawed over by a man obviously interested in nothing but himself.

CONSTANCE: Very well. May?

MAY (*Terrified*): What?

CONSTANCE: Would you read instead?

MAY: You mean out loud right now?

CONSTANCE: You're next. Why not?

MAY: Oh, no! I better wait a little while. I mean, like the flowers I always seem to write about, my story is delicate and needs a little sunshine, and good weather, you see.

BUFORD (*Explosively*): Well, me then! Ah'm willing to read! Ah'm willing to read!

SUZANNE: What a surprise.

BUFORD: Ah mean, if hit's my turn. Ah don't want to step out of line or nothing.

SUZANNE: Out of line or nothing. Jesus Christ.

CONSTANCE: Well, Mr. Bullough, since neither Suzanne or May want to read, go ahead.

BUFORD: Ah will! (*He tears into his huge manuscript, going through its many sections, searching for something*)

SUZANNE: He's like a man changing a tire.

BUFORD: Hit's just where to begin, you see.
MAY: How about the beginning, dear Mr. Bullough?
SUZANNE: Or the end.

Buford finds the portion of his manuscript he wants to read.

BUFORD: Here! Ah got hit.

*Now he plugs his phonograph into a wall socket. From the
box he takes a record in a faded dust jacket. He puts it on the
table face down.*

SUZANNE: Music yet. What are you going to play for us,
Bullough? "Hound Dog?" "Detour?" "The Great Speckled
Bird?"

*Pause. Buford stares at his manuscript. He takes a deep
breath, drinks quickly from his soda can, wipes his forehead
with his kerchief. Then he begins to read. From the moment
he does, Constance, who has been managing all this as best
she can, comes at once to a different life.*

BUFORD (*Reading aloud, at breakneck speed*): On her bed,
beneath the candleflame headboard that guarded her
descent into bitterness and where perhaps madness
overtook her, he lay dreaming, drunk and naked, with a
woman named Edna Craig Somebody blundering around
in the bathroom, picked up at the Paramount Paradise—
SUZANNE: Just a minute.
BUFORD: —Roadhouse four miles out of Ridersberg—
SUZANNE: Just a minute!

Buford stops reading, looks wildly about.

17

BUFORD: Whut?

SUZANNE: The title. You forgot the title.

BUFORD: Huh?

SUZANNE: Title! Name of the thing. What it is called, for God's sake!

BUFORD: Oh. The whole thing is just a man's name. But this part is called F.M.

SUZANNE: F.M. what? I don't understand.

BUFORD: Just F.M.

MAY: You mean F period M period?

BUFORD: Yes, ma'am.

MAY: Then I don't understand either. How can you call something by some initials, and we don't even know if it is a somebody or a something or what it is?

SUZANNE: I mean, is it Frequency Modulation, or Fred Mac-Murray, or what?

BUFORD: Oh, it means something, but that has to come out in the thing itself, you see.

CONSTANCE: Mr. Bullough, you don't have to have your titles yet. Titles are funny. They come before, during and after a book. Let's say F.M. for the moment means Fiction Material. How's that?

BUFORD: That's fine! Fiction Material!

SUZANNE: Or Freak Mouth.

CONSTANCE: Go ahead, then.

BUFORD: Ah'll commence again.

SUZANNE: "Commence again." Then he reads a sentence half a page long.

BUFORD (*Reading aloud, slower*): On her bed, beneath the candleflame headboard that guarded her descent into bitterness and where perhaps madness overtook her, he lay dreaming, drunk and naked, with a woman named Edna Craig Somebody blundering around in the bathroom, picked up at the Paramount Paradise Roadhouse four miles out of Ridersberg, and brought to his mother's small house with shrieks and giggles—

MAY: Mother? Did he say mother?

SUZANNE: I don't know.

Buford makes a change in his manuscript, with a big felt marker.

BUFORD: —with whoops and giggles, while the good neighbors on their porches shook their heads in their chairs and rocked their disapproval—not a day in the ground, they said, not even twelve hours—and he tried now to focus— (*He makes another change*)—he tried to *spend* his whirling powers upon the thin body, the delicate, thorny foxfire woman he had buried that morning, tried to summon her back to him, with all her smiles and rings, her hands on her own breasts, and all her Chinese puzzles, if not to answer his questions framed apart from her for ten years, at least to speak to him who had not heard her voice for ten years, and listening all that time to Edna Craig Somebody, the large and friendly creature in the bathroom.

"How do you turn this light off in here?" said Edna Craig.

"By the wall cabinet."

"Oh, yeah."

May and Suzanne look at each other in dismay.

There was a pause while she found the light, turned it off, and blundered out— (*Change with the marker*) — *came* out of the bathroom into the hall.

19

"Hey! This here old thing a radio?"

"Yes."

"Can I play it?"

"Why not?"

"Let's have some music then. What the hell."

"Go ahead."

"You want me to?"

"I said yes."

Drunk, naked, and dreaming, he lay in her bed, under the candleflame headboard. Mama? Mama?

Which flowers grew where—

SUZANNE: Wait a minute.

BUFORD: —he could never remember—

SUZANNE: Wait a minute!

BUFORD: —and certainly—

SUZANNE: WAIT A MINUTE!

BUFORD: Huh? Whut?

SUZANNE: I don't understand one word of this.

BUFORD: Whut if ah just keep on going? Maybe you will.

SUZANNE: May, do you know what this man is saying?

MAY: Not exactly. There's a man who's brought a woman somewhere—

SUZANNE: And put her in the bathroom, of course, I understand that. But whose bed is it, whose town is it, who is he and what is he doing?

MAY: I certainly don't know.

CONSTANCE (*Quietly*): It is his mother's house. He has buried her that morning. Now to her bed, he has brought a woman from a roadhouse. Is that right, Mr. Bullough?

BUFORD: Yes, ma'am.

SUZANNE: Ugh. That is the most sordid premise for a story in the history of fiction.

BUFORD: Yes, ma'am. Ah got to go ahead with this. Once ah commence reading, hit's awful to stop.

SUZANNE: "Commence" again. Did you really write all that purple prose, Bullough? You don't talk that way. You talk like a hick.

BUFORD: I know it. Hit's whut ah am. But hit's different when ah write. I reckon that's why ah do it.

CONSTANCE: Go on, Mr. Bullough. (*To May and Suzanne*) Take notes and let him read.

BUFORD: Lemme see now.

He finds his place again. May and Suzanne ready their notepads. Buford plunges in once more.

Which flowers grew where, he could never remember, and certainly along that road, that hill, those cowpaths—

SUZANNE (*Writing note*): Cowpaths.

BUFORD (*Reading aloud*): —and between these birches, he cannot remember them all, all the biology bookful of flowers that in his lifetime before he left her passed from his tiny mother's waspish hands to his. (*Pause*) Mama? Mama?

SUZANNE (*Writing note*): Mamamama.

BUFORD (*Reading aloud*): He twists about in her bed, and now reaches up to touch the candleflame headboard and suddenly she is there with him, she speaks to him as he lies naked and dreaming of her, moving toward him through a forest of gigantic flowers, and he sees again their pictures in the books and in the articles she cut out for him, and he sees them lying at their feet during the walks they took through the soft Southern air of his childhood. They walk together past the flowers she points out to him, white baneberry, whose stalks redden with age, whose china-white fruit is poisonous and gleams in the shade, and she says to him, *Oh, my darling, my heart is full of love for you, here, it's in here, touch my breast here*—

MAY: Touch what?

SUZANNE: My God.

BUFORD (*Reading aloud*): —while they walk, over bloodroot poppy, pink as dawn, when crushed giving a scarlet liquid useful, she tells him, as war paint, dye, and it can even change the color of a man's eye, and she says, *Kiss me, my son, my only child, my darling boy,* passing lank green swaths of wild yam and meadowrue, where they stop and he kisses his mother, bereft forever of the passion she seeks in him. They embrace, surrounded by nodding suns of black-eyed Susans, yellow sweet-clover, turkscap lilies and four-leaf loose-strife, Solomonplume orange with stems that zigzag and berries green and red all at once.

MAY (*First note*): They don't zigzag.

BUFORD (*Reading aloud*): And then the laughter, sweet and soft at first, and her eyes not yet wild, her voice not yet hard or cold, *Well, darling, come along, if you don't understand how much your mother loves you, you just don't, it's all right come along.* Her stride picks up, over scarlet fireweed, bull thistle and thimbleberry, and he is desperate to follow her.

MAY (*Note*): Some of those are not even real flowers.

BUFORD (*Reading aloud*): Her laughter becomes shrill now and hard, her step begins to rush along the path above the little town her prison, over crowpoison and Allegheny goatsbeard, whose brownish blossoms become quickly infested with insects. She turns to look back at him, and her stare goes through him now like a needle into cloth.

(*He looks at the phonograph*) Got this music to play right here. It goes with it real good.

He takes the record out of the faded jacket. He puts it on the phonograph. Suzanne picks up the jacket.

SUZANNE: Where did he get this?

She passes it to Constance, who looks at the faded jacket thoughtfully.

MAY: It isn't right to make up flowers any way you want to. Flowers are more important than that. They don't mean anything but themselves. I don't like this.

CONSTANCE (*Looking at the jacket*): Edward Elgar.

The music plays. It is the beginning of the second movement of Elgar's Piano Quintet in A Minor. Buford reads aloud again, slower now.

BUFORD: From the ground, picking them up laughing, she makes for him dreaming as once she did in life, out of three leaves from a fig tree, some cellophane from her purse—laced with pine straw and a rooster's comb of common daisies and with flowers cascading down its back—a bridal crown. She holds it out, laughing at him, the eyes dangerous now, as she tries to put it on his head, saying, *You look like me, son, and I was beautiful, son, beautiful as the day we share in this place of flowers, with our bond singing in our blood. No one, no one, no one can ever alter that, for you look just like me, child, and I was beautiful, child, here, wear this as I did to beget you, so you will always always love me, and the two of us shall be forever one. Let me see, in your face, the bride I was, let me kiss myself upon your lips, angels the two of us, on earth, in gardens of delight.*

May jumps up, exploding.

MAY: I will not have it!! I will not have it!! Shut off that awful music or I will break the damn record!

BUFORD: Please! Ah can't stop now!

MAY: Yes you can! You pervert! (*She takes the arm off the record, stopping the music*) You listen to me, Mr. Bullough. I am a gentle woman. I am not the kind to get mad. But you make me want to blow you up with dynamite. I want to kill you!

CONSTANCE: Sit down, May. Why do you want to kill Mr. Bullough?

SUZANNE: Constance, when you can't even handle a writing course, why start group therapy?

CONSTANCE: Because I feel like it, Suzanne. Let's have it, May.

MAY: I want to kill him because of the flowers. This degraded, obscene writing takes the beauty of flowers and makes them part of some disgusting incest between a crazy mother and an infantile son, and if that's what people want to write about, all right, but leave God's clean sweet gentle flowers out of it! They don't deserve to be in hell where this madman obviously is, but here on earth with the real and the true and the good!

SUZANNE: Way to go, May. I couldn't have said that better myself.

MAY: Thank you, Suzanne.

SUZANNE: I don't think he should read one word more of this. Constance?

CONSTANCE (*To Buford*): Read!

BUFORD: "Hey!" the woman yelled from the hall. "You still there?"

"Yes, Edna Craig."

"I can't get no good music on this God damned radio. Just a lot of fiddles."

"That's short wave. You get Europe with it."

"But not WRD in Ridersberg, huh? What the hell?"

"Forget it. Come to bed."

"Oh. All right."

And she did, to his mother's bed, to lie with him beneath the carved candleflame headboard, where, against linen-slipped feather pillows which clung in the damp Ridersville night delightfully to the skin, he took off her cheap clothes, slowly, while eyes closed, Edna Craig Somebody moaned, breathed heavily, as sudden in lust as in roadhouse friendship, churning through the bed with her large hips until she saw him holding himself back, and staring at her. She folded her hands over the creased flesh at her throat, as if about to pat her hair, set herself somehow right, uncertain of him.

"Honey, come on. Do it. What's wrong?"

"Nothing."

"Yes, there is. Is it me?"

"No. Honest."

"Then is it you?"

"I have trouble sometimes."

"Listen, so do I. Who don't? My old man and me bang together some nights like boxcars and nothing happens. Hush. Don't fret. Put your head here on Mama's tits and get some rest."

MAY: Oh!

SUZANNE: Oh, vomit! Vomit!

BUFORD (*Reading aloud*): He woke from sleeping against her, refreshed, as if both their bodies had undergone a sea-change, and when he reached for her now, it was with purpose. She opened herself to receive him. In mutual relief, and a taking of chance-grafted flesh, they moved each into the other until they were struck, held, then molded again into sleep.

MAY: The end! I hope!

SUZANNE: Is that really the conclusion, finally, of this nauseating exhibition of antifemale pornography?

BUFORD: No! Course not! He has to wake up and see his mama again!

SUZANNE: I knew it!

MAY: I just don't think I can stand that, really, I can't. This course is not for me!

SUZANNE: It's worse than it was last year! I was a fool to take it.

MAY: So was I. And I mean to complain, to the Dean of this college. My trust has been betrayed.

SUZANNE: We'll both complain. (*To Constance*) Which won't do you any good here, I'll tell you that. (*To Buford*) As for you, just one question. What kind of a mother did you have, anyway?

CONSTANCE: What kind of a mother did you have, Suzanne?

SUZANNE: What did you say?

MAY: Well, really!

CONSTANCE: Plant your roses, May. Forget about writing. Suzanne, get yourself a job at the state prison, electrocuting men, and fulfill yourself. (*To Buford*) Buford. Buford.

BUFORD: Whut?

CONSTANCE: The title. F.M. It doesn't mean Fiction Material, does it?

May and Suzanne stare at Constance.

BUFORD: No, ma'am.

CONSTANCE: And it doesn't mean Frequency Modulation, does it?

BUFORD: No, ma'am.

CONSTANCE: It means Fucking Mother, doesn't it?

May and Suzanne stare at Buford.

BUFORD: Yes, ma'am. Hit does.

CONSTANCE: Wonderful!

MAY: Oh, my God!

SUZANNE: That does it!

MAY: Let me out of here! This is altogether intolerable and downright repulsive!

SUZANNE: And you're finished here, Constance! Finished! Come on, May.

May starts after her, stops.

MAY: It's all wrong, what you're doing. Mothers and sons like that, writing like that. It's not decent. It can't be good. If I thought it was, I'd—

Pause. She chokes up, almost weeps.

SUZANNE (*To Constance and Buford*): Now see what you've done. I hope you're satisfied. (*Gently, sweetly*) May. Come on with me.

She leads May off. Pause.

BUFORD: Bye. (*To Constance*) Ah'm sorry to have bothered you. Ah never meant to get you in no trouble.

27

F.M.

Constance walks slowly to Buford. There is a chair tucked against the table. She pulls it out, turns it about, sets it next to Buford, below the table by his chair, about four feet away from him.

CONSTANCE: Give me the bottle.

Buford hands her the bottle of bourbon. Constance starts to drink, stops, puts the needle on the record again, sits. The same music plays again.

Read on, Buford. Read on.

She listens, and when he begins to read, she takes a long slow drink from the bottle.

BUFORD: When he woke, the harsh morning sun was a glare against his mother's bedroom window. He was alone in the bed. He reached above him, and touched the carved flutings of the candleflame headboard, which represented, he now remembered, the Garden of Eden. Rosewood, he recalled. Bought in Tennessee, by his grandfather, and he himself born beneath it. And there, above his ear, his mother called to him once more, in a voice clear, and with laughter quiet, as if it was only a complicated joke they shared together. And he saw her again, in freedom, shorn of all her burdens, his mother within a burning garden of wood, and to the woman whose hands had broken him, but in whose smiles was his hope, and from whose pain came his understanding, he said, *Goodbye.*

Music. Pause. Looking ahead, Constance reaches out her hand, and Buford, looking ahead, takes it.

28

Childe Byron

For Virgil Thomson

Characters

ADA
BYRON
GIRL
BOY
YOUNG WOMAN
YOUNG MAN
MAN
WOMAN

Music

From the works of Hector Berlioz.

Time

November 27, 1852

Place

London, England. The bedroom of Augusta Ada, Countess of
Lovelace.

Scene

A high-backed chair, or a chaise lounge. A table, piled high with books and manuscripts: Byron's poems, Ada's mathematical charts, musical scores, many loose notes and notebooks. Under the table, more books and papers. A model of a curious machine: it looks like the exposed insides of a complicated clock. A violin case. Another chart.

Two other, smaller tables, holding a case of dueling pistols, a broadsword, decanters of wine and water and medicine, glasses, and a drinking cup made from a human skull.

Upstage, the suggestion of a Gothic window, and open air beyond it, where a platform with a billowing sail and a web of rope will create the deck of a ship, sailing under a large and colorful sky.

Below the room, and around it, open space.

This is the London bedroom of Augusta Ada, Countess of Lovelace, on the day of her death. Within the room, and around it, apparitions and hallucinations appear before her.

PROLOGUE

MUSIC: *Harold in Italy* by Berlioz.

A spotlight from the back makes a dark shadow of a woman seated in her chair or on a chaise lounge. She is ill, coughing. Before her is a small glass on a silver tray, with a colored liquid inside it.

VOICE OF BYRON (*Unemotional, cool*):
Is thy face like thy mother's, my fair child?
Ada, sole daughter of my house and heart?
When last I saw thy young blue eyes
They smiled, and then we parted.

The music fades into another sound: the noise of modern electronic computers.

VOICE OF ADA (*Fierce, precise, swift*): Picture a pile of circular metal discs heaped one above the other to a considerable height, each disc having the digits from 0 to 9 inscribed on its edge at equal intervals. That is the essential structure of the Analytical Engine.

The computer noise becomes music again.

VOICE OF BYRON:
> Yet though dull Hate as duty should be taught,
> I know that thou wilt love me: though my name
> Should be shut from thee, as a spell still fraught
> With desolation, and a broken claim:
> Though the grave closed between us——'twere the
>   same:
> I know that thou wilt love me.

The music becomes computer sound. The woman stirs the liquid in the glass, and drinks it.

VOICE OF ADA: Each disc can revolve horizontally, so that any required digit or combination of digits can be brought instantly into view. Theoretically, there can be any number of discs and columns of discs. Therefore, development of the Analytical Engine is limited only by present technical command of size and space.

The computer sound becomes music.

VOICE OF BYRON:
> My daughter! With thy name this song begun.
> My daughter! With thy name thus much shall end.
> I see thee not, I hear thee not, but none
> Can be so wrapt in thee: thou art the friend
> To whom the shadows of far years extend.

The music fades. The spotlight that makes a shadow of the woman also fades, and normal light comes up on and around her. The play begins.

ACT ONE

Ada sits at her table: intelligent, severe, ill. She is looking at her unfinished will.

ADA: I, Augusta Ada, Countess of Lovelace, do enjoin my dear mother, husband and children faithfully to execute this my last will and testament.

She closes her eyes, coughs, presses her hand to her stomach in pain. She breathes deeply, puts the will down and stares at it.

Last will. And testament. But what do I leave?

She takes from a pile of books and papers under her table a well-worn copy of Childe Harold's Pilgrimage.

My daughter! With thy name this song begun.
My daughter! With thy name—

She coughs, closes the book. She leans back in her chair, eyes closed again, as if trying to see something in her mind's eye.

Byron.

Music. Behind Ada, at her window, Byron appears: cloak, collar, romantic.

Speak.

BYRON:
> In Nottingham County, there lives at Swan Green,
> As curst an old lady as ever was seen,
> And when she does die, which I hope will be soon,
> She firmly believes she will go to the moon.

ADA: First poem. At age seven. Against a woman.
BYRON: Yes, that's right.

He comes limping into her room, with a rolling gait that favors the right foot. It causes his shoulders to seesaw as he walks.

How did you know that?
ADA (*Smiling*): It will be difficult to explain.
BYRON: Am I acquainted with you?
ADA: You looked at my face twice, when I was young.
BYRON: And I was young with you?
ADA: No.
BYRON: Oh? I would say we are the same age, approximately.
ADA: Not approximately. Exactly. You are thirty-six. So am I.
BYRON: And I saw your face twice, when you were young, and I wasn't. You don't make sense.
ADA: I make perfect sense, as you will discover. Sit down. There.

She indicates another chair. Byron stares at it, then at her.

If you please.

Byron nods, moves toward the table.

BYRON: My God. It's my claret cup! (*Delighted, he takes up the drinking cup made from a skull*) Where did you get this?
ADA: At Newstead Abbey.
BYRON: What were you doing there?
ADA: Looking for you. Tell me about the cup.
BYRON: You are very imperious. Are you a scholar?
ADA: No. The cup. If you please.
BYRON: I found it the day my mother and I came to Newstead Abbey, to claim my inheritance. The Abbey was a real monastery once. This was no doubt a monk. (*He holds up the skull cup*)

Where once my wit, perchance, hath shone,
In aid of others' let me shine,
And when, alas! our brains are gone,
What nobler substitute than wine?

ADA: Did you think that clever?
BYRON: When I was eighteen, yes. It was soon said to be the hapless skull of a virgin I had ravished.
ADA: Are you sure it wasn't?
BYRON: By the one virgin I ever met, it was hapless me who was ravished, thank you very much. Ah! My pistols! (*He opens the case and takes out his pistols. He points them about with pleasure*)
ADA: You could split a cane at thirty paces.
BYRON: Wonderful things!
ADA: You practiced every day.
BYRON: And never fought a duel.
ADA: Because you were a dead shot?
BYRON: And every bully in England knew it.

ADA: So they imitated you, and shot someone else.

BYRON: Ah! This old thing! (*He puts down the pistols, and takes up the broadsword*) Trim your gullet with this, right enough!

ADA: You took it to Greece. It was your great-uncle's. Whose death made you, his poor relation, Lord Byron.

BYRON: Yes, that's true. (*Pause*) Now, look here.

ADA: If you will only sit down, I will explain.

BYRON: Why do you have all my things—

ADA: Don't talk back to me! Don't argue with me! Just do what I tell you, *exactly* what I tell you! Sit down! There!

BYRON: I thought I knew the worst of them, but you're the damnedest bitch I've ever *seen*.

ADA: Am I?

BYRON: Yes!

Ada grabs up a book.

ADA: *Childe Harold's Pilgrimage*: Canto Three:

I see thee not, I hear thee not, but none
Can be so wrapt in thee: thou art the friend
To whom the shadows of far years extend.
Ada! sole daughter of my house and heart!

I am Ada.

Pause. She tosses the book back on her table.

BYRON: Ada? My little daughter?

ADA: The damnedest bitch you've ever seen, yes. Grown up now. Married. Three children. Not a poet. A mathematician.

BYRON: Like your mother.

ADA: Much more advanced. I surpass the reasoning powers of most men.

BYRON: Is that why you're so pale?

ADA: No.

BYRON: Are you sick?

ADA: Yes.

BYRON: What's the matter?

ADA: I am afflicted with a cancerous growth. It's in my stomach. Doctors tell me they could cut it out, but I would go with it. So.

BYRON: I see.

ADA: It is the usual squalid progression. Once mattresses were nailed to the walls. It hurt me then, and I threw myself about.

BYRON: Does it hurt now?

ADA: No. I am drugged now. With laudanum, every day. I hallucinate, of course. See things. I hope you don't mind. Because that is what you are.

BYRON: I'm what? Hallucination?

ADA: Sorry, yes. Vision, apparition, ghost. I was your creation, now you are mine. Mrs. Shelley had her Frankenstein monster. I have you.

BYRON: What a compliment.

ADA: You are everything I have learned in one year about that dreadful man who died when he was thirty-six, and I was eight. Now I am thirty-six. And.

BYRON: And?

ADA: *I will die!* (*Pause*) I will not, after all, exactly outlive you. It's an equation I cannot quite frame, a problem I can't solve. And I need to.

BYRON: Well, if you're as brilliant as you say you are—

ADA: I am. I will find the solution. The Engine will help me.

BYRON: Engine?

ADA: That's right.

BYRON: Fire? Steam?

ADA: Thought. (*She picks up the model of the machine from her table*)

BYRON: I beg your pardon. An engine run by thought?

ADA (*Swiftly*): Run by clockwork, with digits standing for thoughts. (*She holds the machine, staring at it*) Suppose your every conscious thought is attached to a digit. By arranging them to appear in mathematical combinations, you might have, at your immediate disposal, every idea you ever possessed. Every set of ideas. Every experience. Your whole life, brought to you in a second.

BYRON: No wonder mattresses were nailed to the wall. Are you—

ADA: Some think so.

BYRON (*Looking around*): And the doors—

ADA: Are locked. I am confined. But the Engine is sane!

BYRON: Oh, certainly. (*Smiling*) Does it exist?

ADA: It will. This is only the model. I know its principles, its functions. The possibilities are endless.

BYRON: Did you invent it?

ADA: No. I finance it. A man invented it. Charles Babbage.

BYRON: Babbage, rhymes with cabbage. Perfect name for a mathematician.

ADA: A genius, of the first magnitude.

BYRON: Like a poet?

ADA: Not like a poet, thank you. A genius. The Analytical Engine will surpass all our expectations. It may even write your poems.

BYRON: I might have known that. Well, be careful with it. A machine that thinks is bad enough, God save us from one that writes. (*Pause*) So. My baby daughter, grown up, with a problem-solving thinking machine—

ADA: Yes.

BYRON: Wanting a solution, to me.

ADA: Yes.

BYRON: Pleasant or unpleasant, I suppose—

ADA: Either one—

BYRON: Asking that of a ghost, a vision—

ADA: Of my father.

BYRON: Compounded of drugs, disease, mathematical probability—

ADA: And human nature. It is not unusual, after all, for a woman to trot her father through her head.

BYRON: No.

ADA: That is what I am doing. What is the problem? I lived my life without you. What is the solution? I don't know. Therefore I must tabulate my data. I must become my own Analytical Engine, and discover what you really were. Logically. Without regret, or sentimentality.

BYRON: Ask your mother. She'll tell you, without either one.

ADA (*Fiercely*): Not a word from you about my mother! You leave her alone!

BYRON: All right.

Ada opens a notebook, and takes up her pen.

ADA: I am interested in you now! For the first time, and the last! You, me, the Byron family mystery! So begin! With that! The sword!

BYRON (*Still holding it*): What about it?

ADA (*Exasperated*): You took it to war. It was your great-uncle's, whose death gave you the title. Just talk!

Byron doesn't. He stares at her. Pause.

BYRON: What sort of girl did she make of you?
ADA: Never mind.
BYRON: If you won't, I won't.

Ada sighs.

ADA: A bluestocking. Modern on the outside. Ancient within.
BYRON: Like her.
ADA: Not like her, not quite.
BYRON: But you did what you were told?
ADA: I pleased my mother. I pleased the husband and the children my mother decided I would please. For myself, I study mathematics.
BYRON: So did she.
ADA: Not so well. I also play the violin. She couldn't do that.
BYRON: No.
ADA: I translate French, and recently, collect French music, based on your poems. A man named Berlioz writes a great deal of it. (*She holds up a musical score*) I play the melodies on my violin. Overtures, songs. A sort of symphony, even.

A piece of paper falls out of it.

BYRON: Anything more complicated than a waltz, and my attention wandered. What's this?
ADA: What does it look like?
BYRON: It looks like a racetrack schedule. Week of August 20–27, 1851. Horses?
ADA: Yes, racing. A hobby. My mother didn't do that, either.
BYRON: She most certainly didn't. What else can I find out about you?

ADA: Nothing! The sword! Talk!

BYRON: Your bluestocking notes! *You* talk! (*Pause*) Let the family sword cut both ways.

ADA: Very well.

BYRON: Very well. My great-uncle was the Wicked Lord Byron. I was the Crippled Lord Byron. I was born both feet clubbed.

ADA: Both?

BYRON: The left straightened out. Iron braces, wooden boots, steel screws. The right didn't. The turtle in its shell. Want to see it?

ADA: No. Your great-uncle, please.

BYRON: Well, He had a lifelong friend. They disagreed over the mixture of proper dog food. Of course they had to fight a duel. They took swords into a darkened room, where my great-uncle stuck this into his lifelong friend. Promptly acquitted by the House of Lords. Your turn.

ADA (*Slowly*): You raped my mother, unspeakably, while she was pregnant, with me. Your turn.

BYRON: He was a sort of poet, my great-uncle. One day his coachman talked back to him. He got out of the coach, shot the coachman, threw the body into the coach, where his wife sat also talking back to him, drove the coach to a lake, and threw them both in. Yours.

ADA: When you first proposed, my mother turned you down. "Good," you said. "She is a cold collation. I like hot suppers." And you went off to have a baby by your sister.

BYRON: He sold all the trees on the estate, to ruin it. As an old man, he kept company only with crickets, taking off his clothes and training them to run up and down his body.

ADA: When I was born, you came into the room, took one look at me and said, "Isn't it dead?" Yours.

BYRON: The night he died, all those crickets left his house together, in a river of insects. One hundred and fourteen trees were said to grow up overnight. His only grandson got his head shot off in Corsica. I became Lord Byron.

ADA: Yes, you did. I can just see you.

Music. Enter Boy, limping. He wears a cloak and collar like Byron. He carries a board, paper, pen and a bottle of ink. He settles himself down, to think and write.

BYRON: Is that me?

ADA: Yes. Won't he do?

BYRON: Good God, no!

ADA: Why not?

BYRON: He's too damned pretty! I was fat as a pig! I sat on a tombstone every day, while the other children played, trying to write. Morbid little fat boy, posing. Truth was, I couldn't walk more than a hundred yards at one time. So I sat. And wrote.

ADA: What about?

BOY (*Writing*): Woman!

BYRON: That's it.

BOY:

Experience must have told me,
All must love thee who behold thee.

Me, thee! Right. (*He scribbles, furiously*)

ADA: You had to kneel for your wedding vows. You were mortified. You said to my mother, *after* the ceremony, "Well, Miss Milbanke, are you ready for me?" It was common knowledge that your sexual organ was twice—

BYRON: Oh, three times—

ADA: —the size of a normal man's.

BYRON: Four, maybe five.

ADA: It was calling her by her maiden name instead of Lady Byron she resented, not the size of your—

BYRON: —six, sometimes seven—

ADA: —mythical (perhaps), grandiose (certainly), sexual organ.

BYRON: A clubbed foot, and a grandiose penis. The Lord giveth, the Lord taketh away. People thought it was wit, beauty and literary genius that made my mistresses so reluctant to leave me. Now you know the truth.

ADA: And the truth is my mother made you a perfectly adequate wife. I am here to prove it.

BOY:
Surely experience might have taught,
The firmest promises are naught—

Taught, naught!

ADA: You slept with anyone. Including, I once heard, a pet bear you took to Cambridge.

BYRON: To sit for a fellowship. No, but I think I should have. He was very affectionate. But they hanged you in those days for loving just another man. God knows what they would have done about a bear.

ADA: Moneylenders, prostitutes, pimps. Boys dressed as girls, girls dressed as boys. The scum, the dregs. You drank from the sewer.

BYRON: A Wicked Lord for a great-uncle. For a grandfather, Admiral Byron, who lost so many ships, he was believed to attract storms. (*Pause*) And for a father, Mad Jack Byron. A soldier. He thought he could teach me to walk by floating me in a tub. "It can't even swim," he said, and died when I was three. (*Laughs*) A soldier. I adored him!

BOY:

> O Memory! thou choicest blessing,
> When join'd with hope, when still possessing—
>
> Blessing, possessing!

ADA (*Looking at her notes*): Your father slept with his sister.

BYRON: Yes, I think he did.

ADA: His child by his first wife was your sister.

BYRON: She was.

ADA: And you slept with her.

BYRON: Like father like son.

ADA: Did you love her?

BYRON: Yes. I took refuge in my sister. Make an incestuous little note to that effect. Our souls were one. Her flesh was mine. Cliches like that.

ADA: She was British, while your mother was Scottish.

BYRON: As a burr. (*Scots accent*) The Gordons of Gight. Sexually very proper. (*Pause*) My mother.

The Boy finishes his poem.

BOY:

> This record will forever stand,
> Woman! Thy vows are traced in sand!
>
> (*He smiles, pleased with himself*) I will call my poem:
> To Woman!

BYRON (*Smiles*): To Woman.

ADA: Your proper Scots mother gave you a proper Scots nurse, who read you the Bible, told you about heaven, hell, predestination—

BYRON: And played tricks with my sexual organ. Which wasn't grandiose then at all. Just a fat boy's little treasure, which she found soon enough. I learned the dance of sex to the cadence of Job. I was taught ejaculation and damnation at the same time. I did have the sense to prefer the former, but I still never quite think of one without the other. I was nine years old. Sex was terror. Are you sympathizing with me?

ADA: Your spectacular difficulties as a child do not overwhelm me, sorry. But your mother was a fool.

BYRON (*Softly*): I know it.

ADA: You never wrote about her.

BYRON: I put her in a play. Give me credit for writing about life directly. People I loved and people I hated, not Greek vases, like that idiotic Keats.

Ada looks at her books.

ADA: Oh, yes, true. (*She picks up a book*) *The Deformed Transformed.*

BYRON: That's it.

ADA: A play in verse, about a hunchback boy named Arnold, with a mother named Bertha, who drives him to suicide.

BYRON (*Cheerfully*): That's it.

ADA: But just as he is cutting his throat, Arnold beholds a mysterious tall black man, rising in majesty out of a crystal fountain—

BYRON: Oh, yes—

ADA: —who transfigures him by magic into the shape of Achilles—

BYRON: Yes!

ADA: —and sends him off to accomplish astonishing feats of valor and renown.

47

BYRON: Quite right. How do you like it?

ADA: I don't.

BYRON: You couldn't say that another way, could you?

ADA: Certainly. I like it least of anything you ever wrote I ever read.

BYRON: You could try to see it. It *is* a play.

ADA: All right. (*She reads the stage directions*) A forest. In a far-off country. Enter Arnold, a hunchback.

BYRON (*Points to the Boy*): There.

ADA: And his mother, Bertha.

BYRON: There!

Enter Woman, dressed in a large theatrical cloak.

WOMAN: Out, hunchback, out!

BOY (*Quietly*): I was born so, Mother.

WOMAN:
Out, incubus! Nightmare! Of seven sons
The sole abortion!

BOY:
Would that I had been so
And never seen the light.

WOMAN:
Well, hence! and do thy best!
That back of thine may bear its burden, 'tis
More high, if not so broad as others.

ADA: This is ridiculous.

BYRON: Quiet!

BOY:
It bears its burden. But my heart, will it
Sustain that which you place upon it, Mother?

You nursed me. Do not kill me.
Speak to me kindly. Though my brothers are
So beautiful, and manly, do not spurn me:
Our milk has been the same.

WOMAN:

As is the hedgehog's
Which sucks at midnight from the wholesome dam
Of the young bull.
Call not thy brothers brethren! Call me not
Mother: for if I brought thee forth, it
Was as foolish hens sometimes hatch vipers, by
Sitting on strange eggs! Out, urchin! Out!

BYRON: Exit Boy! Exit Bertha!

They exit. Pause.

ADA: Well, I'm sorry. Hedgehogs don't suckle cows, and hens
don't hatch snakes.
BYRON: You think it's easy, writing a play about your mother?
It's like trying to paint a storm on deck.
ADA: I can do better than that.
BYRON: You?
ADA: Mathematical me. I have my research. I know what your
life with your mother was really like.
BYRON: Oh, do you?
ADA: I do. Change of scene. Garden party. Tea time.

*Music. Enter Man, Young Woman, Girl, Young Man.
While they may appear suddenly, materialized at once out
of Ada's mind, once in the light they stroll on casually,
relating easily to Ada, as a part of their aristocratic family.*

MAN: It was an accident, of course.

YOUNG WOMAN: Receiving the title in the first place.

YOUNG MAN: How to live with it is quite beyond them.

GIRL: Haven't they any money?

MAN: Almost none.

YOUNG MAN: His uncle's estate was ruined when it came to him. He can't even sell it.

MAN: They exist in a sort of genteel squalor, I believe.

GIRL: Here they come.

Enter Boy and Woman, as Byron and his mother. She is a plain, very stout woman who perspires heavily, and is very ill at ease. He still limps awkwardly, but his ardor and confusion have been replaced by a withdrawn and sullen arrogance.

MAN: Dear Madame. You and your son are most welcome here.

WOMAN: Thank you, sir. (*To Boy*) Say thank you, sir.

BOY: Thank you.

YOUNG WOMAN: Will you take some refreshment, after your journey?

WOMAN: You mean food? Now? I never eat, dear lady, except at my meals.

The Boy winces with embarrassment.

But I will take one glass of wine, thank you. The weather here is dreadfully hot. I hardly feel myself. Byron, make your bow, my love. Don't I always tell you, make your bow when you come among strangers? Bow.

The Boy gives them a curt nod.

Now get me my wine.

Ada hands the Young Woman a glass of wine from her table. The Young Woman gives it to the Boy, who takes it, limping, to the Woman.

YOUNG MAN: In spite of the weather, we do hope you enjoy your visit.

WOMAN: I daresay I shall. Your roads, at least, are an improvement on Scotland. Remember, Byron?

BOY: Only when I have to. I hate Scotland.

WOMAN: Nasty thing to say. (*To all*) Did you hear that? (*To Boy*) That was very wicked. Don't I always tell you, hate nothing? Of course I do. (*To all*) The trouble I take, with this boy! I'm sure I don't know why.

MAN: Lord Byron, we have a passable picture gallery in the house. Do you like pictures?

BOY: No, I don't.

MAN: What do you like, my boy?

BOY: I like to be left alone.

WOMAN: What an answer. He can behave, when he wants to, as pretty as a picture.

BOY: Me? Pretty? Rubbish!

WOMAN: Byron, dear, I insist on civil conversation, as befits your station. And don't slouch! Stand up straight, as I teach you, like a man!

BOY: I am not a man yet. I wish to God I was.

WOMAN: Don't provoke me, sir! Stand up properly! Do you hear me?

BOY: Everybody hears you, Woman.

WOMAN: Do not call me Woman! That is no way to address me now. Lady Byron, sir! (*She drinks down all her wine*) More of this, and no more backtalk.

He takes the glass to be refilled.

51

What a life I lead. He's worse than his father.

MAN: Dear Lady, don't distress yourself.

YOUNG MAN: Surely he has no wish but to please you.

WOMAN: Him? He knows how I love him. But how does he talk to me? Contempt! Insults!

The Boy brings her the glass of wine.

BOY: I am not insulting you, Woman!

WOMAN: Stop calling me Woman! You little snake. Or I'll slap the insolence out of you.

BOY: The way you slapped it out of my father?

WOMAN: Don't defend your father to me!

BOY: He can't defend himself!

WOMAN: And you're just like him! Oh, my God!

MAN: Madame, please—

YOUNG WOMAN: Dear Mrs. Byron—

WOMAN: Lady Byron! Lady Byron! I insist on that! I'm not blind. I see what you think of me. Nothing, nobody! Because of him! The way he treats me. Oh, my heart, my soul! Ah, you brat! You damned cripple! (*She throws the wine in his face, and the glass at his chest*) Insults! Insults!

She storms off. Slowly, the Boy wipes his face and picks up the glass.

BOY: I trust no one here will so forget themselves as to slight my mother. She is my friend. She will defend me against anyone in the world, but herself. (*He hands the glass to the Young Woman*) It would please me if you would kindly attend her.

They all move quietly after the Young Woman and exit, all but the Girl. She waits, to one side. The Boy sits again, his head in his hands. Pause. Byron stares at him.

ADA: What do you think of that?

BYRON: Cheap, embarrassing melodrama. Accurate family portrait, and cheap, embarrassing melodrama. Now, what about you? You married, you said. Children? How many?

ADA: Three.

BYRON: Girls?

ADA: One.

BYRON: Boys? I never had those.

ADA: Two. I am a mother myself, and like yours not a very good one.

BYRON (*Moved*): Two boys?

ADA: Yes. Who must escape from me. How did you do that, finally?

BYRON: Don't you know?

ADA: How a boy escapes from his mother? No, tell me.

BYRON: He must fall in love with someone else.

ADA: Oh.

She looks at the Boy. Music: the Boy's theme, repeated. The Girl returns, to stand by the Boy. He jumps awkwardly to his feet, limping. She holds out her hands and he takes them, staring at her.

BYRON:

He has no breath, no being, but in hers,
She is his voice, she is his sight,
He has ceased to live within himself,
She is his life.

BOY (*Passionately*):
> Oh! Might I kiss those eyes of fire,
> A million would scarce quench desire!

GIRL (*Smiling*): Byron.
BOY:
> Nought would my kiss from thine dissever,
> Still would we kiss, and kiss forever!

GIRL: My dear boy.
BOY:
> To part would be a vain endeavor!
> Can I desist? Ah, never! Never!

GIRL: Byron. Are you making love to me?
BYRON: Yes!
GIRL: I am only a friend, my dear. I could never—

He looks down, toward his foot. He covers it quickly.

BOY: Marry a cripple!
GIRL: Marry a boy! A boy!

She kisses him on the cheek, gets up and leaves.

BYRON:
> Girls like those are born in clusters.
> They marry soldiers, like Captain Musters.

BOY: Ah! Ah!

He beats his foot. He lurches to his feet. He writhes in mortification, helpless, furious, twisting himself about in self-loathing. He beats himself.

Oh! Oh!

ADA: That's too much! It's ridiculous!

BYRON: He doesn't think so.

The Boy's anguish is acute, out of proportion to what has happened.

ADA: She was an idiot. He's well out of it.

BYRON: Explain it to him.

The Boy throws himself on the ground in agony.

ADA: What happens to him?

BYRON: Oh, he goes to school. To learn. Like everyone else.

Enter Young Man, as older Cambridge classmate, with a glass of brandy.

YOUNG MAN: Byron! My dear fellow! Don't be a fool. Here. Drink this.

He gives the Boy the brandy. The Boy drinks.

Now look me in the eye. It isn't a tragedy.

BOY: Isn't it?

YOUNG MAN: You're heartsick. Standard for students.

BOY: You're a student.

YOUNG MAN: Almost graduated. Cured. You can talk to me.

BOY: Yes, I can.

YOUNG MAN: Splendid.

BOY: I want to explode!

YOUNG MAN: Because you are a healthy young man. Forget your girl. Her soldier sweetheart is a boor. She must rather like that. Face the truth about women, Byron. That's what a man does.

BOY: Does he?

YOUNG MAN: Another piece, gone for a soldier. If you had really wanted her, you could have had her. You know that.

BOY: What?

YOUNG MAN: Byron, if you had exposed to the young lady something more than poetry, she'd have been interested, all right. Do you think she is different from the rest? They're all bitches.

BOY: I don't believe that.

YOUNG MAN: Yes, you do.

BOY: Then why didn't I—

YOUNG MAN: You didn't want to.

BOY: I don't understand.

YOUNG MAN: You cannot enjoy her. You can enjoy me. I won't let you cry, Byron. (*He holds the Boy by the shoulders*) Women? They are beautifully bound, like books in languages we cannot read, edged, you see, in gilt. There is nothing there for us but dust. Marry one, by all means. Have your children, if you can stomach that. But cry about them? Them? I'll release you, Byron. Face the truth. Be a man.

He kisses the Boy. The Boy, shocked and furious, attacks the Young Man, who handles him roughly and throws him to the ground.

Well, you *are* a fool.

Exit Young Man. The Boy weeps.

ADA: Stop it. Help him.

BYRON: Nothing easier.

He takes up his uncle's sword and tosses it at the Boy. It falls at his feet. The Boy stares at it, picks it up. He makes a few weak passes with it.

Another world. Simple. Manly. Direct. No women at all. Higher. Point up. Thrust! Don't slash! Hack with it! Don't be delicate! Split the shoulder. Aim for the neck. Thrust!

The Boy moves about with the sword. Byron opens the case of dueling pistols.

Keep on! Starve yourself on greens and biscuits, so there's no more weight on that damned foot than there has to be. Play cricket in four overcoats, my lad, bat better than anyone else, and sweat it off! Here! (*He throws the Boy a pistol*) Learn! Hit coins! Split canes! Leave animals alone, but hit your targets. And when a man makes free with you again, put a bullet in his head. Aim!

The Boy aims. His hand shakes badly.

Let it shake! Just bring it down and fire. Coins, canes, and that space between a man's eyes. Let the bastards think about that. Here! Put it down. Come at me.

The Boy puts down the pistol and the sword. Byron takes off his shirt. The Boy also strips to the waist. Byron hops to him quickly.

Left hand up. Right back. Now switch. Don't let me know what you're going to do. Switch again.

57

Both limping, they circle each other. Suddenly, Byron smacks the Boy in the face.

Are you going to cry, or what?

The Boy attacks, clumsily, but with spirit. Byron shoves him back.

Good! Come again! Good!

They box. The Boy gets more and more expert, both in boxing and in moving quickly.

Forget the damned foot! Just push with it! You can! There! That's it! Good! Good!

The Boy hits Byron a good smack in the face. Byron smiles.

Good! Again! Again!

Bells, suddenly. Funeral music. The Boy does not hear them, and keeps on fighting. Byron grabs his fists and holds him still. The Woman, as Byron's mother, walks hands folded through the scene and exits.

ADA: When she died, you would not go to her funeral.
BOY: My mother, dead?
ADA: You stayed at home and boxed, with a servant. You said goodbye to her as you had lived with her, fighting.

Byron hold up his hands. The Boy hits at them savagely.

Poem by Lord Byron, on the death of his mother. There is none.

Enter Man and Young Man, on opposite sides, as critics.

YOUNG MAN: Poems by Lord Byron, a Minor, published today.

Byron and the Boy stop and listen.

MAN: Entitled *Hours of Idleness*, which they certainly become
for the reader.

YOUNG MAN: This first book of poems by a young Lord belongs
to that class neither noble nor pedestrian but quite simply
terrible.

MAN: They are infantile effusions, spread most pompously out
over a dead flat. They can no more rise above that level
than stagnant water.

YOUNG MAN: They consist of embarrassing lyrics, tedious lam-
entations, and ungrammatical translations. They are all
equally preposterous, and equally dull.

MAN: We can only hope that our young Lord, out of respect for
his superior station in life and his own good name, however much he writes in the future, will publish no more.

BYRON (*To Boy*): Well? Come on.

*The Man and the Young Man watch while Byron and the
Boy square off. Byron holds up his palms, while the Boy hits
them again.*

BOY (*Boxing*):
　　　And though—I hope—not hence unscathed to go—
　　　Who conquers me—shall find—a stubborn foe—
　　　I've learn'd to fight—and sternly—speak the truth—
　　　Learn'd to deride the critic's starch decree—
　　　And break him on the wheel he meant for me!

The Boy and Byron land smacking blows on each other, and then turn toward the critics. Exit Man and Young Man.

BYRON: You remember that.

Byron moves away from the Boy, as if to join Ada again, putting on his shirt.

ADA: That isn't all, with him.
BYRON: What?
ADA: Look at him again. Listen.

Byron turns, looks at the Boy again. We hear the high tenor of a choirboy, singing. The Boy stands off by himself, looking at Byron.

ADA: Who is he now?
BYRON: Oh.
ADA: Your choirboy?
BYRON: Yes.
ADA: How did you find him? Surely not in church?

Byron stares at the Boy anew, then moves to him again, slowly.

BYRON: In water. There my foot was as good as any man's. I swam at Cambridge. One day I saw him, far out, waving his arms, in trouble.

The Boy kneels, and bows his head. Byron stands behind him.

I rescued him. We took off our clothes, to dry out in the sun. I found a creature like the animals I took home all my life: my hedgehogs, my turtles, my monkeys, my badger, my tame crow, my ducks and pigeons, my bear. My little dogs. All my helpless, wretched, lonely things. Myself, when young. (*He touches the Boy*) He was a farmer's son, but he sang like an angel. And with him, so did I.

The music stops. The Boy turns to Byron. Byron spreads wide his arms, and kneeling with the Boy, embraces him.

There be none of Beauty's daughters
With a magic like thee,
And like the music on the waters
Is thy sweet voice to me.

When as if its sound were causing
The charmed ocean's pausing,
The waves lie still and gleaming
And the lull'd winds seem dreaming.

They kiss. The Boy rests against Byron.

And the midnight moon is weaving
Her bright chain o'er the deep,
Whose breast is gently heaving
As an infant's asleep.

Byron strokes the Boy's hair, with great tenderness.

So the spirit bows before thee,
To listen and adore thee,
With a full but soft emotion,
Like the swell of summer's ocean.

Music—the voice singing. The Boy leaves Byron, backing away into darkness.

Goodbye.

ADA: What happened?

BYRON: I am a poet. He died, of course. Which you know.

ADA: Of pneumonia, in jail. Waiting to be hanged, for promis-
cuous sex, with many men—

BYRON: —on a gallows built for him alone, so he would not
infect murderers—

ADA: —a pervert.

BYRON: Yes. God bless him.

Pause.

ADA: Choking up? That is to say you are deeply moved?

BYRON: Think what you damn well please.

ADA: How touching. The trouble is: all your boyfriends looked
like you.

BYRON: You don't begin to understand.

ADA: Oh yes I do. You were in love with yourself, as always.

BYRON: I loved him. And I loved him purely.

ADA: Don't. You make me ill.

BYRON: Believe it or not.

ADA: I don't. Not.

BYRON: Suit yourself.

ADA: Guttersnipes. Choirboy guttersnipes, with tenor voices,
but guttersnipes.

BYRON: I loved him. Go to hell.

ADA: And all the rest? You loved them, too? Purely?

BYRON: Well, that was all the rest.

ADA: Of course.

BYRON: What was I to do? Lord Byron. Any decent woman I
breathed on would have a baby the next day. Slovenly,
loose women I could not enjoy.

ADA: Hoo!

BYRON: Except, of course, under stress, and temptation.

ADA: How much stress and temptation did it take?
BYRON: Well, very little, but do you really think that is fun?
ADA: I think it was for you.
BYRON: I was all alone. Father, mother, family, gone. The only one left to me was my sister. I adored her, never happy, except with her. She married, in family tradition, a stupid soldier. I was bereft. It hurt!
ADA: Oh, poor Byron. What a pose. Never to be happy, and no one cares. There was one portrait of you kept in the house. In a back hallway, covered with a green cloth. I found it, of course, and peeked. There you were. On a ship, sailing away. Like every other idiot with nothing to do, you traveled.

Ropes appear, and along them, rising behind Byron a large sail. Behind it: color, a morning sky. Music.

Away from home. Into a scarlet sunrise, under eastern winds, on a ship called the *Lisbon Packet.* Toward mountains of Asia, to seek Vampire Kings with bloody teeth. To desert monasteries, to study Greek and flirt with God. To the marble palaces of Turkish baths, to sink yourself in sherbet and sodomy. For Maids of Athens, Boys of Rome, nights of gin and dawns of verse, set sail, my foolish father: Byron, young!

Enter Man, Woman, Young Man, Young Woman, Boy and Girl. They join Byron as passengers on a sea voyage. The sail now looms above them, and as they prepare for the voyage, it begins to move, to sway and billow. Wind rises, and the people face the excitement and danger of a sea voyage at that time. Byron, apart, moves toward the center of the sail.

YOUNG MAN:

> Off we go to Greece and Turkey
> Lord knows when we shall come back!

WOMAN:

> Breezes foul and tempests murky
> May unship us in a crack!

BOY:

> Now we've boarded, lo! the Captain,
> Gallant Kidd, commands the crew.

MAN:

> Passengers their berths are clapt in,
> Some to grumble, some to spew.

WOMAN:

> Heyday! Call you that a cabin?
> Why, 'tis hardly three feet square!

YOUNG MAN:

> Not enough to stow Queen Mab in,
> Who the deuce can live in there?

*The wind rises. The sail moves and billows out from the
ropes. Sounds of wind, and gulls, and the creak of ropes and
decks.*

MAN:

> Who, sir? Plenty!
> Nobles twenty
> Did at once my vessel fill!

BOY:

Did they?

WOMAN:

Jesus!

YOUNG MAN:

How you squeeze us!

WOMAN:

I will not survive the racket
Of this brutal *Lisbon Packet*.

GIRL:

Now at length we're off for Turkey!
Lord knows when we shall come back!

WOMAN:

Breezes foul and tempests murky
May unship us in a crack.

MAN:

All for this my skill is hired,
Hark! the farewell gun is fired!

*We hear the boom! of a ship's cannon. Lights change. The
people melt away, leaving Byron standing alone, holding
fast to a rope, while behind him the sail shakes and billows.
Another light is on Ada, seated in her chair, but lit with
Byron, traveling as he does. Music.*

ADA:

> Roll on, thou deep and dark blue ocean—roll!
> Ten thousand fleets sweep over thee in vain.
> Man marks the earth with ruin—his control
> Stops with the shore—

Wind again, rising.

BYRON:

> And thus I am absorb'd, and this is life,
> I look upon the peopled desert past,
> As on a place of agony and strife,
> Where for some sin I was cast
> To act and suffer, but remount at last
> With a fresh pinion—

Byron sails, enjoying his freedom. From around Ada, speaking to her, appear Man, Woman, Young Man, Young Woman, Girl and Boy. Each carries a copy of a slim book of verse: Byron's Childe Harold's Pilgrimage. *They read the lines to Ada, all genuinely stirred by Byron's work.*

YOUNG MAN:

> I have not loved the world, nor the world me,
> I have not flattered its rank breath, nor bow'd
> To its idolatries a patient knee—

YOUNG WOMAN:

> Nor coin'd my cheek to smiles, nor cried aloud
> In worship of an echo: in the crowd
> They cannot deem me one of such—

Music. Wind.

BOY:

> 'Tis to create, and in creating live
> A being more intense, that we endow
> With form our fancy, gaining as we give—

GIRL:

> The life we image, even as I do now.
> What am I? Nothing: but not so art thou,
> Soul of my thought, with whom I traverse earth—

Music. Wind.

WOMAN:

> I have not loved the world, nor the world me,
> but let us part fair foes: I *do* believe
> Though I have found them not, that there may be—

MAN:

> Words which are things, hopes which will not deceive,
> That two, or one, are almost what they seem,
> That goodness is no name, and happiness no dream.

Music. Wind.

ADA:

> Childe Byron bask'd him in the noonday sun,
> Disporting there like any other fly,
> Nor deem'd before his little day was done,
> One blast might chill him into misery!

All the others turn to Ada.

YOUNG WOMAN: *Childe Harold's Pilgrimage.* It's beautiful.

YOUNG MAN: Do you know, he swam the Hellespont? I mean, jumped in the open sea, and swam it?

GIRL: He's been to Greece and Rome—

BOY: Albania—Turkey—

YOUNG MAN: Places no Englishman ever went before—

MAN: He's not just a poet. He rides. He shoots.

YOUNG WOMAN: He's a Peer of the Realm.

WOMAN: He translates Greek and Latin.

GIRL: He spoke in the House of Lords.

BOY: For the common man. The worker.

YOUNG MAN: He despises cant. He says what he thinks.

MAN: He's scornful—

YOUNG WOMAN: But tender—

GIRL: He's proud—

WOMAN: And shy—

YOUNG MAN: And mysterious.

MAN: He's lame—

GIRL: And he's beautiful.

ADA: And he's coming home.

They all turn to Byron, who now steps down from his ship, returning to England.

MAN: Welcome home, Lord Byron.

WOMAN: We are glad you have come back to us.

YOUNG MAN: It is our privilege to have you home again.

YOUNG WOMAN: We are proud of you.

BOY: You are everything we want to be ourselves.

GIRL: We love you.

ALL (*Quietly*): Welcome home.

*Long pause. Byron has watched all this with great amuse-
ment, staring with his own curiosity at all these people who
suddenly love him.*

BYRON: Well. I wake up this morning, and find myself famous.

YOUNG MAN: Lord Byron, my admiration knows no bounds. To
me, you are like Jesus Christ!

BYRON: Aren't you taking that a little far?

YOUNG MAN: Of course, I don't mean in person. I mean in
situation.

BYRON: Which means a crucifixion. Thank you very much.
(*He moves away*)

BOY: Is it true, Lord Byron, that like Leander you swam the
Hellespont?

BYRON: Not like Leander, no. He had a girl on the other side,
for motivation. I did not. He was drowned. I was not. (*He
moves away*)

YOUNG WOMAN: Lord Byron, can you describe your ideal
woman?

BYRON: Yes. A female with talent enough to understand mine,
but not enough to sparkle herself. You might do. (*He
moves away*)

MAN: Lord Byron, what are you writing now?

BYRON: A book on British morals. "Sodomy Simplified,
or, Pederasty Proved to Be Praiseworthy." (*He moves
away*)

WOMAN: Lord Byron, if you weren't already sleeping with so
many of us, we would suppose you didn't like women at
all. You won't even take dinner with us! How do you
reconcile such opposites?

BYRON: Very simply. With the exception of lobster salad and
champagne, women should not be seen eating. It spoils

the other appetite. Besides, you always take the wing of the chicken.

BOY: Lord Byron, please don't joke. You mean too much to us. You are fierce and wise and alive. What do you think about life and death?

BYRON: I like one better than the other.

YOUNG MAN: Do you believe in a life after death?

BYRON: It doesn't seem very likely. If we are all going to live again, why die?

MAN: Lord Byron! Have you no fear of God?

BYRON: I have. Not for what he will do to me in the next world, but for what he has already done to me in this one.

WOMAN: We give you our affection and respect, and receive your mockery in return. We are not fools. It is only your fear, in disguise.

BYRON: Absolutely. And since mockery may be the plaything God gives us when we are afraid, as a father makes a toy for a sick child, I cherish it.

GIRL: Lord Byron! I can no longer exist without confessing how my soul burns with recognition of the beauty of your own!

BYRON: Do you write verses too?

GIRL: Yes. Do you think I want to kiss and tell?

BYRON: No, I think you want to fuck and publish. (*He moves away from all of them, holding up his arms*) Now then! From this pinnacle of social divinity, from this apotheosis of Regency perfection, from your caresses and your breath-taking praise, I must detach myself. It is wonderful to be a social lion. I'll not deny that. But I am tired now, lonely among people I cannot trust and among waltzes I cannot dance, and I've fallen in love. Truly, terribly in love. I hope you understand.

MAN: In love?

WOMAN: Well, of course you are in love.

YOUNG MAN: Who isn't?

GIRL: It's the only interesting thing to do.

BOY: Who with?

BYRON: I can't tell you.

GIRL: Why not?

BYRON: It's a deep dark secret.

WOMAN: It won't be for long.

YOUNG MAN: Give us a hint.

GIRL: Do.

MAN: You might as well.

WOMAN: We'll find out anyway.

BYRON: Very well. The creature I love is a goose.

WOMAN: Goose?

MAN: Did I hear Lord Byron say—

BYRON: A goose.

Ada laughs.

ADA: You named me for her! Augusta Ada, Augusta Leigh, Augusta Goose!

The Young Woman now steps forward as Augusta Leigh, Byron's half-sister.

YOUNG WOMAN: My dear.

BYRON: My dear. I need your company. Your joy.

YOUNG WOMAN: It's yours.

They move to each other, embrace gently, savoring a tremendous sexual attraction. They walk away, whispering.

MAN: Oh, dear God. It's his sister.

71

WOMAN: He calls her Goose.

GIRL: Because that's what she is.

YOUNG MAN: Augusta Leigh is an imbecile. Everyone knows
that. She *giggles*!

WOMAN: Married, three children. Attendant on the royal family. And four years older. It's disgusting.

MAN: Well, wait. She's technically his half-sister.

WOMAN: And that makes it half-acceptable?

ALL: Please!

BOY: She isn't even pretty.

YOUNG MAN: All she does is gossip, laugh, have babies—

GIRL: And love her brother.

WOMAN: Lord Byron can have all of us, and sometimes does.
Why her?

*They step back. Byron and the Young Woman come down-
stage. She wears a shawl. Byron is listening to her, delighted
at their silliness.*

BYRON: They said *what*?

YOUNG WOMAN (*Straight face*): Joanna Southcott, the female
evangelist, is going to have a baby.

BYRON: She's sixty years old!

YOUNG WOMAN: It will be a miracle, you see. The baby will be
a boy. The new Messiah. She has already named him.

BYRON: William Wordsworth?

YOUNG WOMAN: No. Shiloh.

BYRON: That's a *city* in the Holy Land. Ridiculous.

YOUNG WOMAN: Listen to this. Ten doctors and ten clergymen
examined her.

BYRON: *What* did they say?

YOUNG WOMAN: Her condition, in a younger woman, would be
entirely consonant with pregnancy!

BYRON: Just in case—

YOUNG WOMAN: Shiloh may be the new Messiah.

BYRON: I long to see what she will deliver. Getting pregnant at sixty is certainly a miracle, but getting someone—

They laugh.

BYRON AND YOUNG WOMAN: —is a bigger one!

They laugh, like children. Their delight in each other physically releases them, like sex.

BYRON: Laughter. I think the great goddess of love, towering Aphrodite, invincible Venus, is first and last, above everything else, simply silly.

YOUNG WOMAN: An idiot. Me.

BYRON: A goddess. You.

They stand very close to each other, but not yet touching.

YOUNG WOMAN: When we were little, you never laughed. You were always angry or sad—

BYRON: And fat and lame and miserable—

YOUNG WOMAN: You had always cut yourself or hurt yourself somehow and—

BYRON: You laughed at me, and—

YOUNG WOMAN: —made you smile, at least—

BYRON: I am still lame. I am still miserable.

YOUNG WOMAN: And you know I can refuse you nothing.

Music: the Boy's theme, repeated. Byron takes the shawl off her shoulders slowly, voluptuously.

BYRON:

> Oh thine be the gladness, and mine be the guilt.

Byron holds her in his arms.

> One sigh of thy sorrow, one look of thy love,
> Shall turn me or fix me, shall reward or reprove,
> And the heartless may wonder at all I resign,
> Thy lips shall reply, not to them, but to mine!

He kisses her with great sexual hunger and she responds. The others gather, and watch.

WOMAN: They don't care who sees them.

MAN: If they'd keep it quiet, who'd care?

YOUNG MAN: But they won't.

GIRL: He won't. He uses her, to insult us.

YOUNG MAN: I suppose it is poetic.

WOMAN: Nonsense. It's one more way of loving himself. It's disgusting.

BOY: It's shameful.

GIRL: Someone must stop them.

WOMAN: Who?

MAN: How?

The Young Woman takes herself out of Byron's arms. She kisses him lovingly on the mouth, but briefly, and then moves away.

YOUNG WOMAN: I can't live with you forever.

BYRON: Why not? I wish you would.

She kisses him again.

YOUNG WOMAN: You ought to get married.

BYRON: Goose!

YOUNG WOMAN: You must sometime.

BYRON: Marry? Live like a fish packed in ice, when I can laugh with you. Live with you. Don't leave me.

YOUNG WOMAN: I must.

BYRON: Leave your husband. Bring the children or leave them, too. I don't care. Your flesh is mine.

YOUNG WOMAN: Indeed it is. I am pregnant. By you.

BYRON: Are you sure?

YOUNG WOMAN: Yes.

BYRON: Good! Wonderful! We will learn how to live with ourselves and love ourselves! Come with me to Greece again! Rome, anywhere!

YOUNG WOMAN: They will know.

BYRON: Let them!

YOUNG WOMAN: You defy them, dearest, if you must. I can't.

BYRON: Goose!

YOUNG WOMAN: I must have my baby at home! (*She embraces him*) Goodbye.

She leaves him. The others move in on him.

BOY: Now then, Byron!

GIRL: I will leave my husband for you!

WOMAN: I will leave my lover for you!

YOUNG MAN: I will leave my wife for you!

MAN: I will leave my mistress for you!

BOY: I will leave my mother for you!

BYRON (*To Boy*): You won't have to! (*To all*) This is all my fault. I have you fighting over Byron because Byron is too weak to refuse any of you anything. I must change that. (*To Woman*) I thank you for your wise bed, your voluptuous mothering, and those astonishing tassles on your nightgowns. (*To Young Man*) I thank you for your endless descriptions of your beautiful wife, the many invitations to dinner, and the great pleasure I took in not sleeping with either of you. (*To Man*) I thank you for the brandy and the bad jokes, which I loved. (*To Girl*) I thank you for the locket, with the strands of our pubic hair clasped within it. That was very dear of you. (*To all*) All of you are dear to me, every one. But every one of you leads me backward, not forward, as if, once inside you, with my eyes closed, time will stop and recede. But of course it won't. A man will age just as fast during intercourse as he will during prayer. Not even our bluest blood, not even our most hare-brained notions of privilege can stop time and feeling. I must do something more with my wretched life than fornicate with you, write verses, and have children by my sister. I must free myself from this gigantic wing of love that o'ershadows me. I must find a wife!

MAN: And by God, sir, you'll regret that!

YOUNG MAN: Unless he takes my wife. He can certainly have her.

BOY: I have a sister for you.

WOMAN: I have a niece.

YOUNG WOMAN: No. He's leaving you.

GIRL: Leave me? Never, Byron! It is I, beloved, who will leave you!

She produces a small knife, and saws at her wrists.

ALL (*In horror*): Ah!

BYRON: You are doing it with a butter knife. Stop. (*To all*) These ridiculous frenzies of love. Surely we all have better things to do. My sister is right. I must move on. I must marry. I want a wife, a home, my children and my good name! I will have them. Now. My wife! Where is she?

The others have moved back. Byron is left with Ada, who has been sitting quietly in her chair. She puts an elegant shawl about her shoulders. It changes her, making her less severe, younger.

ADA: I am here, Lord Byron. Waiting.
BYRON: You? Waiting for what?
ADA: To become my own mother, of course. (*She rises*)
BYRON: Very well. Come ahead.

They face each other. Lights fade.

Act Two

Ada, now playing her mother, Annabella Milbanke, approaches Byron.

MAN:

> She walks in beauty, like the night
> Of cloudless climes and starry skies—

YOUNG WOMAN:

> And all that's best of dark and bright
> Meet in her aspect and her eyes—

YOUNG MAN:

> Thus mellow'd to that tender light
> Which heaven to gaudy day denies.

GIRL:

> And on that cheek, and o'er that brow
> So soft, so calm, yet eloquent—

BOY:

> The smiles that win, the tints that glow—
> But tell of days in goodness spent—

78

WOMAN:

> A mind at peace with all below
> A heart whose love is innocent.

Music: people waltz. Through them, Ada/Annabella and Byron walk back and forth, passing each other. Byron stumbles, falls to one knee. Fiercely embarrassed, he jumps up again, brushes his knees, and finds himself facing her.

BYRON: I beg your pardon.

ADA: What for, Lord Byron?

BYRON: I fell, Miss—?

ADA: Milbanke. You stumbled.

BYRON: I could have hit you.

ADA: You didn't. It can happen to anyone.

BYRON: And they think nothing of it. For me, I am sorry to say, it is a calamity. I beg you to pardon me.

ADA: Lord Byron. I have something I would like to say to you.

BYRON: Miss Milbanke, please do.

ADA: Your dread of your lameness is logical. Your mockery, which hides your feelings, is logical. Your pose as a man—

BYRON: Who—

ADA (*Going right on*): —too proud to accept sympathy for unutterable transgressions—

BYRON: But who are—

ADA: —may also be logical, but in my opinion, you are a logically good man making yourself illogically tiresome. I beg you to pardon me!

BYRON: Who in the world is she?

She has moved away. Not far. They move in directions that will return them to each other.

WOMAN: Well, she's from the country.

YOUNG WOMAN: A provincial heiress.

GIRL: Rich?

BOY: Not very.

YOUNG MAN: What does she do?

MAN: She studies mathematics.

WOMAN: Mathematics?

Byron and Ada/Annabella meet again.

BYRON: Dear Miss Milbanke. White flag. Truce.

ADA: Dear Lord Byron. I see it. Truce.

BYRON: Will you be my friend? My amiable mathematician?

ADA: I would like that.

BYRON: I will call you my Princess of Parallelograms. Our proceedings will be rectangular. Two friends moving side by side into infinity, never to touch.

ADA: This is a London marriage market. Why are we never to touch? Because I am a decent woman, and you must therefore consider me a superior and sexless being?

BYRON: Is that what you think I think?

ADA: It's the general approach, yes.

BYRON: Whatever your sexuality, if your being is truly superior, then you must allow me whatever spiritual advancement I may gain by knowing you.

ADA: A superior being, a little encumbered with virtue. I can't flirt with you. If I tried, it would be the dance of an elephant.

Byron laughs.

Please let us be direct.

BYRON: By all means.

ADA: Why do you waste all your time making up verses?

BYRON (*Jolted*): All right. (*Pause*) I do hope one day to do better things. In the meantime, poetry is the lava of my imagination. Its eruption prevents earthquakes. Why do you study mathematics?

ADA: It is the language of reality. It alone can grasp the underlying facts of the natural world.

BYRON: Like earthquakes.

ADA: But real ones.

BYRON: Mine are real.

ADA: Yours are emotional. Reality is physical. You face the past, not the future.

BYRON: But in the future, what will matter mathematics, steam rockets to the moon, and three-hundred-year-old people, if human emotions, like earthquakes, devour them?

ADA: We will at least understand what we lose.

Pause.

BYRON: You look straight at a man.

ADA: Yes.

BYRON: I cannot laugh at that.

ADA: Because you are a prude.

BYRON (*Astonished*): Me?

ADA: You really condemn the women you enjoy. And for a wife, you want a woman pure and strong, who will never betray you.

BYRON: So I can betray her?

ADA: If you please. But if she is strong enough, you won't care to.

BYRON: What I don't care to do is fall in love again. In spite of my reputation, it is shattering, every time.

ADA: I believe that.

BYRON: I do dream about a companion. I am not a sentimental-
ist. I've seen enough love matches, and what time does to
that.

ADA: So have I.

BYRON: And are you strong, and pure, and faithful?

ADA: I try. Before you go any further, dear Lord Byron, I
must—gently and with respect—forestall your kind offer of marriage.

BYRON: Miss Milbanke, I did not—

ADA: You were considering it. I am already engaged.

BYRON: What?

ADA: This three weeks past, to a Mr. Derks of Devonshire,
where I live. Do you know him?

BYRON: Derks? No.

ADA: Believe in my regard. It can never change to love. But it
does stand above worldly friendship. Goodbye.

*She walks away from him. They take another turn, Byron
very unhappy. The others come forward.*

MAN: My God, she is a mathematician.

YOUNG WOMAN: Proving one minus one may still equal two.

WOMAN: A place for everything and everything in its place. She
put Byron in his.

GIRL: While Mr. Derks of Devonshire conveniently broke their
engagement and went to Canada.

YOUNG MAN: No wonder Byron never heard of him. In Canada
or Devonshire, Derks doesn't exist.

BOY: Some country girl.

MAN: What now?

They move away. Byron and Ada meet again.

BYRON: Well, you really are an icicle. You turn me down before I ask, then don't marry someone else, then write me letters hoping we are still friends.

ADA: Are we?

BYRON: Of course. I thought you ran away.

ADA: I do not run.

BYRON: You are looking at me as if I do not entirely disgust you?

ADA: Yes.

BYRON: I did underestimate you.

ADA: How so?

BYRON: I am a rake. You are not a flirt. Yet you have sunk me in the valley of rivals, frequenting the shadows of frustration.

ADA: I'm delighted. Do you know what's wrong with you?

BYRON: Please tell me.

ADA: You think you would rather be seized and teased, than pleased and eased. There it is, from a superior being, in rhyme.

BYRON: And it isn't true?

ADA: No. You have a great deal to learn. So do I, but so do you.

BYRON: Don't be a fool. I am mad, bad, and dangerous to know.

ADA: I am not impressed. You are simply unable to make an advance to a woman unless you know in advance it will be met.

BYRON: Well, if I make it, will you meet it?

ADA: If you ever make it, I might. What an ordeal! Here you are, my sophisticated rake and dandy, sleeping no doubt with half the society dancing around me, and at the same time nibbling at my hook as timidly as a pet fish. Why? I am as old-fashioned as my virginity. Just take it or leave it.

BYRON: Do you require me to kneel?

ADA: At the moment, no.

BYRON: Later, perhaps?

ADA: Later will never come! You are a fool who considers me a bigger one, when in fact I am beyond your comprehension. You are a coward! You do not love me! Goodbye!

Byron stops her, arms outspread.

BYRON: Stop! Zounds!

ADA: Let me by!

BYRON: No. You come at me straight out of the shrine of Saint Ursula. I saw eleven thousand virgins there, all buried together. Eleven thousand maidenheads of bone, and the effect of all that virtue was overwhelming. (*Pause*) I am very nervous.

ADA: With reason.

BYRON: I need a strong woman.

ADA: You should have her.

BYRON: The truth is, you will do. Miss Milbanke, I offer you my hand and my heart.

ADA: The truth is, Lord Byron, I love you. I accept.

BYRON: Good.

ADA: Good.

BYRON: Soon?

ADA: As soon as possible.

BYRON: Agreed.

ADA: Agreed.

BYRON: My hand?

ADA: And mine.

She shakes with him, like a man, and they part and circle again. The others come forward and join them, the men joining Byron and the women joining Ada. The men spruce

*Byron up, pat him on the back, etc., while the women dress
Ada up like a bride.*

MAN: Well, that's that.

YOUNG MAN: Lawyers go to work. Time is passing.

MAN: Up straight, Byron. Shoulders back.

GIRL: The wedding is announced. Now *she* gets nervous.

WOMAN: You will be beautiful, my dear. Formidable, but beautiful. Smile.

YOUNG WOMAN: Time is passing. The wedding day arrives.

WOMAN: And so does he, only just in time for the wedding,
upsetting everyone.

*They all make a line now, the men ushering Byron, and the
women Ada.*

MAN: The ceremony is even more grisly than he'd imagined.
He has to kneel—

Byron does.

stumbles—

Byron does.

and almost falls on his face.

Byron does, gets up again.

YOUNG WOMAN: He calls his wife "Miss Milbanke" and keeps
holding hands with his best man.

*Byron and Ada are placed side by side and pushed gently
away.*

GIRL: In the carriage, off on the honeymoon, he sings Turkish songs about sex with everything but a woman at the top of his voice.

YOUNG MAN: At the nuptial retreat, before bed —

BOY: There they are.

They place two high-backed chairs at center, each facing out. Byron and Ada sit in them.

WOMAN: Together at last.

MAN: Lord and Lady Byron.

YOUNG WOMAN: She has her man.

YOUNG MAN: He has his woman.

GIRL: Country girl —

BOY: And rake.

YOUNG WOMAN: Mathematician —

YOUNG MAN: And poet.

WOMAN: Until death they do part.

MAN: Until death they do part.

The others retire, leaving Byron and Ada alone. Long pause.

BYRON: Well, Pip?

ADA: Well, Duck?

BYRON (*Smiling*): Why do you call me Duck?

ADA (*Smiling*): You call your sister Goose.

BYRON: So you call me Duck?

ADA: Yes.

BYRON: Curious.

ADA: You call me Pip.

BYRON: I call you Bell.

ADA: Sometimes you call me Bell. Other times you call me Pip. Just now you called me Pip. Why can't you make up your mind?

BYRON: I suppose, Pip, I sometimes call you by different names, imagining you turning into different people, Bell.

ADA: That doesn't make sense, Duck.

BYRON: Oh, yes it does. Goose would understand.

ADA: Goose is a goose! I am a Pip! (*She jumps up, sits on Byron's lap*) You have made me that, bless you! The great thing about being virgin is all one has to learn. And I will learn everything! I absolutely mean to be the best wife—in every way—any man ever had. Do you doubt that?

BYRON: Not for a moment.

ADA: When are we going to do it?

BYRON: I will announce that at the proper juncture.

ADA: Of course. Can we talk while we do it? I hope so. You mustn't spare me coarse details. I'm quite ready for them.

BYRON: Are you?

ADA: Because I am a decent woman doesn't mean I am made of china. I won't break.

BYRON: I am happy to hear it.

ADA: With all your vast experience, you may naturally wish to be gentle and hold things back. Don't. You mustn't be afraid, or timid, or clumsy.

BYRON: Clumsy, timid, afraid. I'll avoid all three.

ADA: The life of the body, like the life of the spirit, must inspire, and redeem.

BYRON: Is that what you think it does?

ADA: With me it will, if you will let it. I am certain.

BYRON: I see you are.

ADA: I love marriage! (*She kisses him again*) Ours is perfect! (*She moves back to her chair*)

BYRON: Perfect.

ADA: Well—

BYRON: Almost—

ADA: Perfect. One little thing. I must speak my mind.

BYRON: Do.

ADA: I'm afraid that going to bed with masterful Byron will be like entering a beautiful palace, sitting down to a grand meal, eating it and leaving, then wondering, faintly, if you were all that time really welcome.

BYRON: What fascinating imagery.

ADA: But do you know that feeling?

BYRON: I do now.

ADA: I ask myself if you will ever say the same about me.

BYRON: I might.

ADA: I beg your pardon?

BYRON: Who can tell?

ADA: Tell what?

BYRON: If I will ever say all that about you.

ADA: All that? All that?

BYRON: Well, whatever you said—

ADA: What I said was, I promise you will never have from me a feeling of not being entirely welcome.

BYRON: That's a relief.

ADA: Then there it is. We will progress.

BYRON: Progress?

ADA: In love, as in all human emotions, one axiom is inexorable: we move forward or we stand still.

BYRON: How about sliding back?

ADA: That we will never do. Come kiss me.

BYRON: God. Where's my sister.

ADA: What?

BYRON: Where's my sister?

ADA: Did I say anything wrong? No, I didn't say anything wrong!

BYRON: Of course not! You never say anything wrong! That you are aware of!

ADA: Do not shout at me. I am not aware I said anything, Duck, that is sufficient cause for shouting.

BYRON: Goose! Goose!

They rise and move away from each other. The others now return. They turn the chairs to face each other.

BOY: So there they were.

YOUNG MAN: That night, hasty and importunate—

YOUNG WOMAN: Or quite possibly frightened—

MAN: He had his wife's virginity before dinner.

WOMAN: On a mohair sofa.

GIRL: Which broke.

YOUNG WOMAN: Now they are at home, in London.

MAN: Trouble in Piccadilly.

YOUNG MAN: For one thing, he's living beyond his means.

BOY: Up to his eyes in debt.

YOUNG WOMAN: For another, he's joined the management of Drury Lane. That means actresses and drinking companions.

MAN: Debased, he says everything.

WOMAN: Noble, she says nothing.

GIRL: And so they see it through—

BOY: With the baby on the way.

Byron and Ada sit in the two chairs facing each other.

BYRON: Why are you looking at me like that?

ADA: You know perfectly well.

BYRON: That wretched girl. Once. You did forgive me.

ADA: Of course I forgive you. Once.

BYRON: Well, what now?

ADA: Your sister is always here. You send me to bed and sit up drinking with her. Night after night.

BYRON: You keep inviting her—

ADA: To please you—

BYRON: —*I* don't—

ADA: I will remedy that.

BYRON: I have to laugh with somebody.

ADA: But not with me.

BYRON: I defy *anyone* to laugh with you.

ADA: You wallow in your misery. I don't.

BYRON: Oh, Bell. What is the matter?

ADA: You have abused me.

BYRON: What do you mean?

ADA: Shamefully. Perversely.

BYRON (*In sudden rage*): You asked for it!

ADA: I did not! I did not!

BYRON: Show me, Byron! Teach me, Byron! That's what you said!

ADA: Only what is done in marriage, rightfully!

BYRON: It *is* rightfully done in marriage—

ADA: It is bestial—

BYRON: —especially when a woman's pregnant—

ADA: Yes, use that! Oh, how vile—

BYRON: —in every healthy country but this frozen fishbarrel! Are you pretending you didn't *know* what we were doing?

ADA: Do you tell your sister about it? Do you drink with her and tell her everything we do? Do you tell your friends in the taverns? I know you do. I am dying of shame.

BYRON: You're not dying of shame, you're dying because you don't have the Byron of your dreams. I told you what I was.

ROMULUS LINNEY

ADA: My dreams? You speak to me about my dreams? After
what you've done to me?
BYRON: Oh, for Christ's sake! I won't do it again!
ADA: You will do it again. You will trample me into the dirt
again, and again, and again!
BYRON: God damn you. I never struck a woman in my life, and
I never will. But God damn you—
ADA: You did strike me! You married me!
BYRON: You married *me*! Bitch!
ADA: Bastard!

*They stare at each other, frozen in shock. The others move
down.*

WOMAN: Yes, yes, of course.
MAN: Nothing new in this.
YOUNG WOMAN: We must help them.
YOUNG MAN: Of course we must.
GIRL: Anything we can do.
BOY: However we can help.

The women move to Ada, the men to Byron.

WOMAN: Lady Byron, what's the matter?
ADA: He is a devil!
MAN: Lord Byron, what's the matter?
BYRON: She is an idiot!
ADA: I thought he loved me, and look.
BYRON: I thought she loved me, and look.
ADA: When I was in labor, having his baby, he shot off pistols in
the room below me. They sounded like cannons!
BYRON: I was knocking off the heads of soda bottles! To drink
that instead of brandy!

91

ADA: When he saw our baby, the first thing he said was, "Isn't it dead?"

BYRON: I am afraid of birth, and deformity. I have reason to be.

ADA: He made fun of my baby, and me. Rhymes. "The child she bore, came sweetly in, with blood and gore, around her chin."

BYRON: That's truth, not mockery. Hate my baby? I dreamed she would be born with wings. Lift the blanket, and there they are, pink as her flesh, tender as the heart of an artichoke, furled close to her little back. My daughter. With wings.

ADA: He turned the baby over and over. "Where are the wings?" he said. "Where are the wings?" I left him the next day.

BYRON: She did not leave me! We agreed she would take the baby to Devonshire, while I closed the house and cut my debts. I have a letter from her, full of affection. Love from the baby.

Ada whispers to Girl.

GIRL: What did you say?

Girl whispers to Young Woman.

YOUNG WOMAN: I can't believe it!

Young Woman whispers to Woman.

WOMAN: Such men should not be left alive!

Byron takes up his pistol, aims it at the wall. The Man approaches Byron, hand outstretched.

MAN: Byron. Dear fellow.

BYRON (*Shaking hands*): What's the news about the estate?

MAN: None. Byron, I'm worried.

BYRON: So am I. Until we sell the damned thing, I can't cut my debts.

MAN: I don't mean the estate. I mean your health.

BYRON: My health?

MAN: You need rest, Byron.

BYRON: What for?

MAN: To become yourself again.

BYRON: You think I'm not myself?

MAN: Your treatment of your wife would indicate it, yes.

BYRON: What the hell do you know about that?

MAN: Everyone knows about it! You would have the best care, the best of consultants. Put yourself in my hands.

BYRON: I am in your hands. You're my lawyer. You represent me.

MAN: No longer, sir. I now represent Lady Byron.

BYRON: What?

MAN: And your treatment of her is so foul—

BYRON: What, represent my wife?

MAN: —so extreme in every disgusting detail, that we can only assume you are the victim of some savage disease.

BYRON: Disease?

MAN: Of the mind. We do not wish to take advantage of you.

BYRON: You mean she says I'm crazy?

MAN: It is the only rational explanation for your behavior. A man who shoots pistols at the wall, inspects his baby for wings, and writes poems to Napoleon, needs to be restrained.

BYRON: My amiable mathematician? She wants me put—

MAN: Yes.

BYRON: My Princess of Parallelograms? Send me to a mad-house?

MAN: To a sanatorium, in her care. That is correct.

BYRON: Well, you're the one who's crazy. You know damn well she can't. I'll shoot my pistols as I please, look at my baby any way I wish, and talk to Napoleon all night long, if I want to! What are you going to do about it? (*He fires his pistol at the wall*)

MAN: I freely admit no hard case for insanity. We had hoped for voluntary cooperation.

BYRON: *Voluntary* cooperation? What for?

MAN: To more easily effect, my Lord, the separation.

BYRON: You son of a bitch. What separation?

The Man steps back. He is joined quickly by the Young Man and the Boy, who carries a legal document.

MAN: We must inform you that Lady Byron and her child—

BYRON (*Roaring*): *Our* child!

MAN: —will never return to you. She is adamant. If you will not admit your behavior intolerable, if pistols, wings and Napoleon are not enough for you, then graver matters may very well be employed.

BYRON: What graver matters?

BOY: Your sexual intercourse with other men is the behavior of a criminal or a lunatic.

YOUNG MAN: Your sexual intercourse with your sister is the behavior of a criminal or a lunatic.

MAN: Your act of sodomy upon your innocent and trusting wife is the behavior of a criminal or a lunatic.

BYRON (*Astonished*): She will accuse me of that?

MAN: All that.

BYRON: Homosexuality, incest, sodomy. Is that all?

YOUNG MAN: As far as we know, my Lord, it is.

BYRON: Little Pip. She tries to prove her loving Lord is mad, but since he has some lucid intermissions, she next decides that he is only bad—

MAN: This issue is no rhyme!

BYRON: And no crime! Our bedroom door was shut! She has no proof for her slander. You have no grounds for your action. Take me to court and see. I will sign no separation.

He turns away from them. The women have been whispering with Ada.

GIRL: Did he? Oh, no. How sad.

YOUNG WOMAN: Oh, my. Unbelievable.

WOMAN: What else?

ADA: Do not ask me to speak further against him. He is the father of my child.

GIRL: Of course.

YOUNG WOMAN: We understand.

WOMAN: Say no more.

ADA: Except this. In the honest trust our union would help him, I endured his rage, guilt, and blasphemy. I discovered there is a place in every woman's heart reserved not for her husband, but for her dearest, most precious sense of herself. When he put himself there, like Almighty God, and said, worship me, I left him, and I will never return.

WOMAN: What strength.

YOUNG WOMAN: What power.

GIRL: What beauty.

BYRON: What cant! (*Pause*) Bell. Don't.

ADA: I will.

MAN: Attend, my Lord, to the business at hand.

YOUNG MAN: This separation must certainly be signed—

BOY: In some amiable arrangement—

YOUNG MAN: Or the name of Byron—child, wife and husband—

BYRON: Bell. Listen to me. This is a great mistake. We can do better than this. Forgive my rhymes. Forgive my rage. I speak calmly now, and plainly. We cannot change our nature. I am warped. That is true. I beg your pardon. But so are you. As much, perhaps, as I. Your lawyers speak of an amiable arrangement. I want the most amiable of all arrangements. I want to be reconciled with my wife. I want to be forgiven where I have offended, and where I may have cause, freely, freely forgive. Bell, come back. I will sign no separation!

ADA: Your heart is a battlefield where I have no gun. Your words are ropes in which I will always be bound. Your soul is a wasteland where I will surely perish. Do you think I will ever bow this head to you again? Do you think I will ever again suffer your idle, careless, puerile, adolescent abuse of my person? Take your pistols and your brandy and your women and play with them in hell, where you belong, and leave me alone! I am a free and powerful woman, and you will feel me, Byron, as *I* felt *you*!

Pause.

BYRON: I see.

MAN: Will you sign?

BYRON: When do I see the child? Bell?

ADA: Never.

BYRON: Never?

ADA: Do you think I will let you take my baby away from me? *I* had her! Never!

GIRL: What did you expect?

WOMAN: She is a mother now. Not a toy.

YOUNG WOMAN: A child's life, in your hands? Impossible!

BYRON: She's my daughter!

MAN: Action against that has already been taken. Your child is a ward of the court. You have no recourse.

YOUNG MAN: Sign for the separation, my Lord.

BOY: Or everything will be published against you.

GIRL: It is your scandal, not ours.

YOUNG WOMAN: You have danced on your crooked foot.

WOMAN: And treated us all shamefully. Now pay the piper.

YOUNG MAN: Your position is impossible.

BOY: In public, no one will speak to you.

YOUNG MAN: Sign.

MAN: Or your good name—such as it is—will be forever dishonored.

BYRON: Bell?

ADA: Never.

ALL (*In unison*): Sign!!

Pause. A chair has been brought to the center of the stage. Byron sits, and thinks. The others stand around him erect and furious. Ada stands opposite him, alone. Byron looks at them all.

BYRON: So. I have committed some sin against you all, so elemental none of us knows what it is. Come now. Why do you hate me so? Because of my boy feelings, which I will not kill within me, and the sweet dreams they bring? For the foolish love of my foolish sister, and in her face and body, the sad family I inherit from God, and will not disown? For my physical bestiality, which, given the in-

credible phallus your gossip has bestowed upon me, not
only would damage my wife's pride, but split her rectum
up to her palate? How do I threaten you? With verse? My
stanzas will overthrow the Church? My rhymes will bring
down Parliament? I am only another guilt-ridden writer,
returning every night like a dog to brandy, verse, and the
vomit of memory, to make my music from it: what has
that to do with you? Because I am rich? I owe my creditors
thirty thousand pounds! Because I am a dandy? Any one of
you can enter a British drawing room gracefully. I must
bobble in, like a cork. Because I am a Peer of the Realm? I
was born to squalor, and you know it. To your great noble
family you must admit me, you have no choice, but
around the accident of my title, you hold your noses.
Because I am both obvious and overpraised, and you can
forgive anything but that? Or, finally, is the cause too
simple ever to be discovered? (*Pause*)

Why, whatever the reason, you monumental gentlemen who tell lies about me and beat your own wives, you
regal bitches who invite me one day into your bodies and
into a social slaughterhouse the next, you are shameless
frauds—*I* blush for *you*—you are priests without religion,
you are saints without morals—you defy burlesque!

(*Passionately*) You are the canker and the worm! You
are the death of the heart! And you will never, ever admit
that you are also, at the bottom of your souls, man and
woman, every last one of you, the same poor *animal* I am:
the slave of your unfound love, as I am the slave of mine!
(*Pause*)

Bell! Still do I cling to the wreck of my hopes, before it
sinks forever. Were you never happy with me? You were.
Did no affection pass between us? It did. We can have our
place in life together. We should. We will. Leave these

people. Say but one word, and I will come to you this moment, and buckle you, Kate, against a million!

ADA: You would quote *The Taming of the Shrew*. My attorneys will speak for me and for our child. As for your sister, she has agreed to tell me not only if you try to communicate with her, but what you say. In your own world, you are cut dead. I am vindicated. I am restored. I am not Miss Milbanke now. I am Lady Byron, and you no longer exist.

MAN: Sign the separation, and be silent.

GIRL: We are sick and tired of you.

YOUNG MAN: Of your poses—

BOY: And your rages—

YOUNG WOMAN: Of your limp—

WOMAN: And your scandals.

MAN (*Enraged*): Do the decent thing for once, man, and sign!

BYRON: All the women in the world, and I marry a moral Clytemnestra. To hell with her. Sign? Why not?

He sits and the lawyers gather around him, with document and pen. He starts to sign, then stops, thinks. Change of light. Short piece of music. The others freeze.

Is thy face like thy mother's, my fair child?
I see thee not, I hear thee not, yet none
Can be so wrapt in thee: thou art the friend
To whom the shadows of far years extend.

Ada, as herself, takes off part of her mother's clothes, and moves to her chair.

ADA: Oh, no I'm not! If you really care about your daughter, you won't leave her. You won't sign.

BYRON: What else can I do? No one in London will speak to me. Even my sister tells me to go.

ADA: Me! Never mind your sister! Me!

BYRON: You are a ward of the court of England! They are taking you from me! Can't you understand that?

ADA: No excuse, hero. I am your child. You could fight for me. You will fight in Greece, why not in England?

BYRON (*Stung*): And will you, my darling, fight in England, ever? When you are faced with their lethal stares and bitter tongues and the everlasting rhetoric of English accusation, what will you do? What you're told, I think we said. England was my home. They knew how to hurt me. How can you demand of your father what you were afraid of yourself?

ADA: Sign it then.

Byron does. A change of light. Ada sits in her chair again, watching Byron, but becoming again the severe, ill daughter. Byron turns to face his former friends and worshipers, now all deadly.

MAN: Goodbye, Lord Byron. Enjoy Switzerland. Enjoy Italy.

YOUNG MAN: Enjoy your paper and your ink.

YOUNG WOMAN: Enjoy your brandy and your gin.

BOY: Enjoy your gondolas and your canals.

WOMAN: Enjoy your pimps and your whores.

Byron moves away from them, proudly and with contempt, but hurt nevertheless. He goes to the table and pours wine into the skull cup.

MAN (*Very quiet and very bitter*): You detestable traitor.

YOUNG MAN: Who betrayed your honor and your privilege.

YOUNG WOMAN: And then dared to joke about it.

BOY: We will have no more of you.

GIRL: We are ashamed of you.
WOMAN: Trivial man.

One by one, they exit.

YOUNG MAN: Never come back.
GIRL: Write your poems.
BOY: Drink yourself to death—
YOUNG WOMAN: Laugh at your country—
WOMAN: Do what you please, but never again—
MAN: Show your face in England.

Exeunt. Byron drinks.

ADA: Exile.
BYRON: Exile.
ADA: What did you write first?
BYRON: Nothing serious. (*Remembers*) Oh. (*Smiles, and thinks of England*)

So we'll go no more a roving,
So late into the night,
Though the heart be still as loving,
And the moon be still as bright.

(*Looking at Ada, he is not so jaunty with the second verse*)

For the sword outwears its sheath,
And the soul wears out the breast,
And the heart must pause to breathe,
And love itself have rest.

ADA (*Breaking the spell.*): Oh God, yes. That. Famous ditty. (*She looks at her notes*) Written, it says here, after you'd exhausted yourself in a week straight of Italian orgies. No wonder you couldn't go no more a roving. Italy. Land of self-indulgence and self-forgiveness. How dull. Why did you go there?

BYRON: Well, the women in Italy kiss better than anywhere else, you see. It is attributed to early habits of osculation induced by rings of Popes and feet of sacred statues, et cetera, et cetera. Now, what about you?

ADA: Me?

BYRON: Yes, you! It's time! I want to know about you!

ADA: Not yet. Look.

Enter Girl, as Teresa Guiccioli, beautifully dressed, with a glass of wine. Music.

BYRON: Oh. Well, I did settle down, finally. With her.

ADA: An Italian countess. (*She consults her notes*) Tempestuous and stupid, given to uttering loud death cries in orgasm. Was she as ridiculous as everyone says she was?

Byron looks fondly at the Girl.

BYRON: There was nothing ridiculous about her orgasms, believe me. Someday everyone will have them, and the world will be saved. She was nineteen when I met her, married to an old man. Not beautiful, but passionate, as I remember my mother. Silly, but loving, as I recall my sister.

ADA: The old folks at home.

BYRON: For seven years. We grew fat together, tame.

He holds up the wine cup. They toast each other.

Amico Amante in Eterno!

GIRL: Amico Amante in Eterno!

They blow kisses to each other. Exit Girl.

BYRON: That's what we called each other. You want to say
something?

ADA: I want to throw up. Romantic atmosphere notwithstand-
ing, answer me this: did you or did you not leave her, too?

BYRON: Yes, but—

ADA: Did you or did you not leave all the *other* women you had
in Italy?

BYRON: Yes, but—

ADA: Did you or did you not leave the woman who gave you
another child—another *me* if you will—

BYRON: Yes, but—

ADA: And that child did you or did you not put away, at the age
of five, in a convent, where she *died*, of neglect? Yes-but
me *that!*

Pause. Byron, head bowed, is silent.

Christ. You are the most selfish man who ever lived. You
deserted everyone, betrayed everyone— (*Pause*) I think
I've had enough of you, too. It's time for you to go.

BYRON (*Quietly*): No, wait.

ADA: Why?

BYRON: You want the truth, I believe? For your solution, to me?

Ada waits. Byron moves closer to her.

I did leave her. And Italy. But there was a reason.

ADA: Certainly. Like me, like everyone else, she bored you.

103

BYRON: No. I saw something. A shape, a form.

Byron sits closer to Ada, with his skull cup of wine. He pours some wine in a glass and gives it to her, and she takes it. Talking to his daughter, he becomes very compelling: ironic, truthful, and seductive. In spite of herself, Ada is slowly drawn to him, and they create together a sudden intimacy.

I lived with my countess and her husband, for a while. That is the custom in Italy. You become a cavaliere servente. Rhymes with plenty. A flatterer of tenors, a fan-carrier of dowagers, an expert in the arrangement of shawls and lace. It was life as it really is: the opera. Five notes of pleasure, one scene of hysteria, and four acts of boredom. The count left his countess. I remained, stead-fast. Shelley came, with his hopeless poems, his radical self-righteousness, and his talented wife he constantly dreamed about choking. Visions of dead babies in the foam of the sea, huge breasts turning into eyes, staring at him. Shelley's wife brought along her younger sister, who climbed in bed with me—and, I suspect, with Shelley—until finally she could say, like her sister, she'd also had a baby by a poet. Which poet? I couldn't tell. The baby was beautiful, like me, crazy like Shelley, and nobody knew. I took her in, at their request. A little girl, like you. I fed her cake. (*He drinks*)

Shelley was a good critic. We read our poems to each other, talked the candles down, rode with our women through the forests, by the lakes. I began—with great pleasure—*Don Juan*—

ADA (*Smiling in spite of herself*): Your new one, your true one—

BYRON: Which everyone insisted I stop writing because it was obscene. It was only funny. (*He drinks*)

Our little natural baby died in the convent school where I put her, to grow up as she should, with other children, and her mother accused me of murder, Shelley had fits. She died of a fever, asking a nun for a piece of cake. (*He drinks*)

I wasn't Childe Harold anymore. I got fat again. My skin turned sallow. My teeth came loose. My curls went limp. On hotel registers, where it said Age—

ADA: You wrote, one hundred.

BYRON: The form, the shape began to emerge. My life—I saw it plainly—what a mess. A man's soul, *parboiled* by his youth. (*He looks at the wine in the skull cup*)

Like poor Shelley's brains in the cauldron of his skull, seething, bubbling, boiling there, when we dug him out of the sand of an Italian beach, and cremated him in a tin oven, making a ceremony out of a suicide, which is what he was. And what I would be, too. (*Pause*)

The shape of his life, and mine. Complete. But how to do it? I had always been the great swimmer, so it would really be too embarrassing to drown, like Shelley. Or put a bullet in my head, since I had pointed so many pistols so many times elsewhere. But there it was, like a ship in the fog, waiting to take me—where? (*He puts down the skull cup*)

I began to diet again. Make up verses. Rhyme again. I wrote *The Deformed Transformed.*

ADA: A play about a suicidal boy, redeemed by death in battle.

BYRON: Yes. Then, suddenly, out it came, in a jingle. "When a man hath no freedom to fight for at home—"

ADA: "Let him combat for that of his neighbors. Let him think of the glories of Greece and of Rome—"

BYRON: "And get knocked on his head for his labors." Yes. And there it was. The ship in the fog. The return to Greece. And there I was.

ADA: Fat, philosophical, faithful, retired, rich, and suicidal. Some Don Juan.

BYRON: Don Juan. If I'd finished him, he'd have died a miser, which I was becoming, and a Methodist, which is next.

ADA (*Smiling*): A miser and a Methodist? You?

BYRON: It is called poetic justice.

ADA: But you didn't die a Methodist, did you?

BYRON: No.

ADA: Or a suicide.

BYRON: Not exactly.

ADA: And you went to Greece. You weren't a miser there.

BYRON: No.

ADA: Because of Byron, Greece is free. That's what peasants say now, on Mount Olympus.

BYRON: Is it, really?

ADA: Yes. (*Pause*) Suppose you hadn't gone to Greece. Suppose you'd come home. You would be an old man now. I would go to see you twice a month. I would take you magnesia and tooth powder. Vinegar and greens, for your diet. Paper, ink, and gin.

BYRON: Yes.

ADA: There we'd be, father and daughter. I would put you to bed, tuck you in, kiss you on the cheek, and then, no doubt, like the vampires you wrote about, sink my teeth into your throat—

BYRON: Suck my blood—

ADA: And spit it into your face.

BYRON: Yes.

Pause. Suddenly Ada throws herself into Byron's arms. She embraces him fiercely. She weeps.

Hush.

They hold each other. Then, just as suddenly, just as fiercely, Ada tears herself away from him. They stand apart, trembling. She dries her eyes with a handkerchief.

ADA (*Coldly*): I beg your pardon.

Byron smiles.

BYRON: And how is your mother?

Pause. Then Ada also smiles.

ADA: Oh, thriving, thriving. England adores her. (*She laughs*) My God. You for a father, a British Saint for a mother. Her greed for virtue and dominion is worse than yours for sluts and gin.

BYRON: Or yours for engines that think?

ADA: Yes. She's forgiven me that, finally. She even reads my book.

BYRON: Your *what?*

ADA: I didn't mean to tell you. I wrote one.

BYRON: You?

ADA: Nothing glamorous. Not very long.

She takes a slim volume from her table and hands it to Byron. He opens it eagerly, and becomes immediately absorbed. Ada looks away, then, in spite of herself, watches him read.

Nothing to do with war, or love affairs.

Byron reads, fascinated.

Just a poor old impossible engine that thinks.

Byron reads.

Of little interest to a layman. Or a poet.

Byron reads.

You won't like it.

BYRON (*Reading aloud, slowly*): "For mathematical truth is that superb language through which alone we may adequately express the great facts of the natural world, and what is written there." (*He looks at Ada*) You wrote that?

ADA: You don't find it passionate? Not poetic enough?

BYRON (*Reading aloud*): "This language alone, spoken by a great engine, may finally trace among the agencies of our creation, the unceasing changes of mutual relationship, far too complicated for the human mind."

ADA: That's enough! Give it back!

She reaches for it. Byron pulls away.

BYRON (*Reading aloud*): "And while such an engine can never create the eternal conditions of human being, it can return to us the truth we forget."

ADA: Stop! My mother thinks it absurd. I suppose you do, too.

BYRON: Ada, what happened to you?

ADA: I got sick, that's what happened to me!

BYRON: Before that.

ADA: What do you care?

BYRON: Oh, darling Ada—

ADA: Darling Ada? Ada, darling? Am I to be your little angel now? Your precious heart, sitting on Daddy's lap? Whatever the reasons, you left me! To my mother! I could have killed her a thousand times! Any kind of life, anywhere else, would have been better! (*Ferociously*) Ah! I hate my mother! I hate my—

Long pause. Ada stares at Byron, and shudders.

You. Get away from me.

BYRON: What's the matter?

ADA: There I was, in your arms. Wanting to kiss you. Wondering what you thought of my *book*!

BYRON: Ada—

ADA: Hating my mother and loving you? My God, you are a vampire, after blood.

BYRON: Ada, listen to me!

She grabs his sword and points it at him.

ADA (*Fiercely*): Don't touch me! You've made your conquest! You've *had* me!

BYRON (*Surprised at her vehemence*): What's the matter with you? All I did was look at your book. What's wrong with that?

ADA: Everything!

BYRON: Look here. (*He picks up the copy of* Childe Harold *and puts the two books together, to Ada's horror*) Don't you see—

ADA: No, no—

BYRON: How much alike they are? They even sound alike.

ADA: They don't!

BYRON (*Holding out her book*): You: "the language through which alone we may express the great facts of the natural world."

ADA: Stop!

BYRON (*Holding out his*): And me:

Though dull Hate as duty
Should be taught,
Though my name
Should be shut from thee
As a spell—

He pushes the blade of the sword aside and she drops it.

Both great facts of the natural world.

ADA: Put them down! Put them down! (*She knocks both books from his hands*) Poet! Liar!

Byron seizes her, holds her.

BYRON: Ada, it's time! I want to know what happened to you!
ADA: Nothing! Go away!
BYRON: Ada, I command you—

Ada breaks away from him.

ADA: You? Command me? You don't even exist! You are a dead man I have pulled out of his grave! You are dust and ashes! And I don't give a damn what you did with your life! You can take your silly poems and *swim* to Greece!
BYRON: Tell me what happened to you!
ADA: Achilles!
BYRON: Ada—
ADA: Napoleon!
BYRON: Ada!
ADA: *Cripple*!
BYRON: Bitch!
ADA: Bastard!

Ada takes a glass from her table and throws water in his face.

BYRON: I wish to God you had never been born!

ADA: So do I!

Ada stares at Byron, moves back. She puts her hands to her stomach. She groans.

Ah. Ah.

She coughs, puts a handkerchief to her mouth. Blood. She looks at Byron.

Papa. Papa.

Byron moves toward her, reaches for her.

Ah, get away! God damn you! *Be gone!*

BYRON: I will not!

ADA: Oh, yes, you will. (*She goes to her table and rummages through her notes and books, finding this passage and that*) Here. I'll send you to Greece. I'll kill you, by God!

BYRON: Not before I find you out. Because that is what you want! Your father, finding you out! All right, he will! Here, this thing! A thinking machine. Logic. All right.

Byron picks up the model of the Analytical Engine.

ADA: Off you sailed to glorious war, with your bankbook and toadies, your doctors and crates of gin, and a boy—a boy!—so much for true love in Italy, Don Juan!

BYRON: You are confined in here, you said. Padded walls and locked doors. But you're not crazy. Why, then?

ADA: Greece free, because of you? Because of your money, you fake, because of your name, you fool!

111

BYRON: So what do you do, about a machine that doesn't exist? You build it!

ADA: And Greek rain turned your fields of glory into stagnant mud! The only battles you ever fought were with your own soldiers, over paychecks!

BYRON: That's what you'd do, build it! But you'd need a fortune.

ADA: And you rode out into the rain with your pistols and your sword, and you came back with fever!

BYRON: Did you lose all your money? And then some?

ADA: And you died in bed, soldier! With your Italian-opera doctors sticking leeches on your head!

BYRON: You'd borrow, I know you! Try again! Go in debt! Gamble! You'd gamble!

ADA: Three pounds of blood out of you, three times a day. That's what killed you, hero! Your own doctors!

BYRON: The racetrack! That schedule! You gambled on the races!

ADA: And you begged at the end. "Let no one see my foot." Everyone did!

BYRON: To keep building the machine, you bet on the races and lost. How much? Everything?

ADA: "Publish my memoirs, the story of my life!" My mother had them burned!

BYRON: Scandal, was there a scandal? Of course there was!

ADA: "Leave my body in one piece." You were split open and pickled in alcohol!

BYRON: What did you do then, steal? You *stole*?

ADA: "Bury me in Greece!" You were shipped home, in a box!

BYRON: And if you weren't sick, Ada, would you be in jail?

ADA: Home to England, where Shelley is the great poet now, and you are an overrated balladmonger!

BYRON: Would you be in *prison*?

ADA: Yes, I would!! And they buried you, at last, in that filthy country church!

BYRON: And they buried you, in here!

ADA: Down there in the vault, with Mad Jack Byron, and all the rest of them!

BYRON: A madwoman yourself!

Ada tears wildly into her books and notes, throwing them to the floor.

ADA: And you're dead, that's the end, it's over!

BYRON: A criminal!

ADA: You're back in your grave, vampire!

BYRON: A disgrace, like me!

ADA: You're dead, and I have killed you, finally and forever, you're dead, dead, dead!!!

She sweeps all her notes and books off the table.

BYRON: And so are you!

ADA: Yes!

Ada sits in her chair, exhausted. Long pause.

BYRON: I see. (*He picks up Ada's book from the floor. He looks at it, then at her*) Your death, at least, will be free from me, as it should be. You have put the vampire in his tomb, with the family sword through his heart.

ADA: Yes, Father. I have.

BYRON: Good. I approve. (*He puts her book on her table*) And I must say, you became an astonishing creature.

ADA: Like you. (*Pause*) Like you.

BYRON: Yes, like me. (*He goes to her, slowly*) For my life, and what it did to you, my child, I beg your pardon.

ADA: Don't.

She holds out one hand. Byron takes it in both of his. He stares at his daughter.

Thank you for coming to see me.

BYRON: You are welcome.

He kisses her hand. He backs away, toward the window where he first appeared.

ADA: Wait. There is something I want to give you.

BYRON: What?

ADA: My answer.

BYRON: To me?

ADA: I have found it. The problem is solved. (*She takes up her will and her pen. She writes*) I, Augusta Ada, Countess of Lovelace—

BYRON:
Though to drain my blood
From out thy being
Were an aim and an attainment—

ADA: —do enjoin my dear mother, husband and children faithfully to execute this my last will and testament.

BYRON:
All would be in vain.
Though my name
Should be shut from thee—

ADA: My body is to be placed in no other place—no other place—but the vault containing the body of George Gordon, the Sixth Lord Byron—

BYRON:

Though the grave
Closed between us
'Twere the same—

ADA: Who perished bravely in Greece, restoring to that ancient country, and to his good name, their former glory and renown.

BYRON:

I know that thou wilt love me.

Ada puts down her will. Byron is now barely visible behind her.

ADA:

My father. With thy name this song began.
My father. With thy name this song shall end.

The lights fade.

I see thee not, I hear thee not, but none
Can be so wrapt in thee. I am the friend
To whom the shadows of far years extend.

Tennessee

For Janet Fish

Characters

HERSHEL
MARY, his wife
CARDELL, his son
THE OLD WOMAN
GRISWOLD PLANKMAN
NEIGHBOR

Time

1870.

Place

The Appalachian Mountains of North Carolina.

*The porch of a log house, facing us straight on. A young
woman in a homespun dress stands nursing a baby and
gazing out over the slopes. She sees someone, and waves.*

MARY: Whoo—oo!
VOICES (*Offstage*): Whoo—oo!

*Mary nurses her baby, sings to it. She makes a face, wincing
as the baby's gums pinch her nipple, then she smiles again.
Enter Hershel, her husband, and Cardell, her son, carrying
axes. They are hot and tired.*

MARY: Well, it's about time.
HERSHEL: We're here, ain't we?

*The men drop their axes, stretch, and go to a bucket sitting
on the porch. They reach in it and throw water on their
faces. Hershel mops his face with a kerchief. His son does
the same.*

MARY: Oh, goodness me. Just so tired and all wore out. I bet you
both been laying on the creek bank thinking about
supper.

119

HERSHEL: See Cardell, what you got to look forward to? You go out into the world. You get yourself some land, a house and a wife. Then you keep careful note of ever minute in the day, because you're going to account for ever damn one. Yes, ma'am. That's it. We been laying on the creek bank, counting clouds.

MARY: I ain't surprised.

HERSHEL: How about you? We going to watch you feed that baby all night, or do we get something to eat, too?

MARY: There might be something in the pot for you, if you don't ask for it too often. Ouch. Ow-ee! Baby, go easy on me! Ow!

HERSHEL: Eating you up, is he? Well, why not?

MARY: You'd know why not, you had him pulling on you. There now. Shoo. That's better. All right, supper's ready. Come on.

HERSHEL: Hold it. Take a seat.

MARY: What?

HERSHEL: Take a seat, I said. Cardell, you too. I want to sit here and watch the sun go down. Supper can wait.

MARY: I never heard you say that before. Cardell, what's wrong with your father?

CARDELL: I don't know. Feeling good, I reckon.

HERSHEL: That's it. I'm feeling good. Sit.

They sit in slat chairs. Hershel props his feet on a crate, fills a pipe. He is suddenly relaxed, expansive, thinking about something that is important to him. They sit for a while.

So tell your mother what we did today.

CARDELL: We girdled a stand of them tulip trees. I still say we didn't notch them deep enough, though.

HERSHEL: Oh, yes, we did. Just so the bark's cut through, they'll die. And come down dry wood. We'll have us a new porch and a whole new floor, with boards that won't warp. What about that, Mary?

MARY: That'll be all right.

HERSHEL: Yes, by God, it shore will. We're coming along. Four years a-groaning and sweating on another man's land, and now we got our own. This here is our estate, you know that? Be yours, Cardell, one day, if you want it. And the baby's. 'Cept it'll look different then. I aim to build out this porch half again as wide. How about that?

MARY: That'll be nice.

HERSHEL: I aim to cut into that brush yonder and add it to my slope field. Then we can look out over fifty damn acres. All of it cleared. All of it ours. How about that, by God?

MARY: Ain't you hungry, yet?

HERSHEL: Yeah, I'm hungry! Hungry for what's mine! And I got it, too! It cost me, but I got it.

MARY: Hush. Cost you what?

HERSHEL: The getting of it. Not so easy. Your son can tell you about that. He's commencing to want his own in this life. He's commencing to think on that, worry about it. He'll pay for it, just like I have. Yes, you will, Cardell. Son, you're getting about the age now where you and me are looking slantwise at each other. I notch a tulip tree, and you stand there thinking how much better you could do it yourself. That right?

CARDELL: I didn't mean nothing about them trees.

HERSHEL: The hell you didn't!

MARY: Hershel. Don't swear at the children.

HERSHEL: But that's all right, son. That's the way it ought to be. That's the way you'll get *your* estate. Pretty soon here, you'll get fed up with the way I do things. Turn red about to bust wanting them your own way. You'll say no, and I'll say yes, and I'll say yes, and you'll say no, and then you won't give a damn what I say. And that's the way it ought to be. That's good. When you can go, Cardell, you can go. Understand?

MARY: All right, wise grandpa. Enough of this. Supper's ready.

HERSHEL: Stay right where you are! Look at this estate! Drop a penny in that ground, and grow yourself half a dollar. North Carolina bottom land! Whoo-pee!

MARY: I declare, Hershel. What's got into you?

HERSHEL: Satisfaction's got into me! I'm taking time to think about it! House, land, a new baby, a son standing up to me like he should, a wife with sore tits but otherwise all right—

MARY: I certainly am glad I'm otherwise all right, Hershel. You took a big load off my mind.

HERSHEL: Yeah. I growed up crawling over a dirt floor in a shack, like a God damned ant. Going to work with my daddy, Cardell, for a man lived in a big white house on a hill. People up there in the shade, eternally fanning theirselves, and yelling at my old man, do this and fetch that, me getting hauled about and swore at. Then, when I got just big enough to tell my daddy, enough of this, having to go serve in the God damned Confederate Army. So I crawled some more and got hauled around and swore at some more. Ended up lying in a pine forest watching shells set them pines on fire. Men scared to death, running ever which way, and me, lying there waiting to fry like a piece of bacon, thinking, I'll never get out, never.

MARY: But you did.

HERSHEL: Yeah, I did.

A cowbell is heard, ringing not far away.

I ain't there no more. I'm where I dreamed I'd be, someday.

The cowbell is heard again.

On my estate, by God! I got it! And it's mine!

The cowbell rings again, closer.

MARY: Well, you can enjoy it on an empty stomach, if you have to keep on bragging. (*She points offstage*) Cardell, split me some more wood. I got to heat everything up again.
HERSHEL: Never mind, son. You just sit there and think about what you want in this life, too. I'll go get the damn wood. How about that?
MARY: Hershel, that will be right nice.

Exit Hershel in the yard, and Mary into the house. Cardell sits dreaming, thinking about his father. The cowbell is heard again, much closer. Cardell looks up. A light flashes in his face, making him blink. It plays about him, a strange reflection of the afternoon sun, jumping about. He covers his face, blinks. He shades his eyes, stands, and looks out into the brush. Enter the bent figure of an Old Woman. Her dress is ragged and torn. Her white hair, unbound, is stringy and wild. She carries a cowbell in one hand, ringing it. In the other hand, she carries a piece of shattered mirror glass, holding it up, reflecting the sunlight into Cardell's astonished eyes. She stares at Cardell.

OLD WOMAN: Didn't expect to see me. Did you?

CARDELL: Who're you?

OLD WOMAN: What?

CARDELL: I said, who are you?

OLD WOMAN: Where's everybody else? Where'd they go to?

CARDELL: What?

OLD WOMAN: Wait. Hold on. Let me figure something out. You're just a boy. Do you live here?

CARDELL: Yes, I do.

OLD WOMAN: Since when?

CARDELL: Since a year ago. My daddy bought this place a year ago.

OLD WOMAN: Who from?

CARDELL: Nobody. From the county, I think. There was some old man living here, but he died. He didn't have nobody to leave it to, so it was for sale.

OLD WOMAN: What was his name?

CARDELL: Larman.

OLD WOMAN: I know that. I mean his first name.

CARDELL: Abner, I think it was. Wait a minute, you can ask my daddy.

Exit Cardell, running. The Old Woman rings her cowbell. She looks at the house. She gazes into the piece of mirror. She laughs. She drops the piece of mirror on the ground. She looks at the house again, studies it. She rings her cowbell. Enter Mary, carrying the baby.

MARY: Listen now. Enough of this. Put that cowbell down and come on in to supper— (*She sees the Old Woman*) Oh.

OLD WOMAN: Well, I guess that's that.

She laughs. Enter Hershel, with wood, and Cardell with him.

HERSHEL: Don't get so excited, son. Where—

He sees the Old Woman. They stand staring at her. She chuckles and rings her bell, and stares right back at them.

OLD WOMAN: Heh, heh.
MARY: Hershel, say something to her.

Hershel puts down his load of wood, approaches her cautiously.

HERSHEL: How do you do?
OLD WOMAN: Hidy.
HERSHEL: What can we do for you?
OLD WOMAN: Nothing. You can't do nothing for me at all.
HERSHEL: Well, I'm sorry, then. Uh—
OLD WOMAN: This here your boy?
HERSHEL: Yes.
OLD WOMAN: He says you bought this place from a man named Abner Larman.
HERSHEL: I bought this house, and fifty acres, yes. But I bought it from the county. Mr. Larman died here all alone.
OLD WOMAN: All alone, you say? That figures. Fifty acres, you say?
HERSHEL: Right.
OLD WOMAN: You got cheated. There was over seventy.
HERSHEL: How do you know that?
OLD WOMAN: Never mind. It has been pleasant talking to you.

She rings her cowbell, and starts off.

MARY: Hershel, she's so old. It's getting dark, and she ain't got no light. She'll fall down. Ought'n we to do something?

HERSHEL: Yeah. Let me see. (*He catches up with her*) Ma'am! Just a minute!

OLD WOMAN: Yeah?

HERSHEL: Don't you want to come sit with us a minute? It's a piece from here to the roads. You live near here?

OLD WOMAN (*Laughing*): Oh, yes! I live near here. About seven miles, over the mountain. That's close.

HERSHEL: You got somebody waiting on you hereabouts?

OLD WOMAN: Nobody's waiting for me nowhere, mister.

MARY: Come sit with us, then.

HERSHEL: You look tired out.

OLD WOMAN: I do feel a mite puny.

Hershel leads the Old Woman up onto the porch, and seats her in his chair. She holds onto her cowbell.

HERSHEL: Like something to eat? Mary?

MARY: I got some spoonbread you might like.

OLD WOMAN: Sounds good. Got any tea?

MARY: I brew boneset tea. Want some of that?

OLD WOMAN: Boneset. I made it myself, once. Here. I'll help you. (*She tries to get up, but slips back in the chair*)

MARY: Stay right there. I'll bring it out to you. Cardell, take the baby, and come on with me.

Exit Mary, Cardell and the baby. The Old Woman smiles, nods, and rocks in the chair. Pause.

OLD WOMAN: So.

HERSHEL: You say you live seven miles from here?

OLD WOMAN (*Nodding and thinking*): In Tennessee.

HERSHEL: Oh. (*Pause*) You know, I thought the Tennessee border was a good eighty miles over the mountains there.

OLD WOMAN: So did I.

HERSHEL: You sure you live in Tennessee?

OLD WOMAN: That is the only thing in this world I am sure of, mister. I live in Tennessee, all right.

HERSHEL: No wonder you're tired, then, walking all the way from Tennessee.

OLD WOMAN: Only seven miles. (*Laughs*) Figure it out. I can't.

HERSHEL: Where'd you stay last night?

OLD WOMAN: Well, let me see. Oh, I found a stand of pines, and went in and lay down. Pulled the needles up around me. Dry, mostly. I was cold, but I slept. No, wait. That was the first night. Last night, there was this stream I knowed from a long time ago, it seemed. Comes down the mountain undercutting the rock. Sand underneath. Dry again. Slept there. Made me a gig out of a hickory stick. Had frog legs for breakfast.

HERSHEL: You're on a trip of some kind?

OLD WOMAN: That's right.

HERSHEL: Where you heading?

OLD WOMAN: Back to Tennessee, now.

HERSHEL: I mean, where were you heading?

OLD WOMAN: Here, mister. Right here.

Enter Mary, with a bowl of spoonbread, and a jug of tea.

MARY: You see if this don't do you some good.

OLD WOMAN: Nice people. Nice people.

She eats and drinks. Hershel and Mary move aside to talk. Cardell, holding the baby, comes onto the porch and watches the Old Woman.

MARY: Hershel, what are we going to do with her? She's too old just to let walk out into the night.

127

HERSHEL: I know. She can stay with us tonight.

MARY: You think she's a mite crazy?

HERSHEL: She's a mite something. I almost got her to say who she is and all, but not quite. She slept on the ground last night, and the night before that. She gigs frogs.

MARY: How old you think she is?

HERSHEL: Hard to say. I suspect she was a handsome woman once.

MARY: When Cardell seen her, he said she had some kind of a flashing thing in her hand.

HERSHEL: Flashing thing?

MARY: Said she was grinning at him, and it was like she was holding a star in one hand.

HERSHEL: She's something else, all right.

The Old Woman finishes her meal. She seems stronger.

OLD WOMAN: Listen, that was good. You ought not to boil the boneset so much, but it was good anyhow.

MARY: I'm glad you liked it.

HERSHEL: You feel better?

OLD WOMAN: Well, of course. I had me a good meal, on this porch. Sure I feel better.

HERSHEL: Did you tell me awhile ago that you were coming here, to this house? All the way from Tennessee?

OLD WOMAN: That's what I said. I see you put in new post beams. Some of this flooring is all different. Not much of a job, though. You do it?

HERSHEL: Did the beams, not the flooring. I reckon Abner Larman did that.

OLD WOMAN: No. Ab wouldn't bother. It must have been Billy. I suppose he's dead, too.

HERSHEL: Billy?

OLD WOMAN: Poppa's joy. He was always the one. It would have been him. He put the first floor in with Poppa, when we built this place. Ab cared about the farm, not the house. And I guess lasted longest, died last of all, in the house. Well, all except me. You know, mister, this here estate of yours, it ain't rightfully yours at all. It's mine.

HERSHEL: What? I got the deed, lady!

OLD WOMAN: Look at him jump. Men. Fuss and fume. Think everybody wants what you got. Sit still, I ain't no bandit. You're welcome to it, this here estate of yours.

HERSHEL: God damn right it's mine.

MARY: Hershel.

OLD WOMAN: Men. How old you think I am? Come on. Guess.

MARY: We were wondering. I can't tell. Sometimes you look right young.

OLD WOMAN: Nice people. Sometimes a pea will shrink so tight it's smooth. I'm the same age as my tongue, and a little older than my teeth. Comfort me. Guess. Mister?

HERSHEL: Sixty-five?

OLD WOMAN: I'll never see that again. Way off. Son?

CARDELL: Two hundred.

OLD WOMAN: Whoa now. Don't kill me. I got a little time left. (*To Mary*) How about you?

MARY: I would say you are either nineteen or ninety.

OLD WOMAN: Nineteen or ninety! That's comfort. You hit it. Nineteen or ninety. That's me! Yes, sir. (*She steps off the porch. She stands in the yard, facing out, speaking to the family on the porch directly behind her*) When I was nineteen. I stood right here. Right where I'm standing now. And I wasn't no shriveled-up pea then. I was a choice item. The best-looking woman in these mountains. And the meanest. Mean and proud. Damn men. I didn't like 'em. Said so. Drove Momma crazy. You're wild, she said.

Settle down. Like you? I said. Marry when you're a child.
Work and slave for men who don't care one spit what you
think or how you feel. Who never listen. Don't talk like
that, Momma said, but I did. I give men hell. They'd
come, and I'd spit, and they'd go. You didn't like it, either.
You, you up there. You didn't. (*She is speaking to the
family without looking at them, as if, now, they are her
own*) Ab and Billy. Rachel and Poppa. Momma. You don't
know what to do, do you? You just sit there, shake your
heads. Watch me fight. Damn men. (*She stands straighter.
She strokes her white hair*) Heavy-footed, tongue-tied,
bug-eyed horsefaces, coming here looking for a slave.
Wanting to lie on top of me one minute, and work me to
death the next. And take me away from you. And you
hoping one of them would. Clucking your tongues, saying,
"Lands sakes, what will become of her, treating men like
this." Wanting me to go. Well, I won't! I won't leave this
house, and you, to be plowed under like dirt by some
sweating, groaning, boneheaded man! Hell, no! (*She
stares offstage. She sees someone coming*) And then, he
came by. Griswold Plankman, the joke of the world. He
came my way.

Enter Griswold.

GRISWOLD (*Slowly*): Mr. Larman. Mrs. Larman. Billy. (*Pause*)
Miss Larman.
OLD WOMAN: Hello, Griswold. You out of debt yet?
GRISWOLD: Well—
OLD WOMAN: You going to say: getting there, getting there.
GRISWOLD: Well—
OLD WOMAN: And what fine land it is, all eight acres of it.

GRISWOLD: Well—

OLD WOMAN: Now if I wait here a few days, you'll wonder how come I know so much about you. I know enough, Griswold Plankman. You're too poor to paint, and too proud to whitewash.

GRISWOLD: Well—

OLD WOMAN: I'd sure like to buy you for what you're worth, and sell you for what you think you're worth. I can look right through you, and a little piece on the other side.

GRISWOLD: Well—

OLD WOMAN: Get it straight, Griswold. We are as different as cheese from chalk. To speak plainly, as far as I am concerned, you are as ugly as homemade sin, and as welcome here as the bastard at the family reunion.

Griswold smiles and shakes his head.

GRISWOLD: You know what made the river angry? It got crossed so many times. (*He laughs*)

OLD WOMAN: Huh?

GRISWOLD: You know why lightning shocks people? It don't know how to conduct itself. (*He laughs*)

OLD WOMAN: Oh, my God.

GRISWOLD: When is a door not a door? When it's ajar. (*He laughs*)

OLD WOMAN: Man, this is pitiful. Will you just shut up?

GRISWOLD: Why is a pig the strangest of all animals?

OLD WOMAN: I don't know, Griswold! I don't care!

GRISWOLD: Because a pig gets killed before he gets cured.

OLD WOMAN: I wouldn't have you, man, off a Christmas tree! Go home!

GRISWOLD: Know why life is the hardest riddle?

OLD WOMAN: Home!

GRISWOLD: Everybody has to give it up. (*Pause*) What is this I hear about you wanting to be took to Tennessee?

Pause.

OLD WOMAN: Who told you that?

GRISWOLD: Hensley Edwards.

OLD WOMAN: Hensley Edwards is a fool.

GRISWOLD: I know that. But you told him the only man you'd marry was the man who would sell his farm and take you all the way to Tennessee. How come you want to go to Tennessee?

OLD WOMAN: Never you mind.

GRISWOLD: But you did say it?

OLD WOMAN: All right. I said it. It's my word, and I mean it.

GRISWOLD: Long trip. Awful hard country. Eighty-odd mile, here to the Tennessee border. Just mountains. How come you want a man to take you there?

OLD WOMAN: Griswold, stop going around your elbow to get to your thumb. What business is it of yours?

GRISWOLD: This. Come with me. I will take you there.

OLD WOMAN: What?

GRISWOLD: I will sell my land, and take you to Tennessee.

OLD WOMAN: Griswold, you don't know what you're saying. You ain't got the sense God promised a billy goat.

GRISWOLD: If you think marriage is necessary, all right. If not, all right.

OLD WOMAN: You think I'm fool enough to go somewhere with a man, and *not* be married to him?

GRISWOLD: Then we can get married.

OLD WOMAN: Oh, Griswold. You are so green, when it rains, you'll sprout.

GRISWOLD: I'm taking you at your word. You're the one who said the thing.

OLD WOMAN: And what's wrong with my word? It's just as good as any damn man's. But that don't mean you get to put your shoes under my bed.

GRISWOLD: You want to go to Tennessee. I will take you there. I'm not asking you why. No questions. Hard country. Dangerous and powerful lonely. No dances, no parties. And I give up my bottom land. But if that is what you want, we'll go. Think it over.

Exit Griswold. The Old Woman speaks to the family.

OLD WOMAN: Oh, hell. I didn't care nothing about no Tennessee. I only said that to keep off that fool Hensley Edwards. Cross all them mountains? Great God Almighty. But I did say it. My word. Well, I'm safe enough. Not even Griswold Plankman is dumb enough to sell off North Carolina bottom land and go farm a wild Tennessee mountain. (*Pause*) Yes. I know. You want me gone. Have done with this eternal squabbling over men. Well, I won't. I won't go!

HERSHEL (*Very softly*): But you said you would. You'd marry the man who'd take you to Tennessee.

OLD WOMAN: And I will! No man's idiot enough to do that, never mind try to marry me.

Enter Griswold. He puts some flowers in her hands. He turns her gently but firmly so she stands beside him, facing out. Pause.

Well, go ahead and say it.

HERSHEL: I now pronounce you man and wife.

OLD WOMAN: God damn.

GRISWOLD: I'll put your boxes in the wagon. Say goodbye.

Griswold stacks several wooden boxes together, making a sort of wagon seat.

TENNESSEE

OLD WOMAN: Well, Poppa. Billy, Ab. Rachel. Momma. There's more to say. I don't know about Tennessee.

HERSHEL: You will get there all right.

OLD WOMAN: Yes, I know. But it seems like there was something else I had to say. Listen—

GRISWOLD: Honey, it's time.

He takes her to the wagon seat, sits her there. He sits beside her, flicks imaginary reins.

OLD WOMAN: Poppa!

She resigns herself. They travel. Pause. They travel.

Can't you drive this thing no faster than this?

GRISWOLD: In a hurry, are you?

OLD WOMAN: I'd like to get to Tennessee before I die. Who sold you this wagon? Did you look at it at all before you bought it? Don't expect me to fix it when it breaks down. When are we going to stop, and spend the night?

GRISWOLD: Anytime.

OLD WOMAN: What do you mean, anytime? Griswold, where are we going to spend our wedding night?

GRISWOLD: Right here.

OLD WOMAN: You mean *in the wagon?*

GRISWOLD: I don't mean no boarding house.

OLD WOMAN: Oh, God. I've married a miser. Go through the thicket, then pick a crooked stick. He's so tight, when he walks, he'll squeak.

GRISWOLD: I don't want to be shut up in a tiny little room, with neighbors, and a good-looking bride like you. I figure we'll want to make some noise about it.

134

OLD WOMAN: Oh, you do, do you? You God damn man! You coarse, dumb, stupid, God damn man! You wouldn't give a lady air in a jug! I'm going home! They should have buried you, Griswold, and raised the afterbirth!

She starts to get out of the wagon. He grabs her, and holds her.

GRISWOLD: And you are as hot as a hen in a wool blanket.
OLD WOMAN: *What?*

She beats at Griswold with her fists. There is a considerable scuffle.

Man! Man! God damn man!

He holds her until she is tired, and a little frightened.

All right. You can let go of me now.
GRISWOLD: Honey, I ain't never letting you go. How about that?
OLD WOMAN: It is what's happened to me. I confess it, Lord save me. Let go, I won't hit you again.
GRISWOLD: You can if you want to. I think I like it.
OLD WOMAN: Stop! Wait! Stop the wagon!
GRISWOLD: Now what? You aim to run off again?
OLD WOMAN: No, you fool. We knocked over a box. It fell off in the road. Stop the wagon, and I'll go get it.
GRISWOLD: All right. Don't run off.
OLD WOMAN: Just shut up about that, and will you stop the wagon?

He stops the wagon. The Old Woman gets down and stoops over an imaginary box, fallen from the wagon, and broken open.

GRISWOLD: Yours or mine?

OLD WOMAN: Mine. My box of dressing things. Oh, Lord, look here. My mirror's busted. (*She picks up a piece of shattered glass. It is the piece she herself brought with her and dropped. She holds it now in one hand, looking into it sorrowfully*) My mirror. My good mirror. Busted. Oh, me.

Griswold puts the imaginary box back onto the wagon.

GRISWOLD: Come on, honey. You ain't going to need many mirrors in Tennessee.

OLD WOMAN: Oh, me.

GRISWOLD: All right, I'll get you another one, somewhere. Now, come on.

OLD WOMAN: Just wait a minute! My hair's messed up.

GRISWOLD: It wouldn't be noticed on a galloping horse.

OLD WOMAN: Just wait one damn minute!

GRISWOLD: All right! A minute!

The Old Woman holds the mirror, looking about for a place to prop it, so she can look into it with her hands free.

Stick it in the burl of that tree there.

OLD WOMAN: What?

Griswold takes the mirror and sticks it into a burl on the tree stump in the yard, or into one of the logs Hershel brought on and set down. The Old Woman kneels before it, touching up her hair. Griswold gets back into the wagon. The Old Woman does too, looking back at the mirror in the wood.

Look at it shine in the sun. Like a star in the daytime. Well, goodbye. Let's go, Griswold.

They travel. Time passes. They travel. Griswold is placid.
The Old Woman gets more and more oppressed. She looks
about, frightened. She holds it in. She can't stand it. She lets
it out.

Yiiiiiiiii!

GRISWOLD: What's the matter?

OLD WOMAN: Mountains. Nothing but mountains. My Lord.
Nobody nowhere. No cleared land. Nothing. Just mountains.

GRISWOLD: And more to come. It's eighty miles to the Tennessee border, up and down. You should have thought about
that.

OLD WOMAN: If I had, I might not be no Mrs. Plankman.

GRISWOLD: That's possible.

OLD WOMAN: Oh, me.

GRISWOLD (*Pointing*): Sourwood. That gold is birch poplar.

OLD WOMAN: Don't nobody live in these mountains at all?

GRISWOLD: Not many now. Maybe some later, but not so
many. It's wild up here. Steep. Worse in Tennessee. Not
much water on the slopes. You got to look hard for decent
land. But come fall, when the slopes turn, Tennessee is
beautiful. Like a big fire a-burning, all your own. Red and
orange and silver leaves, too, and gold and green, and God
knows what all.

OLD WOMAN: Oh, shut up, Griswold. You ain't never been to
Tennessee, no more than I have. What do you know about
it?

GRISWOLD: Let's say I understand the nature of Tennessee.
I've heard people talk about it. I've thought about it. A lot.

OLD WOMAN: You're crazy.

GRISWOLD: Maybe.

They travel. The Old Woman looks about, more and more frightened. She squirms, holds her hands in front of her eyes. She explodes again.

OLD WOMAN: Yiiiiiiii!!

GRISWOLD: Now what?

OLD WOMAN: How long is this going to last? I can't stand it no more! We been on these God-forsaken trails past six weeks now. Ain't we done eighty miles yet? When are we going to get there?

GRISWOLD: Eighty miles, but up and down. Mountains. Yes, it's a hell of a trip we're taking, you and me. A long ways from your momma and daddy's house. Wilderness. But not so long now. Pretty soon.

OLD WOMAN: Better be pretty soon. (*Pause*) You know why?

GRISWOLD: Why?

OLD WOMAN: Guess.

GRISWOLD: Just tell me.

OLD WOMAN: You best get me there sometime inside the next eight months. I just say that.

GRISWOLD: Well, hoo-pee! Then I sure will. We ain't wasted the time, have we?

OLD WOMAN: Part way to Tennessee, and a baby already. Oh, me.

GRISWOLD (*Happy*): Yeah.

He whistles. They travel, they travel. Then, looking about, Griswold stops the wagon.

OLD WOMAN: Well, what now?

GRISWOLD: We're in Tennessee. Look.

OLD WOMAN: But it's just the same. Mountains and mountains and nobody here but us.

GRISWOLD: All three of us.

OLD WOMAN: Oh, me.

GRISWOLD: But it's open land. I can clear about over there. Hush, hear the water?

OLD WOMAN (*Listening*): It's over there.

GRISWOLD: No, over there. But it's water. Might near a creek.

OLD WOMAN: Well, build next to it.

GRISWOLD: And get flooded out in the spring? No, you'll have to walk for it. But here we are, honey. You get the pot. I'll get the wood. We'll go down to that creek tonight, and gig us some frogs, for breakfast.

OLD WOMAN: Oh, me.

GRISWOLD: It's where you wanted to go, and here we are. Hop, honey!

Exit Griswold, whistling.

OLD WOMAN: I hopped, all right. Hopped while you built the house. Hopped while you sat aching and sweating, waiting for your supper. Then you hopped while I had Sally, and we lost Malcolm, and again when Sarah came. And we lived there, alone. At least I did. There was a store, finally, eight mile off. I didn't get to go much. When I did, I knowed Griswold didn't want me saying nothing. We lived, like a man and a woman can, sometimes speaking, sometimes not. Oh, I took the skin off him now and then. (*Smiles*) He come home once saying there was this girl Polly something working at the store, and it was unfortunate, the girl was pregnant. (*Pause*) And they were trying to blame it on us. (*Laughs*) Us. Men. Well, I made him pay for that. (*She looks at the mountains around her*) And it went by. Slow. Fast. Slow. My God. (*She smiles at the family*) Alone in the mountains. Maybe I saw fifty people all my days there. Three families only we saw more than

139

once a year. I'd sweep my dirt yard smooth as the palm of
my hand, they'd come sit, and the shadows danced. Ten-
nessee. Them neighbors we had, oh, they all loved the
place. Never stopped saying how lucky we were to be
there. Griswold smiling, saying, well it's where she
wanted to go. Everybody nodding, good, good. I wondered
why they always did that, but they just always did. Days
went by. (*She looks about, fearfully. She stoops. She ages*)
Griswold.

Enter Griswold, aged now too. He stands partly in shadow.

GRISWOLD: What's on your mind?

OLD WOMAN: It's hard without the girls. I miss my children.

GRISWOLD: They got good men. They had to go off too, like
you did.

OLD WOMAN: If Malcolm had lived, he'd be farming for you
now.

GRISWOLD: But he didn't.

OLD WOMAN: No. (*Pause*) Sarah. Sally. What's left?

GRISWOLD: I'm left. Tennessee's left.

OLD WOMAN: Then they will have to do.

GRISWOLD: Think we will?

OLD WOMAN: Well, I got my complaints.

GRISWOLD: About me or Tennessee?

OLD WOMAN: Tennessee's all right. And you did bring me here.

GRISWOLD (*Smiling*): That's right. I did.

He whistles. Exit Griswold.

OLD WOMAN: Smiling at me. Saying, "That's right. I did bring
you here."

Griswold's whistling stops.

We both outlived our children. They died young, worn-
out wives. Their children melted away into other kin's
families, and after a while, we didn't hear of them no
more. (*She sits on the edge of the porch*) Griswold was
eighty-nine when he fell and cut hisself on his sickle. I did
what I could, but he'd lost too much blood. So I got him to
a bench he'd made, and sitting there, he looked at me
sideways—a funny sort of look—and then closed his eyes.
I couldn't hold him up no more, so I let him slide off.
There was some linen left in my mother's wedding-
present box. I made Griswold a winding sheet of some
quality, and I buried him there in Tennessee. (*She stands.
Thinks*) That was—a few days ago. I think it was. Can't
tell, exactly. When my neighbor come, she stayed a few
days, that's right. The she commenced to leave, and
something was bothering me. Something I didn't feel bad
about. But I didn't know what it was.

Enter, slowly, Neighbor, a woman her age.

I tried to tell my neighbor about it, when she was going
back home.

NEIGHBOR: You sure you're all right, now?

OLD WOMAN: Oh, yes.

NEIGHBOR: Something. What?

OLD WOMAN: You're my only friend now. And you live four
mile off. Nobody else is left. Something is just not right.

NEIGHBOR: Natural feeling.

OLD WOMAN: Not Griswold dead. Something else. Not plumb-
line straight. I'm powerful uneasy.

NEIGHBOR: You're a-grieving.

OLD WOMAN: Yes, but why does it seem nothing's level. I want
to move. Walk. Got the figits, bad. Go where? Why now? I
don't know.

The Neighbor puts a hand on the Old Woman's arm.

NEIGHBOR: Listen. You stay here. Don't try to leave Tennessee.

OLD WOMAN: Why not? What's to hold me?

NEIGHBOR: Nothing, but don't leave. Don't think about it.

OLD WOMAN: What could happen?

NEIGHBOR: You could get lost.

OLD WOMAN: What difference would that make. Something is eating in me never was there before. Says go. Do it. Move.

NEIGHBOR: And I say, don't. Stay. You've had a good life here.

OLD WOMAN: Sometimes.

NEIGHBOR: No woman can ask for more. (*She backs away*) Listen to me now. Don't leave. Stay here. In Tennessee. (*She is gone*)

OLD WOMAN: But it kept eating on me. I still don't know what, or why. I commenced taking little walks. Ever day a little further. Then I didn't go back. I was loose, in country like country I'd never seen before, that I *had* seen before. I kept on. Slept in my pine needles. Gigged my frogs. Didn't know nothing, except I know this now. I was coming here.

HERSHEL: Wait a minute. Here, from Tennessee? You know yourself, Tennessee is eighty miles—

She rings her cowbell.

OLD WOMAN: I heard this, see? And it seemed like they was all around me, in the woods. I couldn't see quite through the bresh, but I knew they were there, Mama, Poppa, Rachel, Billy, Ab. And Griswold. All of them talking about me. I'd try to hear but couldn't, no more than their whisperings, and I'd find myself standing in places of powerful remembrance, places I'd stood before. Two days of that walking, when I heard this. (*She rings her cowbell*) I'd follow Poppa to the barn, a little girl as pleasant as the flowers are made. Hearing this. I heard it again, and went for it again, and what do you think I found?

HERSHEL: Lady, I sure don't know.

OLD WOMAN: Guess.

CARDELL: A cow?

OLD WOMAN: One for you, sonny! Big Jersey.

CARDELL: I thought that was our cowbell, Daddy. You missed that.

HERSHEL: So I missed it. (*To Old Woman*) You found our cowbell. Then what?

OLD WOMAN: *Your* cowbell? (*Rings it, then suddenly throws it to him*) Look inside!

Hershel does.

What did you see?

HERSHEL: You see a ringer, that's what you see.

OLD WOMAN: What else? Damn man.

CARDELL: Daddy, that's the cowbell was lying on the ground when we come here. There's a big L cut on the inside of it.

HERSHEL: Oh, yeah.

CARDELL: You missed that, too, didn't you?

HERSHEL: All right! I missed that, too! (*He gives the bell back to her*)

OLD WOMAN: L! You damn right L! Larman! I took this bell off your cow. Only one bell in the world sounds like this one. I rang it and rang it, and I found the road, and came walking, not understanding nothing. Poppa's cowbell, on some cow two days' walk, not hardly seven miles, from my yard in Tennessee? What about this, I thought. What about this? Am I dead, or what? Is this heaven? What's going on? (*She moves about the yard, ringing the bell*) Then, on the road, I seen the bend again, and came round it. There it was again. I seen it almost buried in the tree, but not quite. Enough left sticking out of the burl so's it could flash at me. Just one little wink in the sun, but I seen it. (*She goes to her mirror again, where Griswold stuck it. She pulls it loose*) I pulled open the growth of the burl, and there hidden was my star in the daytime. I pulled it loose, my mirror, where I'd left it on the way to Tennessee. (*She looks at herself in the mirror*) There I was. Old woman. Two flashes of a mirror. Little girl, old woman. Good God Almighty, I thought, when I took my bridal mirror out of the tree where he put it, broken, on my wedding day.

HERSHEL: Whew.

MARY: Hershel, she's crazy, none of this makes sense.

OLD WOMAN: It makes sense, all right. I can see it! Why, that man. That damn man. I left the road, took the trail, lightheaded and dizzy. One day in Tennessee, the next day Poppa's cowbell, and my mirror? Then I come out of the brush, into the clearing, and I seen the house. A boy on the porch. And you. You nice people. (*Pause*) And I am still not sure, not even now while I'm a-talking to you. Are you the strangers give me spoonbread and tea? Or are you Poppa? Are you Rachel, Billy, and Ab? Is my mother back in the house, making me my wedding dress?

HERSHEL (*Gently*): I am afeared we're the strangers give you spoonbread.

OLD WOMAN: Ah, I know it! Oh, that man! Griswold, you damn man! What did you do to me?

HERSHEL: Listen, you best come inside and lie down now. You must be awful tired.

OLD WOMAN: Oh, my God! Don't you understand? What's wrong with you? Don't you see it yet? I do! I do! Good God! Great God A-mighty!

The family stands watching her, alarmed. The Old Woman shakes her head, swings her arms. Wheezing, coughing, hopping up and down, ringing her cowbell and flashing her mirror, she stamps out a sort of dance in front of them.

That man! That bloody scoundrel! He never took me to Tennessee at all! He put me in a wagon, and he drove me around these mountains over a month! These same mountains! Around, in circles! Then he settled where he'd meant to all along, in a valley *seven miles off!* And I thought I was in Tennessee! Oh! My God! All them people, my neighbors, they was in on it! Oh! My children, my own children, *they* was in on it! And—oh, no. To get me gone, was it? Poppa? Momma? You, too? Oh, Griswold! You never told me. You never would have told me. By God, you *died* without telling me! What kind of a joke was that? Griswold! My whole life! You damn man!

She rages. Her passion pours out of her. She hacks and coughs and stamps her feet. Slowly, her convulsion subsides. She gets her breath.

Whew. Shoo. Well, that's that. Think you lived your life in Tennessee. Find out you didn't. You, up there. Nice people, with your fine estate. House, land, yard and porch. It's all yours—for a while. Good luck. (*She looks at the cowbell and the mirror*) Poppa. Griswold. (*She drops them both*) Bye. (*To the family*) So long.

MARY: Wait! Don't go now. It's dark.

OLD WOMAN: I know it.

MARY: Hershel! Stop her.

HERSHEL: Wait, now. Where you going?

OLD WOMAN: Back to Tennessee. Where else? That man. That damn man. (*She is gone*)

MARY: Hershel?

HERSHEL: Let her go.

Hershel and Mary look at each other. They shiver. Hershel looks out at his land, then back to the house.

I'm hungry. Let's go eat now. Give me the baby.

He takes the baby from Cardell, holds it tightly, then pushes his wife ahead of him, in to supper. Cardell stares off after the Old Woman. He picks up her mirror, and sees his face in it.

2

For the Actors Theatre of Louisville

Characters

COUNSEL

COMMANDANT

SERGEANT

CAPTAIN

HERMANN GOERING

PSYCHIATRIST

GOERING'S WIFE

GOERING'S DAUGHTER

VOICES OF JUSTICE ROBERT JACKSON

　　　　　　　PRESIDENT OF THE TRIBUNAL

　　　　　　　BRITISH PROSECUTOR

　　　　　　　OTHERS

Place

Palace of Justice, Nuremberg, Germany.

Time

May 1945—October 1946.

Scene

A large room, partitioned down the middle. A wire fence is suggested above its center, without actually splitting the room as was done at Nuremberg. The walls are roughly plastered and newly painted off-white.

Upstage, two doors, right and left of the wire fence. On one side of the stage-left door, an American flag draped on a stand; on the other side, another flag, with a curious device: against an azure background, a large key suspended above a scales; below them, a German eagle fallen into a pit.

At center, a sturdy mahogany table, with a wooden chair on each side. The wire fence hangs above this table, as if it continued down and cut the table in two, separating anyone there.

On each downstage side of the room, a sink and mirror, and a small washstand table, with soap and towels.

Two double windows, high on the stage-left wall, through which light falls.

On the table, lit by a spotlight, is a thick black book.

II

ACT ONE

The spotlight on the black book fades.
Lights come up quickly. The room is empty. Stage-left
door opens suddenly. Pause.
 The Counsel, a German in his late sixties, small, thin and
rather frail, enters the room. The door closes behind him.
He waits.
 Stage-right door opens. Enter a black Infantry Sergeant
and a white Infantry Captain. Both have pistols in holsters,
carry white billy clubs, and wear the white belts and
helmets of American Army Guards at Nuremberg. The
Sergeant chews gum. They stand at ease. Pause.
 Enter Commandant, a Colonel in the American Cavalry.
He is very spit-and-polish, in a perfectly pressed and
creased uniform. He carries a swagger stick, and he wears a
gleaming black helmet, on which, as on his shoulder
patches, are a key and a scales.
 The door closes swiftly behind him. The Captain and the
Sergeant snap to attention.

SERGEANT: Ten-shun!!
COMMANDANT (*To guards*): At ease. (*To Counsel*) Good
 morning.

COUNSEL: Good morning, sir.

COMMANDANT: You will represent the prisoner?

COUNSEL: I will, sir.

COMMANDANT: You will confer with him here. This wire fence will separate you at all times. You are never to touch him. Never. Understood?

COUNSEL: Yes, sir.

COMMANDANT: When papers are exchanged between you, a Sergeant in the Army of the United States will inspect each transaction, himself overseen by a Captain in the Army of the United States. Nothing, say again, nothing, but paper is to pass between you. Understood?

COUNSEL: Absolutely.

COMMANDANT: If you need assistance, you inform the guards.

COUNSEL: Thank you, sir. When do I see the prisoner?

COMMANDANT: When I have finished talking to you.

COUNSEL: Yes, sir.

COMMANDANT: The Military Tribunal has instructed me, as Commandant of the prison within the Palace of Justice at Nuremberg, to give defense counsel free access to the prisoner, and ample time to prepare a defense. Here is a complete and official copy of the Indictment. (*He points to the black book*)

COUNSEL: Thank you.

COMMANDANT: Your notes will be in hand only, no briefcase. You will be searched before and after every meeting. Understood?

COUNSEL: Yes, sir.

COMMANDANT: Any questions?

COUNSEL: No, sir.

COMMANDANT: Bring in the prisoner.

CAPTAIN: Yes, sir.

The Sergeant opens the stage-right door and exits after the Captain, closing the door behind them.

COMMANDANT: You may sit down.

COUNSEL: Thank you. (*He sits in his wooden chair*)

COMMANDANT: I understand you never met him.

COUNSEL: No, sir.

COMMANDANT: Ever seen him, in person?

COUNSEL: Everyone did.

COMMANDANT: When was the last time *you* did?

COUNSEL: A year ago. He gave a speech here.

COMMANDANT: What was he like then?

COUNSEL: He wore a great white-and-green uniform, with many medals, as usual. He was—ah—overweight, as usual.

COMMANDANT: A great white pig.

COUNSEL: Ah, yes.

COMMANDANT: What did he say?

COUNSEL: He told us the war would be won. And laughed.

COMMANDANT: When he walks in that door, you won't recognize him. The day I got here, he weighed almost three hundred pounds. Can you believe that?

COUNSEL: Ah—yes, I can.

COMMANDANT: He was eating forty morphine pills a day. I cut them out one at a time. "I'll kill myself!" he said. "Oh, no you won't," I said. No suicide with me. His pill was a little cylinder of glass—this big—inside a cartridge case. Prussic acid. Turns a man green in thirty seconds. I found it, in his storage-room gear. I gave him three months of G.I. rations, healthy exercise, and shaped him up. He's a model prisoner now.

Enter Sergeant, holding the door open. Enter Hermann Goering. It is startling to recognize in him the familiar,

153

*obese, often-cartooned figure. Goering weighs a hundred
pounds less than he did at the end of the war. He still wears
his pearl gray Luftwaffe uniform, which, though altered for
him, is now too large. It hangs on him loosely but does not,
oddly, look bad. He has kept his high military boots, of the
finest leather. His skin is clear. His eyes are bright. He has
indeed been restored to health. The Captain enters, closes
the door, takes up his position with the Sergeant, one on each
side of the door.*

Good morning, Goering.

GOERING: Good morning, my Colonel.

COMMANDANT: Here is the counsel you requested.

GOERING: A million thanks.

COMMANDANT: Under the rules we have discussed, you are
now free to consult with him. Gentlemen.

*The Sergeant opens the door. Exit Commandant. The Ser-
geant goes to parade rest again.*

GOERING: Good morning.

COUNSEL: Good morning.

Goering smiles, looks at the Sergeant.

GOERING: I knew I was in trouble when I saw soldiers standing
around me, chewing gum. (*He laughs*) You don't recognize me?

COUNSEL: You've—lost weight.

GOERING: It is a first-class health resort, this place. Seventy-
one pounds, gone! I'm fit! Are you wondering why I
picked you?

COUNSEL: Yes.

GOERING: That Swagger-Stick Colonel handed me a list of lawyers in Nuremberg. I said I didn't know any lawyers. I never needed one. He said, shut up, you need one now. I closed my eyes and picked you. How old are you?

COUNSEL: Sixty-eight.

GOERING: Do you want to defend me?

COUNSEL: Yes.

GOERING: Why?

COUNSEL: I do not like the charges.

GOERING (*Laughing*): Neither do I!

COUNSEL: You are being tried for breaking laws that did not exist when you broke them. Ex post facto.

GOERING: What did you do during the war?

COUNSEL: I was a civil court judge. Appeals, mostly.

GOERING: Can I trust you?

COUNSEL: I will defend you to the best of my ability.

GOERING: I don't mean that. What I mean is, do you love Germany?

COUNSEL: I do love Germany. Can I trust you?

GOERING: How?

COUNSEL: Will you tell me the truth?

GOERING: Always.

COUNSEL: Then I will do my best for you. But—

GOERING: What's the matter?

COUNSEL (*Smiling*): What do I call you?

GOERING: Anything! Hey, you! Whist, *hey Buddy!* Fatso!! (*Laughs*) While chewing gum! (*He smiles, regains his composure*) I thought the Reichsmarschall of Germany would make peace with the Supreme Commander of Europe, man to man. But no. General Eisenhower throws me in prison and calls me a war criminal. Is that what you call me?

COUNSEL: No.

GOERING: So what am I? Just another client?

COUNSEL: No.

GOERING: *Hermann?*

COUNSEL: I was fifty-six years old when you came to power. I watched my country—led by Hitler and by you—become one with itself, strong and vigorous. When you stood up— in those childish uniforms, with all those gleaming medals, dancing over a belly getting bigger and bigger every day—you made no bones about any of it. We were dazzled by Hitler, but we loved you. You were human, sometimes harsh but good at heart. A mirror for Germans. Then, with our cities in flames, we still loved you. I don't know why, but we did. I do now. I will defend you with all my heart but—I will never know what to call you.

GOERING: Good old man! I couldn't have made a better choice. I will be simply what you defend. Man to man.

COUNSEL: Defendant.

GOERING: Counsel. So.

COUNSEL: So.

GOERING: Begin!

COUNSEL: The indictment. You and twenty-one associates are specifically charged with Crimes Against Peace, War Crimes, and Crimes Against Humanity. The Tribunal will be composed of two judges each from France, Russia, Great Britain and the United States.

GOERING: They're wrong already. That's not a tribunal.

COUNSEL: It will function as one.

GOERING: Who prosecutes?

COUNSEL: A representative of each country, in turn.

GOERING: Four to one. Who is leading all this?

COUNSEL: The Chief Prosecutor is an American. Robert Jackson, a Supreme Court Justice of the United States. Very eloquent man. He has declared this trial an opportunity to outlaw all future wars.

GOERING: Has he, really?

COUNSEL: The Tribunal claims it will convict on hard evidence alone. But it will use the records kept by us.

GOERING: That cooks me, does it?

COUNSEL: Not completely. You were so far up in the structure of command, I do not think it will be so easy to pin you to individual events so far down.

GOERING: Can I call witnesses?

COUNSEL: Yes.

GOERING: Shift responsibility down to subordinates?

COUNSEL: Yes.

GOERING: And up to the top?

COUNSEL: We can shift a great deal of the blame.

GOERING: We shift nothing! Not a word against Hitler.

COUNSEL: What? But we must!

GOERING: Not one word!

COUNSEL: The other prisoners will do exactly that!

GOERING: No, they won't. I won't let them.

COUNSEL: This will make things very difficult! Please understand—

GOERING: I *do understand!* I will not deny! I will debate! I will *challenge!* I know more about what happened in Germany than any man alive! I am not TWO now! I am ONE!!

COUNSEL: Very well. (*Pause*) One!

They smile. Change of light. Sounds of an American military band, playing a Sousa march, "El Capitan." Counsel's door opens. Exit Counsel. Goering walks around the room. Door opens. Enter Psychiatrist. He is a Jewish Army Major, in his thirties, intelligent and formidable.

PSYCHIATRIST: Good morning, Goering.

2

GOERING: Doctor Freud? Is that right?

PSYCHIATRIST: That's right. How did you know?

GOERING: It's time for you. You are my sixth Doctor Freud. You have that quietly receptive look about you.

The Psychiatrist puts his briefcase down on his side of the table, takes out some notes and a pad.

What happened to the Irishman?

PSYCHIATRIST: He went home.

GOERING: Why?

PSYCHIATRIST: His tour of duty was over.

GOERING: Please, Doctor Freud.

PSYCHIATRIST: Okay. I'll be honest with you, if you will be honest with me.

GOERING: With all my heart, now and forever. What happened to him?

PSYCHIATRIST: The Irish psychologist you liked, liked you, too. In fact, he hated the British so much, he ended up loving you. Ever read Shakespeare?

GOERING: In English, thank you. I love the theatre. My wife was an actress.

PSYCHIATRIST: Then maybe you saw *Richard III.*

GOERING: Several times.

PSYCHIATRIST: He was powerful because the people around him wanted to be corrupted.

GOERING: Richard III being me, corrupting Irish psychologists?

PSYCHIATRIST: Yes.

GOERING: So they send him home and replace him with— what? A Jew? Are you a Jew?

The Psychiatrist makes notes.

PSYCHIATRIST: Yes.

GOERING: Congratulations.

PSYCHIATRIST: *What?*

GOERING (*Smiling*): You won.

Deadly pause. The Psychiatrist takes a deep breath.

PSYCHIATRIST: At a price.

Goering shrugs.

GOERING: We all paid a price. What's the matter?

With a great effort the Psychiatrist controls himself.

PSYCHIATRIST (*Briskly*): There are tests to give you. I must ask about your psychological background. I must consult with you about your interpersonal relations with the other prisoners. I must be of help to you in a situation that will be difficult for both of us. But first, I've brought you this. (*He holds up a packet of letters and starts to hand it to Goering*)

CAPTAIN: Sergeant.

SERGEANT: Hold it! (*He moves swiftly to Goering's side*) Hand 'em over.

CAPTAIN: Sir.

SERGEANT: Sir.

The Psychiatrist hands the letters to the Sergeant, who flips through them roughly. Goering, closing his eyes, looks away.

GOERING: Who from?

PSYCHIATRIST: Your wife. And your child.
GOERING: Oh, my God.

He looks at the Sergeant, ruffling through the letters. Pause.

Where are they?
PSYCHIATRIST: Safe.
GOERING: WHERE?
PSYCHIATRIST: In an Army prison. Just for interrogation.

The Sergeant hands the letters to Goering.

SERGEANT: Okay. Here.

Goering takes them. He closes his eyes. The Sergeant goes back to his place. Pause.

PSYCHIATRIST: Aren't you going to read them?
GOERING: I will read—these letters—in my cell alone or not at all.
PSYCHIATRIST: Being observed reading your family mail is intolerable?
GOERING: Yes!
PSYCHIATRIST: I want you to know that I am in favor of your communication with your wife and daughter.
GOERING: Why should you care?
PSYCHIATRIST: I think it is a key to my understanding of you and your understanding of yourself. I will make sure your letters are sent and theirs received. Just be reasonable and talk to me. Okay?
GOERING: Okay! (*He puts the letters in a pocket*) Shall I tell you about my childhood? My father and mother?
PSYCHIATRIST: Good.

GOERING: Fine. My first memory of my mother's face. Age four. I was bashing it in with my little fists.

PSYCHIATRIST: Why did you do that?

GOERING: I didn't like her. What does that mean, Doctor?

PSYCHIATRIST: Let me explain something to you. I am an officer in the American Medical Corps. My orders are One: gather psychological information about Hermann Goering, and Two, when I can, relieve his distress. I am a Jew and I am a Pole and I am a citizen of the United States! Unlike the Irishman, I don't like you now and never will. But on duty, I am your friend! So don't try to get my goat.

GOERING: Get your what?

PSYCHIATRIST: Goat. American expression, meaning make me mad.

GOERING: Good, thank you. I don't get your goat. You relieve my distress. I do beg your pardon, and bang my head upon the floor.

PSYCHIATRIST: Will you take some tests?

GOERING: What kind of tests?

PSYCHIATRIST: Standard I.Q. Army Intelligence.

GOERING: I want to be as helpful to you as you do to me. (*He laughs*) Which means I want to live, you want me to die and we hate each other to death. Doctor. You aren't the war criminal. I am. If I can joke a little, why can't you?

PSYCHIATRIST: You aren't funny. And I saw *Richard III.* "I can smile and smile, and murder whilst I smile."

GOERING: You are a hard case, but you're right. The Irishman was fudge. All I had to do was be a good fellow—man to man to man—and he'd believe anything I said. You won't.

PSYCHIATRIST: You are God damn right I won't.

161

GOERING: Fine. Give me your tests, and ask me your questions—my family excepted—and I will answer. And I will try to get a smile out of you somehow! Doctor Freud? Agreed?

PSYCHIATRIST: Okay.

GOERING: Okay.

Change of light. Sounds of GIs marching. Psychiatrist's door opens. He exits. The door closes. The Captain whispers to the Sergeant, opens the door and the Sergeant exits. Goering sits in his chair, watched by the Captain. Outside, GIs are being marched in cadence.

GIs (*Voiceover*):
Hup, toop, threep, four!
Hup, toop, threep, four!

CADRE (*Voiceover*):
Ain't no use in writing home—

GIs:
Ain't no use in writing home—

CADRE:
Jody's got your gal and gone.

GIs:
Jody's got your gal and gone,
Hup, toop, threep, four!
Hup, toop, threep, four!

CADRE:
Ain't no use in feeling blue—

GIS:

> Ain't no use in feeling blue—

CADRE:

> Jody's got your sister, too!

GIS:

> Jody's got your sister, too!
> Hup, toop, threep, four!

CADRE AND GIS (*Fading away*):

> Left, your left, your left, right, left!
> Hup, toop, threep, four!
> Your left, your left, your left, right, left!
> Hup, toop, threep, four!

> *Goering listens, trying to understand them. The counting and the marching fade away.*

GOERING: So, who was Joe-dee?

CAPTAIN: Shut up. You're not supposed to talk to me.

GOERING: The Commandant said if I had a question, ask. You are a Hauptmann, is that right. Ah, Captain?

CAPTAIN: That's right.

GOERING: You see I pay attention to your rank. Hauptmann, who is Joe-dee? You must answer, no? Orders from the Commandant?

CAPTAIN: Well, all right. Just don't expect me to call you sir.

GOERING: Man to man to man.

CAPTAIN: Jody's a guy who 4-Fs. That means he don't get drafted, put in the Army. Has flat feet or knows some Senator or something. So he stays home, and screws my girl. That's all, now shut up.

2

GOERING: Screw? (*He gets it*) Ah! Joe-*dee!* Bang, bang.

CAPTAIN (*Nodding*): Bang, bang. Like everwhere else.

GOERING: Not in Germany. No Hans-ee or Fritz-ee in Germany.

CAPTAIN: How come?

GOERING: Nobody stayed home. I saw to that.

CAPTAIN: That's what you say. Reckon I'll believe whatever you say?

GOERING: Reckon?

CAPTAIN: Means guess, suppose.

GOERING: Ah. Slang. Brooklyn?

CAPTAIN: God, you're dumb. No, the South.

GOERING: Oh. Red neck?

CAPTAIN: Me? Do I look like a redneck?

GOERING: Of course not. But where?

CAPTAIN: God's country!

GOERING: Ah! Great Smoky Mountains? I know. "Daniel Boom kill'd a bear." Carved on a Smoky Mountain tree by the great hunter Daniel Boom. No?

CAPTAIN: Sort of.

GOERING: You see!

CAPTAIN: He was Daniel B-o-o-n-e, Boone. From Kentucky.

GOERING: Ah! Kentucky! Deadly shots! Blood feuds! The uh— um—

CAPTAIN: Hatfields and the McCoys.

GOERING: Tough men, hard! Shoot on sight!

CAPTAIN: Sometimes.

GOERING: I had once a rifle like Daniel Boone's. Hessian Grenadier musket. You know them, ah, here, the lock, the—

CAPTAIN: Flintlock. Had to put your powder in every shot.

GOERING (*Miming*): Like this!

CAPTAIN: Like that, yep. Bang!

GOERING: Bang!

CAPTAIN: Then reload.

GOERING: One shot. I like that. Turkey, deer?

CAPTAIN: One shot.

GOERING: Bear, man?

CAPTAIN: One shot!

GOERING: Ho-ho! Don't miss!

CAPTAIN: Deadeye.

GOERING: You a deadeye?

CAPTAIN: My great-grandaddy could hit a pheasant with a flintlock. In the *air*.

GOERING: Americans are best with rifles. The British with shotguns. Germans bang-bang firepower. No aim. What is the best hunting rifle you ever saw?

CAPTAIN: A 460 Weatherly Magnum. I'll tell you—

Right door opens. Enter the Sergeant, who takes up his place. The Captain looks stiffly ahead. The Sergeant glances at him, looks at Goering. Goering smiles at the Sergeant, man to man. Change of light. Sounds of airplanes flying over Nuremberg. Enter Counsel, who sits in his chair.

COUNSEL: The Tribunal is doing something never done before. It is holding individuals responsible for the acts of nations. Each prisoner will be tried separately, in turn, and judged individually, at the end of the trial.

GOERING: Can we call friendly witnesses?

COUNSEL: Yes.

GOERING: Bodenchatz, Milch, Dahlerus?

COUNSEL: Yes, men like that, who respected you.

GOERING: They will tell the truth. I didn't want to invade Poland! I didn't want to invade Russia!

2

COUNSEL: Did you tell Hitler that?

GOERING: I did! He saw my point, listened to Ribbentrop, and we lost the war! If I'd had my way, there wouldn't have *been* a war!

COUNSEL: So you say, Defendant. But we must answer the indictment, without self-serving testimony. (*He picks up the black book*) Allow me to prepare a defense.

GOERING: I beg your pardon.

COUNSEL: Basically, there are three indictments.

GOERING: All right! One, two, three!

COUNSEL: One. Crimes Against Peace. Conspiring to wage war in violation of international treaties.

GOERING (*Laughs*): What treaties? *Versailles?*

COUNSEL: Among others.

GOERING: That wasn't a treaty. That was a death sentence. Two!

COUNSEL: Two. War Crimes. Violations of the laws or customs of war.

GOERING: What crimes?

COUNSEL: Murder, slave labor, plunder, hostages, reprisals, wanton destruction.

GOERING (*Laughs*): What every soldier does! Or be shot himself! Three!

COUNSEL: Three. Crimes Against Humanity.

GOERING (*Laughs*): Against *all* humanity? What?

COUNSEL: They mean extermination on racial or political grounds.

GOERING: Extermination?

COUNSEL: Races. Slavs, gypsies—and—well—

GOERING: Well?

COUNSEL: Jews.

GOERING: Me? Exterminate Jews?

COUNSEL: I think they may accuse you of that, yes.

GOERING: What could be more grotesque, or untrue? I did everything I could for the Jews. So did my wife. Actor after actor from her old theatre days we got out. And many others. Let me tell you—

COUNSEL: None of that matters.

GOERING: I WAS SPEAKING TO YOU!!

COUNSEL: And talking nonsense! You wrote the Nuremberg Laws, that stripped them of their citizenship. *You* were what the Jews ran away from!

Pause.

GOERING: My dear man, I beg your pardon. Please proceed, as you think best.

COUNSEL: One. Crimes Against Peace. Here you can defend yourself. You simply restored a country to prosperity, under the legal orders of a Chancellor. Just don't brag about it.

GOERING: But of course I am going to brag about it. I am proud of what I did.

COUNSEL: I wouldn't put it quite like that, if I were you. You will be asked if you created the Gestapo.

GOERING: What does that have to do with crimes against peace?

COUNSEL: Hostages, reprisals, conspiracies, infiltration of other countries, murder.

GOERING: Every country has a Gestapo. I established ours, then did more important work. It ran itself, until Himmler got it in 1934.

COUNSEL: You will be asked if you created the Air Force.

GOERING: As Germany's greatest flier, who else?

COUNSEL: Bombing civilians, machine-gunning evacuees, and so on. Wanton destruction.

2

GOERING: Wanton destruction? Me?

COUNSEL: Yes, Defendant, you!

GOERING: Britain's Dresden? America's atom bomb? The Russians?

COUNSEL: No accusations against Great Britain, the United States or Russia are to be admitted as testimony.

GOERING: *What?*

COUNSEL: Two. War Crimes.

GOERING: Absolutely not guilty! Never!

COUNSEL: Prisoners of war?

GOERING: Yes, some prisoners were shot, I know it happened, but I did not do it, and no genuine document will say I did!

COUNSEL: So war crimes, none?

GOERING: None. Now, Himmler, Heydrich, I don't know.

COUNSEL: I thought we weren't shifting blame.

GOERING: To subordinates. Himmler was no subordinate of mine, no matter what it looked like. Listen. When Adolf Hitler gave somebody something to do, he gave somebody else the same thing to do, so they would fight each other for his approval. That is the way he kept control of his staff. So I hated Goebbels and he hated me and we both hated Himmler and everybody hated Bormann and so on.

COUNSEL: It was really that simple for Hitler to control the leaders of the Reich?

GOERING: He did it in other ways, too. He had a photographic memory. Purely mechanical. He could recall how many ball bearings were packed to a crate twenty years ago in May. Not June! May! He ridiculed everyone that way. Generals, Ministers, me, everyone. He knew. You didn't.

COUNSEL: Tell the Tribunal that!

GOERING: Never. That's all about Hitler. I will not hide behind him. The truth is, I was his war hero, who stood up to Hindenburg for him. I made him Chancellor. But whenever he looked at me, my heart jumped out of my chest. If he scolded me, I became a little boy. I stood up when I talked to him on the telephone. I was his, get used to it. Any order I signed I am responsible for, no matter what. Period.

COUNSEL: Very well. Plunder?

GOERING: Of course I plundered. I stripped Europe of everything we needed to win the war!

COUNSEL: Paintings? Statues? Altarpieces? Tapestries? To win the war?

GOERING: All right, art collections. Everything was bought. Bills of sale exist for each transaction. I paid a fortune for a collection of art that would bear my name and be left to the German people! Hitler did the same!

COUNSEL: Legitimate purchases?

GOERING: Absolutely. Hitler, lucky for me, bought naked women with snakes around their navels, sleeping monks and perfect children, for God's sakes! I left him all that and found my Cranach Adam and Eve! I bought Rubens and my Van Dycks, the best! Bargains, but legal! Next!

COUNSEL: Three. Crimes Against Humanity.

GOERING: None! Never! None! I was hard, yes! I did my duty twice over! But humanity I love!

COUNSEL: You will be asked if you created the concentration camps.

GOERING: Using as models the British enclaves in South Africa and the Indian Reservations of the United States, yes I created concentration camps.

COUNSEL: And if you put Jews in them.

GOERING: Along with others, when they threatened us, yes.

COUNSEL: What do you think happened to them there?

GOERING: They worked hard. To death, sometimes, yes I understand that, and regret it, and always did what I could to stop it.

COUNSEL: As the creator of those camps, you can say that was all that was done in them?

GOERING: In the beginning, some camps presumed to disobey my humane directives. I made short work of them, and closed them down. Later, Himmler and Heydrich, and a Major—ah—Eichmann, who became very competent, took them over.

Pause.

COUNSEL: Defendant. You asked me if I loved Germany. I said yes. I asked you if you were going to tell me the truth. You said yes.

GOERING: I *am* telling you the truth!

COUNSEL: You can't be. Everyone knew terrible things happened in those camps. First in Germany, then in Poland, and the east. No one said a word, since we could all be in one the next day.

GOERING: So where did you hear such things? Gossip?

COUNSEL: Yes, gossip, and the radio! It was everywhere! How can I tell the Tribunal that the second-most powerful man in Germany knew nothing about the camps? You knew!

GOERING: Before 1934! After that, I was busy rebuilding the German economy, and creating the Air Force. What Himmler did then was none of my business.

COUNSEL: You expect me to say that in court?

GOERING: If you won't, I will! (*Pause*) I only ask you to believe in me!

COUNSEL: I will try.

GOERING: Thank you.

Right door opens. Enter Commandant, Psychiatrist. Captain and Sergeant snap to attention.

SERGEANT: Ten-shun!!

COMMANDANT: At ease. Gentlemen, morning session convenes in fifteen minutes. We will wait here for exactly five, then proceed, arriving in place one minute before nine.

Exit Captain.

COUNSEL: But, my God, we've hardly begun!

GOERING: My Colonel is a Prussian! Exact! So! So!

COMMANDANT: No, I'm not. I'm a Swagger Stick. Right?

GOERING: How did you know I call you that? Very clever!

COMMANDANT: You will sit at the head of the dock.

GOERING: Number One?

COMMANDANT: Number One.

GOERING: Who's next to me?

COMMANDANT: Hess, then Ribbentrop.

GOERING: The madman and the fool. Then?

COMMANDANT: Keitel.

GOERING: A lackey. Doenitz?

COMMANDANT: On the back row.

GOERING: Bravo. Where is Speer?

COMMANDANT: In the back.

GOERING: Where he belongs! Perfect, my Colonel!

COMMANDANT: I'm glad you're happy.

GOERING (*To Counsel*): What happens first?

COMMANDANT (*Looking at his watch*): Tell him.

171

COUNSEL: Aides will read the Indictment. The prisoners will declare themselves guilty or not guilty. Lunch, probably. This afternoon, the American prosecutor will make his opening speech and I think there is a film.

GOERING: Movies! Good! And I will see the great Robert Jackson, of the Supreme American Court, at work?

COUNSEL: He will no doubt make a devastating speech.

GOERING: Speeches. Yes, I remember speeches. I listened to too many of them. You know what we should say? Two words. With that eloquent gesture taught me by GIs.

COUNSEL: What is that?

GOERING: Military Tribunal says, "What is your defense?" One. Prisoners stand up. (*He does*) Two. Prisoners hold out their right arms. (*He does*) Three, prisoners say "UP YOURS!"

Goering hits his right arm at the elbow, sending his fist up into the air in the American "up yours" gesture, then roars with laughter. The Sergeant chews his gum. The Commandant and Counsel stare at him.

Don't you think that would be funny?

Enter Captain, with a red-on-white polka-dotted aviator's scarf.

CAPTAIN: Got it. (*He holds out the scarf to the Commandant*) Sir. He asked for this.

COMMANDANT: Where'd you get it?

CAPTAIN: Through Quartermaster. In his gear.

The Commandant looks at it a moment.

COMMANDANT: Okay.

The Captain gives Goering his aviator's scarf.

GOERING: Ah, Great American Hunter! (*With great pleasure, he puts on the scarf and tucks it under his collar. To Commandant*) I thank you for this small decoration, as I go to battle. Wonderful. There. (*He goes to the washbasin, throws some water on his face, runs his hands through his hair*) Wash my face! Look my best! (*He rubs his face and hands with a towel*) Staring at me, aren't you. Well, guards look through a hole in my cell door every minute of the day and night. The only time they can't see me is when I take a shit. Which is the only time I wish they *could* see me! (*He sits again, his towel draped over one shoulder, and looks about at everybody waiting*) Very well! The great Inter-Galaxy Armies of Venus and Mars are packed into gigantic Space Ships. The Universe itself is to be invaded and conquered by these invincible forces, and the first planet to be conquered is Earth. The Supreme Leader of this overwhelming Air Force has studied the situation thoroughly. He sends his Ambassador, a great Martian soldier, to issue an Ultimatum, to the first man on Earth he sees. The Ambassador lands—at a filling station in Cleveland, Ohio, by a large gas pump. "Well," says the Supreme Leader, when he returns, "did you find an Earthman?" "I did," says the Ambassador. "Did you issue our Ultimatum?" "I did," says the Ambassador. "What did he say?" says the Supreme Leader. "Nothing," says the Ambassador. "He just stood there, with his dick in his ear."

Goering roars with laughter. The others stare at him. Goering jumps up.

Oh, come on, gentlemen. Laugh! Why not? Scarf! Uniform! Boots! I'm ready! Once Hermann Goering was known and loved all over Germany! And by God, years from now, he will be again! All right, not loved maybe, but known, and admired!! (*He hands the towel to the Sergeant*) Thank you, nigger.

The Sergeant starts to hit him. Captain grabs the Sergeant.

I beg your pardon! That *is* what they call you? You'll end up in a camp, too! Just watch!

COMMANDANT: Goering!

GOERING: Yes, sir!! My Colonel, sir! Tell me, my Colonel, sir, where are all the Generals? Eisenhower and Patton? Montgomery and Zhukov and De Gaulle? As far away from this travesty as they can get, where *they* would be on trial if they'd lost, and so would you. Doctor Freud, make a study! Who thought up this monkey trial!

COMMANDANT: Time!

GOERING: Time, gentlemen! Let's go to the movies!

Blackout. Band music ends. All move to the back wall and stand in shadow. Downlight on Goering's chair, which becomes his place in the dock at the trial. Goering walks down and sits proudly in his chair. A flickering of light plays on him: it is a film being shown. Its horrible and familiar huge images wash behind Goering on the white back wall. They are images of the concentration camps. Piles of wasted, naked bodies being dumped out of carts. Faces whose teeth have been torn out. Great rows of people being shot and falling into ditches. Crematoria with burning smokestacks. Human skin, a shrunken head. Mothers and children. Goering stares at the film, bolt upright, in mounting anger. Blackout.

Lights come back up on the interrogation room. It is empty. Enter the Psychiatrist slowly, a handkerchief over his mouth. Then the Counsel, stunned. Enter Goering, the Captain and the Sergeant. Goering sits. There is a very long, shocked pause when no one can speak. Then Goering breaks the silence.

GOERING: Well *that* was a bad movie!

Long pause.

COUNSEL: Is that all you can say about it?

The Commandant appears at the door.

COMMANDANT (*Grim*): You have an hour. And this dreadful day is over.

Exit Commandant.

PSYCHIATRIST: You never blinked.
GOERING: No.
PSYCHIATRIST: People wept, turned away, hid their faces. I almost got sick.
GOERING: I can't blame you for that. Saw your family, did you?
PSYCHIATRIST: I could have! Don't you understand what you saw?
GOERING: One, I don't believe those films tell the truth. Two, even if they do, I had nothing to do with it!
PSYCHIATRIST: That isn't the point! It happened! For God's sake, didn't you see what we saw?
GOERING: I saw it. I had nothing to do with it.
PSYCHIATRIST: We'll see about that, you bastard. I leave you to your counsel.

175

2

Exit Psychiatrist.

GOERING: You sick, too?

COUNSEL: And you aren't?

GOERING: I've been a soldier since 1914. I have seen it all before.

COUNSEL: Not what we just saw, you haven't.

GOERING: It was a film! Propaganda!

COUNSEL: And the teeth? The eyeglasses? The hair? The *shoes?* Propaganda?

GOERING: Oh, really! I had bigger things to do than worry about mattress stuffings or little gold fillings or old shoes!

COUNSEL: There'll be more.

GOERING: Of what?

COUNSEL: Films. Testimony. They have the Commandant of Auschwitz. What will he say? Please tell me now!

GOERING: He'll say Himmler and Heydrich and Heydrich and Himmler! Which is true!

COUNSEL: You didn't know? *Hitler* didn't know?

GOERING: NO! Hitler would never have tolerated such atrocities. Never! If I thought he had, I would—be—very—very—

COUNSEL: WHAT would you be?

GOERING: Very upset!

COUNSEL: Oh, you would, would you? (*Pause*) I don't think I can do this anymore.

GOERING: Can you believe Hermann Goering had anything to do with such horrors? I was never cruel! I had men shot, yes, that was military duty! Women? Children? Never! Hitler? Never! You will *never* find my name or his on anything like that!!! You do believe me! I can see it in your eyes! You want to, and you can!! (*Pause*) Innocent life is sacred! Like animals! You know if a fox or even a

176

rabbit got caught in a steel trap under my game laws, or cut open for some experiment, the guilty man went to a camp! Boom, like that!!

COUNSEL: And got cut open instead? I will see you tomorrow morning, before trial.

GOERING: Wait. All right, yes. The film will make a difference. I can admit that. Prison, maybe. What do you think?

COUNSEL (*Weary*): Good afternoon, Defendant.

GOERING: What am I to *do* until tomorrow? Twiddle my fingers? Think about my *soul?*

COUNSEL: Right now, I don't care what you do.

Exit Counsel.

CAPTAIN: Chow time, Goering.

A sound of airplanes, flying over Nuremberg. Goering looks up at them. Change of light. Exit Captain. Sound of airplanes. Pause. Goering waits in his chair, drumming his fingers on the table. Only the Sergeant stands guard. Pause.

GOERING: Getting any? (*He laughs*) That's what all soldiers say. American, German. No? Well, I understand, from the waiters in the mess, German women have an especial penchant for black gentlemen from the States. Not, I understand, because you are demon lovers, so much. You are kinder to them, gentler, more understanding. You both know what it means, being niggers. I hope you enjoy them and are good to them. Do the Americans still have your women, and hang you from trees with crosses burning?

Enter Psychiatrist.

177

2

SERGEANT: Ten-shun!
PSYCHIATRIST: At ease. Mail call, Goering.

He holds out the letters. The Sergeant steps forward and the ritual examination is repeated, smoothly this time. Goering pockets his letters without reading them.

The psychiatrists of Nuremberg have all come to the same conclusion. Your intelligence level is very *very* high.
GOERING: Higher than Speer?
PSYCHIATRIST: Much.
GOERING: Ha-ha! I knew it! Speer's a dummy! I win!
PSYCHIATRIST: Yes, you do. But tell me something. Purely factual.
GOERING: I'll do my best.
PSYCHIATRIST: When Hitler became Chancellor, one of the first things to happen was the restoration of a medieval custom of execution. Decapitation, by the blade.
GOERING: Yes.
PSYCHIATRIST: *Beheading,* with a *sword?*
GOERING: Yes. Often a messy business, since it is very hard to cut through the neck at one blow. Many times, there was hacking. Like this. (*He hits a palm with the edge of a hand*)
PSYCHIATRIST: Did you do that, or did Hitler?
GOERING: Ah, *that,* Hitler did.
PSYCHIATRIST: And the family of the dead man, or *woman,* I understand, was billed about fifty dollars for the beheading and a hundred for the burial?
GOERING: That part of it might have been my idea. Why do you ask?
PSYCHIATRIST: I should think that a man with your great intelligence level could see something wrong when the first thing Germany's new Leader did was—literally—

178

start cutting off heads. Then euthanasia executions. Then death squads shooting a thousand people a day. Then, what we saw in that horrible film.

GOERING: I wasn't interested in any of that!! No! All I wanted to do was fight, win what we needed, and then stop. Hitler hated the Jews. All right, I didn't, but—

PSYCHIATRIST: Oh, come *on!*

GOERING: I wanted them somewhere else, out of Germany, so they wouldn't be standing there in your job somehow every time you turned around. Everyday anti-Semitism, yes, hatred, no! Hitler felt otherwise, so I did my duty. In my place you would have done yours, you to Germans as we to Jews.

PSYCHIATRIST: I would not! I would die first!

GOERING: Oh, now *you* come on!

PSYCHIATRIST: Can't you even imagine it? Just stopping something that is dragging you down to hell? Can't you?

GOERING: I imagined losing the war. The last two years, as much as I could, I stayed with my family, paintings and morphine. But what I didn't do was betray Germans, just as you wouldn't betray Jews and don't tell me you would.

PSYCHIATRIST: I certainly will tell you I would! I am a human being first and a Jew second.

GOERING: Horse shit. You are a pack animal first, a human being second, just like everybody else.

PSYCHIATRIST: No. Not everybody. Some see heads cut off and do their best to end it. And by God, someday we will!

Pause.

GOERING: But not quite yet. I'm not going to prison, am I? You're going to shoot us, aren't you?

PSYCHIATRIST: I don't know.

GOERING: Yes, you do. Your orders are to relieve my distress. Tell me the truth, Doctor Freud. Man to man.

PSYCHIATRIST: I think we will. (*Pause*) I hope we do. (*Pause*) You wanted the truth.

GOERING: Thank you. I'll be shot first of course. Well, I can pull in my stomach now. I'll look very good. Put my head under the tap, comb my hair, march right out to it. No blindfold. When you shoot, I'll say, "Heil Hitler!" Okay with you?

PSYCHIATRIST: Okay with me!

Door opens. Enter Commandant and Captain. The Sergeant snaps to attention.

SERGEANT: Ten-shun!!

COMMANDANT: Goering!

GOERING: My Colonel!

COMMANDANT: Now hear this!

Goering salutes, American Army style.

GOERING: Yes, my Colonel!

COMMANDANT: You will *not, say again, not,* bully the other prisoners further. It is one thing for you to assume command as their ranking superior, and since they seem to accept that, all right, but when they don't you leave them alone!

GOERING: My Colonel, please understand. That pig-dog Albert Speer wants to blame everything on Hitler! We were all seduced by him!

COMMANDANT: Let them say what they please!

GOERING: I won't have it!!

COMMANDANT: Yes, you will—

GOERING: It's wrong!

COMMANDANT: —if *I* say you will!

GOERING: But can't you see—

COMMANDANT: And don't you forget it!

GOERING (*Quickly*): I beg your pardon, my Colonel! Whatever you say.

COMMANDANT: And another thing! Sitting on the end of that dock, you keep turning in and talking to the others during the trial. No more. Shake your head, bounce up and down, but not a whisper, not a sound! You leave everybody alone!

GOERING: Yes, *sir!!*

COMMANDANT: And if you call me "Swagger Stick" again, I'll have you on your knees cleaning grease pits.

GOERING: Joking! Kidding!

COMMANDANT: You'll turn green without that suicide pill, understand?

Goering claps his hands to his mouth.

GOERING: Never again!

COMMANDANT (*To Captain*): Carry on.

Exit Commandant.

PSYCHIATRIST: Does it turn you green, that pill?

GOERING: Oh, yes. Potassium cyanide. Makes your skin look like a cucumber.

PSYCHIATRIST: Green, eh?

GOERING: You are thinking what a wonderful cucumber I would make.

PSYCHIATRIST: You would have been a good psychiatrist. If you need me, let me know.

2

Exit Psychiatrist. Exit Captain. Goering sits and thinks. The Sergeant watches him.

SERGEANT: Cranach.

GOERING: What?

SERGEANT: The painter. Cranach.

GOERING: What about him?

SERGEANT: Never mind.

GOERING: Go ahead, talk. We are alone. I give you my word, no one will know what you say to me.

SERGEANT: You bought his pictures?

GOERING: I did.

SERGEANT: Had 'em in your house?

GOERING: Yes. How did you come across the paintings of Cranach, if you don't mind my asking.

SERGEANT: My daddy's a preacher. He showed me.

GOERING: In a museum?

SERGEANT: In a book. Did you buy his picture about Mary, Jesus and Joseph?

GOERING: Which one?

SERGEANT: I don't know.

GOERING: There were many.

SERGEANT: It looked like this. Mary and Joseph were on a road, under some pine trees. Joseph had that worried look an old man'd get with a wife real young, like Mary was. Baby Jesus was reaching out to a lot of little angels, messing around like any bunch of kids. One caught a bird and, see, had that bird fluttering by the wings and didn't know how to get it to Jesus. Me and my daddy liked that.

GOERING: The Flight into Egypt. You have good taste. So does your father.

Pause.

182

SERGEANT: There's something you ought to know.

GOERING: My dear man, what is it?

SERGEANT: They're not going to shoot you.

GOERING: Oh?

SERGEANT: I was at Personnel, and I saw orders cut. Dated two months ahead but cut. For a Master Sergeant, the U.S. Army executioner. They already know. They going to hang your ass.

Doors open. Enter Counsel, with a copy of Stars and Stripes.

COUNSEL: Great news!

Goering whirls about. He stares at his Counsel.

It's in the Army newspaper! Senator Taft, in the Congress of the United States, has condemned the trial. Justice Black of the Supreme Court calls it Jackson's lynching party. And Churchill has begun making speeches against the Russians! It's all falling apart!

He hands the newspaper to Goering, who glances at it calmly and then looks at the Sergeant. Goering smiles at the Counsel.

GOERING: Perhaps.

Overhead, heavy airplanes fly over Nuremberg. Goering listens, looks up.

Act Two

The Captain and the Sergeant on guard. Goering and the
Counsel are sitting down at the table to confer. The Counsel
is wearing his black court robe.

COUNSEL: Your wife is very calm, very possessed. You would
be proud of her, and of your daughter. They are staying
with me now.

GOERING: That is very good of you.

COUNSEL: It has finally been decided when families may visit
prisoners.

GOERING: For God's sake, when?

COUNSEL: Before the verdict, but after the trial.

GOERING: All right. So. The trial.

COUNSEL: You may carry notes, but only as cues. After our
witnesses testify in your favor, I will lead you through
your life and career.

GOERING: Then Justice Jackson cross-examines me?

COUNSEL: Yes. He's dangerous.

GOERING: I don't think so. His mind isn't on what he's doing.
Why?

COUNSEL: He expects to be the next Chief Justice of the
American Supreme Court.

GOERING: Politics. All right, good.

COUNSEL: He will insist on yes-and-no answers. Which you must give, but then, whenever you can, insert the statements we have worked out. And whatever else you can. Remember, you are still a famous man. The judges are human. They will be curious.

GOERING: So speak to Jackson but aim at them. And the whole world will hear what Hermann Goering has to say. Good!

Drumbeat. Downlight on Goering, as if now in a witness chair. Softer downlight on the Counsel, standing by him. The rest of the stage is dark.

COUNSEL: And finally, when did you first meet Adolf Hitler?

GOERING: November, 1922, Munich. Everything he said was spoken word for word as if from my own soul. I bound myself to him, with my sacred oath, which I have kept.

COUNSEL: And what was the last you heard from him?

GOERING: A telegram in April of this year, ordering my execution as a traitor.

COUNSEL: And the execution of your wife and child?

GOERING: Yes.

COUNSEL: And you still maintain that loyalty to Adolf Hitler? Now?

GOERING: You swear an oath in good times so you will keep it in bad. Otherwise, why swear an oath at all?

COUNSEL: Which brings us to the last questions. Under Hitler, Germany was run by the Leader Principle. How would you define that?

GOERING: Authority moving from above downward, while responsibility moves from below upwards. It was the only choice for us. As it still is, I might add, for the Union of Soviet Socialist Republics, the Empire of China, the Roman Catholic Church and the nations of Islam. Western

Democracy is not for everyone. I do not think it ever will be.

COUNSEL: May it please the Tribunal, this concludes my defense of this witness.

Drums. Light intensifies on Goering alone.

VOICE OF THE PRESIDENT OF THE TRIBUNAL (*British*): Mr. Justice Robert Jackson, of the United States, may now cross-examine.

VOICE OF ROBERT JACKSON: You are perhaps aware that you are the only man alive who can tell us the whole truth of the Nazi Party?

GOERING (*Smiling*): Not perhaps, absolutely.

JACKSON: You fully intended to overthrow a democracy and establish a dictatorship?

GOERING (*Pleased*): And did so.

JACKSON: To abolish parliamentary procedure and rule by the Leadership Principle?

GOERING: Germany was a sovereign nation. What we did with our government was nobody's business but ours.

JACKSON: So you did not permit government by the consent of the governed?

GOERING: That is not entirely correct. From time to time we called upon the people to express themselves with votes of confidence.

JACKSON: But you never permitted the election of anyone who could act with authority?

GOERING: Quite right. Elected officials simply acknowledged the authority of the Leader.

JACKSON: Now, was this Leader Principle adopted because you believed no people are capable of self-government, or because you believe some may be but not the German people, or even if some of us can use a democratic system, it should not be allowed in Germany? Briefly, please.

GOERING: I beg your pardon, but may I untangle your rhetoric so I can understand your question?

Drums. Light change, time passes.

VOICE OF JACKSON: Now, in order to suppress opposing parties and individuals, you created a secret police to detect opposition.

GOERING: I said that in my opening testimony. It was on a bigger and stronger scale than ever before.

JACKSON: You created the concentration camps as well?

GOERING: I said that, too. We had many enemies. Camps are necessary. You are going to have to put all the people you can't handle somewhere. We had to do it. You will, too. It's obvious.

JACKSON: Not so obvious to us. You are explaining a system to men who do not understand it very well and want to know what was necessary and what was not.

GOERING: You are asking me if I considered it necessary to establish concentration camps to eliminate the opposition. Is that what you are trying to get me to say?

JACKSON: Yes or no!

GOERING: Yes. For my Leader I eliminated his opposition. Yes.

JACKSON: Were there no public trials? The Gestapo was subject to no court review?

GOERING: You must differentiate between two categories of enforcement. I was both Prussian Prime Minister and Reich Minister of the Interior—

JACKSON: Let's omit that. I have not asked for that. Just answer my questions. Your Counsel can go into details for you later.

2

GOERING: I have answered your questions, but I want to make an explanation in connection with my answer.

VOICE OF PRESIDENT OF THE TRIBUNAL: Mr. Justice Jackson, the Tribunal thinks the witness ought to be allowed to make what explanation he thinks right in answer to this question.

Pause.

JACKSON: I bow to the Court. Explain then.

Goering smiles a brief smile, and launches into a huge digression.

GOERING: In connection with your question—

Drums. Light, time.

VOICE OF JACKSON: You were opposed to the invasion of Russia?

GOERING: I was.

JACKSON: And said nothing against it.

GOERING: I said a great deal against it.

JACKSON: And nothing happened. You were a "yes man" to Hitler.

GOERING: I would be interested to meet a "no man" to Hitler.

JACKSON: What I mean is, you gave no warning to the German people about this grave danger, you brought no pressure to bear to prevent this step, and you did not even resign to protect your own place in history.

GOERING: These are not only not questions, they are statements all at once and I would like to try and separate them.

VOICE OF PRESIDENT OF THE TRIBUNAL: The Tribunal will hear the answer to each.

JACKSON: May it please this Court, the witness is using the same tactic over and over. He says the question is not clear, then rephrases it to suit himself, and answers as he pleases!

GOERING (*On his feet*): I am not an echo! I cannot answer statements! Or vague questions with exact responses!

COUNSEL: I apologize for the witness's outburst, but I submit he has a point, and I beg the Tribunal to consider it.

PRESIDENT OF THE TRIBUNAL: Mr. Justice Jackson, I must say I find your cross-examination unusual. Simply turning statements into questions and expecting yes-or-no answers does not do justice to the complexity of these situations. Continue, please!

Goering smiles and sits back down.

JACKSON: Very well. (*To Goering*) Separate my questions.

Drums, light. Time. The Captain hands Goering a sheet of paper.

GOERING: This document has just been handed to us.

COUNSEL: I repeat my objection to the prosecution introducing documents in evidence that we have not yet seen.

VOICE OF PRESIDENT OF THE TRIBUNAL: Your objection is noted. Proceed.

GOERING: This contains alternating statements of various individuals.

VOICE OF JACKSON: Third paragraph from the end.

GOERING: Yes.

JACKSON: "These plans must be kept in the strictest secrecy." Do you see that?

GOERING: Yes.

JACKSON: "They include: A: The liberation of the Rhine."

GOERING: Wrong. The word is not liberation. It is preparation. Of the Rhine River. Technically that means clearing it. Of *tugboats.*

JACKSON: These preparations were not military preparations?

GOERING: To develop the country generally, yes, but to occupy the Rhineland, no.

JACKSON: But it *was* military action you were keeping secret from foreign powers? Yes or no!!

GOERING: I do not recall ever seeing publicized the mobilization plans of the United States. Do you?

Pause. Jackson loses his temper.

JACKSON: I submit to the Tribunal! This witness is not being responsive—

GOERING (*Up, simultaneous*): I certainly *am* being responsive, as well as I *can*—

JACKSON: It is futile to waste our time if the witness—

GOERING (*Simultaneous*): —in the face of such inept and confusing questions *nobody* can answer—

JACKSON: —will not answer the questions!

GOERING (*Simultaneous*): —in any reasonable cross-examination!

PRESIDENT OF THE TRIBUNAL: Mr. Justice Jackson, you are making too much of a small point. Every country keeps certain things secret. Proceed.

JACKSON (*Furious*): I protest! We are losing control of a crucial situation in the history of law!

PRESIDENT OF THE TRIBUNAL: You may speak for yourself, sir, about losing control of a situation. *Continue, please!*

Goering, smiling broadly, sits back down.

JACKSON: Is this Tribunal unaware that outside this courtroom lies the great social question of the revival of Nazism? What defendant Goering is trying to do—as I think he'd be the first to admit— is to create propaganda here that will revive it!

COUNSEL: I object!

Goering gleefully nods.

PRESIDENT OF THE TRIBUNAL: Counsel for the Defense.

COUNSEL: My client is hardly in a position to attack the United States with propaganda. Mr. Justice Jackson is possibly confusing him with Goebbels, who has been dead since April. Hermann Goering is fighting for his life, and should be allowed not only to answer "yes," and "no," but if a question is confusing, clarify it!!

GOERING: Bravo!

PRESIDENT OF THE TRIBUNAL: Quite so. Mr. Justice Jackson, the defendant's reference to the United States is a matter you might well henceforth ignore. We have won the war, sir, and are hardly threatened now. Let us adjourn, and compose ourselves!

Drums. Lights change back to the interrogation room. Goering, Captain, Psychiatrist, Sergeant. Goering swings about in his chair, clapping his hands in delight.

GOERING: Got *his* damned goat, by God! In front of the whole world! (*Claps his hands*) I don't think he'll be Chief Justice of anything now, do you?

PSYCHIATRIST: You did very well.

GOERING: With my little flock watching it all! They were proud of me! I saw it! I put some fight back in them!

2

PSYCHIATRIST: All but Speer. He says what you're doing is terrible.

GOERING: Oh, yes, Speer! He doesn't want me making Americans look stupid. He wants me to fall on my face, and say Hitler did it! Well, I'll take care of him. After what I did to Jackson, we'll be all right!

PSYCHIATRIST: The Commandant of Auschwitz testifies tomorrow.

GOERING: I'm on the stand! He can't!

PSYCHIATRIST: The tribunal has voted to suspend your testimony, and interrupt it for his.

GOERING: More films?

PSYCHIATRIST: More films. You are a formidable witness, but those cameras say you tried to exterminate whole races of human beings. That won't go away.

Goering laughs.

GOERING: Oh, won't it?

PSYCHIATRIST: No, it won't!

GOERING: Well, why should it? When the devil is right, he is more right than all the sanctimonious angels in the world. Hitler was wrong about the war, but right about people. You, me, *everybody* lives despising others. The Americans and the British, unfortunately for us, get along, sort of, because one country came out of the other, but the rest? You'll see, or your children will. There won't be countries anymore, just races, all hating each other. Hitler knew. We all hate our rivals, and the first chance one of us has to dominate them, boom! Tell me it isn't so!

PSYCHIATRIST: That is the past. How can I make you understand it is the purpose of this trial to change exactly that!

GOERING: Because it won't. People are what they are, no better.

192

PSYCHIATRIST: Then we will make them better.

GOERING: Oh, Doctor Freud. Is that your insipid answer to the struggle of life?

PSYCHIATRIST: I don't know what the answer to the struggle of life is! But I know it isn't *you!* I don't care if you love your family! I don't care if you tried to stop the invasion of Poland! I care about the blood you shed, which would drown Nuremberg! Your grand cosmic pessimism is an excuse for murder! The hell with you! You're done for, over with, a dinosaur, gone! After this terrible war, the world must come together, and give up its racial stereotypes.

GOERING: Oh, Doctor Freud! Tell that to the rabbis!

PSYCHIATRIST: Rabbis don't murder children, you son of a bitch!

Exit Psychiatrist, opening the door himself and slamming it shut. Goering chuckles.

GOERING: Got his goat, too. Hauptmann? What am I to do now?

CAPTAIN: I don't know. I'll find out.

SERGEANT: You want me to go?

CAPTAIN: If'n I'd a-wanted you to go, I'd a said so, boy!

SERGEANT: Yes, sir!

CAPTAIN: Carry on.

Exit Captain. The Sergeant stands at ease, but he is very upset. Goering smiles at him.

GOERING: He insulted you, didn't he?

SERGEANT: Yeah.

GOERING: Calling you a boy?

SERGEANT: Way he did it, means nigger.

GOERING: Ah. I see. (*Pause*) All my fliers respected each other.

SERGEANT: Glad to hear it.

GOERING: I taught them that. Would you like to know how?

SERGEANT: Just leave me alone!

GOERING: Shhh. My dear sir. Not another word.

SERGEANT: Don't need you to tell me about it.

Pause. Goering goes to the washbasin and puts some water on his hair.

What did you say to your men?

GOERING: Do you really want to know?

SERGEANT: I wouldn't mind.

GOERING: Don't say I'm just being nice to you.

SERGEANT: I said I wouldn't mind.

GOERING: In the First War, officers looked down on enlisted men. We broke up that caste system and made everyone equal as a man. I told my fliers this. "You are young and you will pay for it. Go have your fun. I want you to. But when you get into that plane, you will be comrades, each respecting the next, so that in battle you will be warriors, destroying all resistance, and if it must be, dying for each other."

The Sergeant nods.

No man in my command called another man "boy."

Pause. Goering sits back down in his chair.

SERGEANT: How many Cranachs did you have?

GOERING: Fourteen.

SERGEANT: Lord. Think of that.

GOERING: They will say I stole paintings just for plunder. Well, some, yes. But not Cranach. He gave me—a great freedom.

SERGEANT: Me, too.

GOERING: Would you like me to describe them for you? The Cranachs I owned? I remember every inch of every one.

SERGEANT: Yeah, I would.

GOERING: Let's start with the Madonna and Child.

SERGEANT: All right.

The Sergeant leans forward. Lights change. Sounds of a basketball game: shouts, thud of the ball, squeaking of sneakers in a gym. Passage of time. Lights up. Sergeant and Captain at the door. Enter Commandant, on Goering's side of the partition, the Psychiatrist and the Counsel on the other.

SERGEANT: Ten-shun!

Goering stands up, smiling.

COMMANDANT: At ease.

GOERING: Good morning, my Colonel!

COMMANDANT: Good morning. Gentlemen, we have something to get straight right now! Coercion, in my prison!

GOERING: Oh, my Colonel! How can that be?

COMMANDANT: Goering, you're not a damned Reichsmarschall anymore. (*To Counsel*) During his exercise and at meals. Get it straight with him.

COUNSEL: The Commandant is concerned—

COMMANDANT: Not concerned, God damned furious!

COUNSEL: God damned furious, over his perception of a— slight manipulation—

COMMANDANT: Bullying!

COUNSEL: Bullying—

PSYCHIATRIST: Sir, it's best not to put words in their mouths.

COMMANDANT: *What* did you say, Major?

PSYCHIATRIST: I beg your pardon, sir. It weakens your own position.

COMMANDANT: When I need your advice, I'll ask for it!

PSYCHIATRIST: I beg your pardon, sir! (*To Counsel*) Sorry!

COUNSEL: Bullying—the other prisoners. They have complained.

GOERING: About me, complained? Who?

COMMANDANT: That's not the point.

GOERING: Speer! Speer!

COMMANDANT: That's not the point!

GOERING: Speer, the bastard!

COUNSEL: Actually, it is Ribbentrop who is most concerned.

GOERING: Ribbentrop! Who told Hitler, go! Poland, everywhere! No one will do anything! Now he's sniveling on his knees! God, you can shoot me fifty times over before I'll do that!

PSYCHIATRIST: No one's asking you to do that. What's being asked—

COMMANDANT: God damn it, Major!

PSYCHIATRIST: I beg your pardon!

COUNSEL: What is being asked, as I understand it, is that you refrain from further influencing the opinions of the other accused.

COMMANDANT: You're going to leave them alone, you understand?

GOERING: How *can* I leave them alone? They are my responsibility! I am the leader of Germany now, and I refuse to let other Germans disgrace their country! They are Germans and they are mine, and I will lead them!!

COMMANDANT: No, you won't! You're in solitary, mister. From now on, you eat by yourself!

GOERING: I protest!

COMMANDANT: To who? Me?

GOERING: Not to you, *SWAGGER STICK!* To the Tribunal! Counsel!

COUNSEL: I do feel this prisoner's rights are being abused!

COMMANDANT: The Tribunal has no jurisdiction over me! *I* run this prison!

GOERING: In the eyes of the world, Colonel! And the world will call you what you are, you ridiculous little, *petty* little, *pig-dog bastard!*

Goering, in a rage, moves toward the Commandant. The Captain and the Sergeant rush him, strike down his arms with their billy clubs, seize him and force him face-down to the floor. Pause.

I beg your pardon! I apologize!

COMMANDANT (*Shaken*): Do that again and I'll lock you in a cage! Let him go.

They do. Goering backs away, swallowing his rage.

PSYCHIATRIST: Sir, this is an issue here.

COMMANDANT: Major, you're out of line!

PSYCHIATRIST: No, sir, I'm not!

COMMANDANT: Jesus Christ!

PSYCHIATRIST: You've got the most thankless job any officer in the Army ever had. I know that! But this man is world famous! And you aren't!

COMMANDANT: I'll court-martial you, by God!

PSYCHIATRIST: All right, do that! But that's Hermann Goering! He's hateful and he's hideous and I have more right to despise him than you do, but if you are unfair to him, you'll get hurt! Don't underestimate him!

COMMANDANT: I've given my orders. Consult all you want. Then carry them out, Major, or you're on charges. That's all.

Exit Commandant.

PSYCHIATRIST: Congratulations, Goering. You've got us fighting among ourselves.

GOERING: Don't let him do this to me. I must not be separated from—Germany.

PSYCHIATRIST: Breakfast, lunch and dinner in your cell. That's it. I did my best. Here, I brought your glasses.

He holds up a pair of dark eyeglasses, for the Captain to see. The Captain nods. The Psychiatrist sets them down on the table. Goering picks them up, looks them over.

GOERING: Well, German lenses, good. (*He puts them on*) Now I look like an old woman in Florida.

PSYCHIATRIST: Right.

GOERING: No laugh? Not even a smile?

PSYCHIATRIST: No.

GOERING: I understand. It would violate your high moral position. I must be a monster. Gas-pump creature, with my dick in my ear. You think you can march me into a courtroom, find me guilty, kill me, and change the course of human nature. But I am a man just like you. You are a man just like me. Pretending otherwise is a great mistake.

PSYCHIATRIST: Nuts. Just give me back the glasses. You'll get them going into court.

GOERING: I can't keep them?

PSYCHIATRIST: You could cut your throat with good German lenses.

GOERING: So I could. Okay. (*He takes off the glasses, hands them back*)
Thank you.

Exit Psychiatrist.

(*To Counsel*) If I can't eat with them, I can't talk to them. You must negotiate for me.

COUNSEL: How can I?

GOERING: Through their lawyers! They'll listen to you!

COUNSEL: Perhaps.

GOERING: Tell them I will not implicate anyone, not Ribbentrop, not even Speer, if they will stand fast, and not break ranks! Germans together, or else! Understand!

COUNSEL: Or else what?

GOERING: I know enough to send them all to hell a hundred times over.

COUNSEL (*Quietly*): Oh, do you? And how much of that do I know? Nothing?

GOERING: Yes. Do you want to quit?

Pause.

COUNSEL: No. You want me to—threaten other prisoners— with exposure of crimes known only to you. Is that it?

GOERING: That will do. It is your duty as a lawyer.

COUNSEL: I have three duties. To my client, to the law, and to Germany. But not, evidently, to myself.

GOERING: Thank you.

COUNSEL: The British cross-examine tomorrow. Only a staff lawyer, but be careful.

GOERING: I beat Jackson, didn't I?

COUNSEL: Yes, you did.

GOERING: So. You do your duty and I'll do mine. Until tomorrow.

COUNSEL: Good afternoon.

Exit Counsel. Pause. Goering sags, wipes his face with his hands.

CAPTAIN (*To Sergeant*): You got a break.

SERGEANT: What?

CAPTAIN: I said you got a break. Take ten. Move out!!

SERGEANT: Sir.

Exit Sergeant. Pause. Goering becomes aware that he and the Captain are alone in the room. He regroups his forces.

GOERING: I am sorry to see a Hauptmann standing guard with a black man. They aren't quite human, are they? No wonder you call him boy.

CAPTAIN: Yeah, well never mind that.

GOERING: None of my business.

CAPTAIN: Right. (*Pause*) So what was the best rifle you ever had?

GOERING: Ah, well! My old bolt-action Dryse! It had a birch stock to it, fit my chin like a woman's hand. Fifty years old but lead a stag, and it fired itself! Bang! Clean through the heart!

CAPTAIN: I shot a 460 Weatherly Magnum once.

GOERING: And it kicked!

CAPTAIN: Nearly tore off my shoulder!

GOERING: High power, short range. Not my old Dryse. With it, easy, follow, lead—

He mimes hefting a rifle to his shoulder and leading a stag. The Captain does the same.

GOERING AND CAPTAIN (*Softly*): Bang.

Pause.

CAPTAIN: People say you raised lions. I mean, had them at home, in the house.
GOERING: Oh, yes.
CAPTAIN: *Lions?*
GOERING: Delightful creatures. Full of love and trust.
CAPTAIN: What do you do when a lion, all full of love and trust, jumps on your lap?
GOERING: You keep still.
CAPTAIN: I reckon. (*Pause*) I hear you shot down thirty planes in the First War.
GOERING: Twenty-two.
CAPTAIN: One time, in this dogfight, you got this plane dead to rights. You saluted the man, and flew away. Really?
GOERING: His guns had jammed. He was helpless.
CAPTAIN: Oh.
GOERING: Hauptmann, why are you disobeying orders talking to me?
CAPTAIN: I'm proud to know you.
GOERING: And I you, American Hauptmann. Salut.

Goering salutes, with the American Army salute. The Captain returns it.

CAPTAIN: Sir.

Drums. Downlight on Goering again. Accent light on the Counsel.

2

VOICE OF THE PRESIDENT OF THE TRIBUNAL: The Prosecutor for Great Britain may now cross-examine.

VOICE OF BRITISH PROSECUTOR (*Dry and deceptive*): A few minor questions. In 1944, fifty British Air Force Prisoners of War, upon their escape from Stalag Luft III, were captured and shot. Upon your orders?

GOERING: Absolutely not. I was on leave.

PROSECUTOR: It was Hitler's decision?

GOERING: We had a very bitter argument about it.

PROSECUTOR: As Minister of the Air Force, you had jurisdiction over medical experiments on captured aviators?

GOERING: I knew nothing of this.

PROSECUTOR: Then let me tell you about it. Men were frozen on the ground at sky-altitude temperatures. Then they were put in a bed with naked women. They were allowed to come alive if they could, and, if they could, have sexual relations. Then they were gassed. Air Force experiments!

GOERING: I never heard of anything like that in all my life!

PROSECUTOR: Do you consider it serious?

GOERING: It is an atrocity, whether in the name of aviation *or* science! I consider *nothing* more serious!!

PROSECUTOR: Atrocities upset you?

GOERING: Yes!

PROSECUTOR: Let us see about that. This document, numbered 786–QS. A letter addressed to Obergruppenfuhrer-SS Reinhard Heydrich. Would you read the last paragraph?

The Captain gives Goering a paper.

COUNSEL: I have not seen this document before. I object.

PROSECUTOR: Last paragraph, or I will read it.

COUNSEL: I appeal to the Tribunal!

VOICE OF THE PRESIDENT OF THE TRIBUNAL: Letter addressed to Obergruppenfuhrer-SS Reinhard Heydrich. Last paragraph.

GOERING (*Reading*): "I further instruct you to present to me at once all logistical preparations for the Final Solution of the Jewish Problem."

PROSECUTOR: That is your signature?

GOERING: It's only a formality, an enabling act. Drafted by Himmler, or Heydrich.

PROSECUTOR: Not Hitler?

GOERING: Never!

PROSECUTOR: Not you?

GOERING: No!

PROSECUTOR: You have boasted and boasted to this Tribunal that you are responsible for whatever you signed! Well? Who signed it?

GOERING: Signed, Goering, Reichsmarschall! But translated wrong. Final solution should read complete solution.

PROSECUTOR: Oh, please! What is the difference?

GOERING: Emigration, not liquidation! That's the difference!

PROSECUTOR: I don't believe you. I believe Number One gave Number Two a verbal order to murder eleven million Jews and Number Two put it in writing for him. Then Number One left Number Two holding the baby. How could you be so stupid? Of all the Germans, you were the only man with the power to oppose Hitler and his inhuman policies, and you can't even do it now, while he is putting the rope around your neck! Never mind your sacred oaths and heroic poses! Why didn't Number Two *ever* say no to Number One?

GOERING: To him?

PROSECUTOR: To him.

2

Pause. Then Goering holds up both hands, shakes his head, and smiles. Drums. Lights change. The interrogation room. Goering sits at the table, handcuffed to the Sergeant, who stands by him. Across the table sits his Wife, a handsome woman in her forties, dressed in stylishly made-to-do threadbare clothes.

WIFE: But I must ask you.

GOERING: No, please!

WIFE: Even now! I must! For God's sake, he was going to shoot me! Kill your child! The whole world knows he was the devil! He brought all Germany, and us, to ruin! Say so!!

GOERING: Never.

WIFE: Why not? It's the only chance you have!

GOERING: I have no chance at all.

WIFE: You don't know that!

GOERING: Of course I do. Don't fool yourself. Tell our child that I am going to die. Is she afraid they'll kill you, too?

WIFE: Always.

GOERING: Tell her I will die, but not you. Maybe it will help.

WIFE: Please.

GOERING: What?

WIFE: Hitler! Hitler!

GOERING: My dearest, Hitler is not to blame for what I did. I am.

Pause.

WIFE: All right.

GOERING: Thank you.

Pause.

WIFE: We would have been very happy, in the theatre.

GOERING: Do you think so?

WIFE: You would have been a marvelous actor.

GOERING: Yes, I would. Falstaff!

WIFE: You could have worn your costumes and been bigger than life. After performances, in the evening, we would drink, with the other actors, and then go home.

GOERING: But I wasn't acting. Unfortunately for me.

WIFE: You are the best husband any wife ever had. We have the most beautiful child in the world. Whatever happens, I am content.

CAPTAIN: Time's up.

The Sergeant moves back, forcing Goering up by the hand-cuffs. The Wife rises, too. Goering reaches out for his wife and she moves toward him, as if they would kiss through a screen. The Sergeant jerks Goering's arms down roughly. Goering waves a goodbye to his wife. She to him. Exit Wife, the Counsel opening the door and closing it after her. Then he moves down to her place. The Sergeant unlocks the handcuffs and joins the Captain on guard. Goering sits very still. Then he sees the Counsel staring at him.

GOERING: You will help her?

COUNSEL: All I can.

GOERING: In spite of what you think of me.

COUNSEL: Yes, in spite of that.

GOERING: What you think of me is very important to me.

COUNSEL: Some will admire you.

GOERING: But not you!

The Counsel goes to the washbasin on his side of the room, to wash and dry his hands and face.

205

COUNSEL: At first, I thought the Tribunal unjust. Then the horrible realities of those camps wiped out everything. The trial is no longer about guilt as we ever knew it. It is about the absolute worst in human nature, and it looks squarely at you. I don't know how guilty you are anymore, or how guilty I am, for that matter. Yes, it's my turn too. You awed me, charmed me, in spite of everything, made me admire you, and I blackmailed men on trial for their lives. Right here, in this prison. For you!

GOERING: You were right to do so. They broke their vows.

COUNSEL: I had no right to do so. Men can change their minds.

GOERING: If that is what you think duty is, you know nothing of men and never will.

COUNSEL: At sixty-eight, I'm learning. And one of the things I am learning is that of all the ideas men have ever had, duty is the worst!

He throws the towel into the basin.

GOERING: So, verdict tomorrow. What do you think?

COUNSEL: No one believes anything good about you now.

GOERING: Not even you?

COUNSEL: You are courageous. Everyone says that. You dominate the courtroom, and everyone says that, too.

GOERING: What do you say?

COUNSEL: You *still* don't think anything wrong was done!!! (*Pause*) Your wife was right. You should have bullied and pillaged and murdered in the theatre, where you belong.

GOERING: Well, you did your best.

COUNSEL: Thank you.

GOERING: I have one more thing to say to the Tribunal.

COUNSEL: Yes?

GOERING: Shooting I will accept. Hanging I will not.

COUNSEL: You hardly have that choice.

GOERING: I must have that choice. Think. What will be best for Germany? For its Reichsmarschall to be hung, like a dog, or shot, like a man?

COUNSEL: To be shot like a man.

GOERING: You said you loved Germany.

COUNSEL: I do!

GOERING: Then you must do *your* duty as I must do mine.

COUNSEL: What duty now?

Drums up. Lights change. Spots on Goering and the Captain.

GOERING: You alone will know. Only a great hunter, wise and cunning, can do it. Are you that man?

CAPTAIN: I could be.

GOERING: Will you do it?

CAPTAIN: I might.

GOERING: They don't search the guards, do they?

CAPTAIN: No, they don't.

Spots on Goering and the Sergeant.

GOERING: The mother of Jesus holds him firmly. His infant hand lingers on her cheek. It can be yours.

SERGEANT: Nobody'd believe me.

GOERING: With my signature, they would legally have to. (*Pause*) You might keep it. Or sell it for a fortune.

SERGEANT: What you want me to do?

GOERING: A few steps, a moment alone with my gear, slip something in your pocket, and give it to me. They don't search the guards, do they?

SERGEANT: No, they don't.

207

2

Drums. Lights change. Spot on Goering. The drums continue, muffled.

VOICE OF THE PRESIDENT OF THE TRIBUNAL: You were the second only to Hitler in the Nazi movement—

GOERING: I did not want a war, nor did I bring it about—

PRESIDENT OF THE TRIBUNAL: You created the Gestapo and the concentration camps—

GOERING: Except as a military duty, I never ordered the execution of anyone—

PRESIDENT OF THE TRIBUNAL: You designed the German Air Force, and began the bombing of cities instead of military targets—

GOERING: Compared with Dresden and Hiroshima, my Air Force was a model of restraint.

PRESIDENT OF THE TRIBUNAL: You looted Europe of its cultural treasures as no other man in history—

GOERING: I paid for everything—

PRESIDENT OF THE TRIBUNAL: You persecuted the Jews, first by devastating economic laws—

GOERING: When my duty allowed, I was always a friend to the Jews—

PRESIDENT OF THE TRIBUNAL: You then issued orders to Himmler and Heydrich—

GOERING: I utterly condemn these terrible mass murders!

PRESIDENT OF THE TRIBUNAL: To exterminate the entire Jewish population of Europe!

Drums are silent.

Six million died.

Pause.

208

There are no excuses for you. The Tribunal finds you guilty, on all counts. You may address the Court before sentence is pronounced.

GOERING: I speak to the German people. The winner will always be innocent. The loser will always be guilty. This trial changes nothing.

PRESIDENT OF THE TRIBUNAL: Defendant, on the counts by which you have been indicted, this Tribunal sentences you to death by hanging.

Burst of drums. Blackout. A young girl's voice is heard in the darkness.

DAUGHTER (*Voiceover*): "A Lady Stood," by Dietmar von Aist.

Lights up slowly. Goering is standing by his chair. He is handcuffed to the Sergeant again. His eight-year-old daughter is standing across the wire fence, in front of her mother, whose hands are on her shoulders. The Counsel and the Psychiatrist stand in the background, as does the Captain.

DAUGHTER:
A Lady stood on a turret stone
Looking away o'er the moorlands lone,
To see her love come riding there.

She saw a falcon in the air:
Oh, happy falcon, flying free,
Flying where your heart would be!

My eyes have singled out a knight.
What though his arms have lost their might?
For him I cry.

Though all my prayers be answered never,
My love for him will live forever.

Do you like it?

GOERING: It is perfect. So are you.

Pause. The Wife presses the Daughter's shoulders.

DAUGHTER: I am to say goodbye now.
GOERING: I know.
DAUGHTER: God bless you.
GOERING: God bless you.
DAUGHTER: Goodbye, Daddy.
GOERING: Goodbye.

*She turns and walks out, followed by the Wife and the
Counsel. The Sergeant unlocks the handcuffs, steps away.
Goering wheels away, hiding his feelings, which are intense
and genuine. He turns back, to face the Psychiatrist.*

PSYCHIATRIST: You killed her. *Her.* A million times. Can't
you understand that?

A terrible pause. Goering struggles with himself.

GOERING: *UNDERSTAND IT? YES!! I UNDERSTAND IT!*
(*Pause*) And it makes no difference whether we understand it or not.

PSYCHIATRIST: Why?

GOERING: Because we are men, and men will do what men will
do.

PSYCHIATRIST: My God! That's all you have to say?

GOERING: What do you want me to say? I am a fool? Yes! I
would do it all again? Yes? That there is nothing worse
than a man? ABSOLUTELY!!! *Why* did it happen? I don't
know! *You* can tell everybody that, Doctor! What will you
put in your book?

PSYCHIATRIST: The truth about the war, as I saw it!

GOERING: Authoritarian regression, psychological sadism, the
household origins of global treachery, and that explains
everything. So much for psychologists. What else do we
have to say to each other?

PSYCHIATRIST: One more thing.

GOERING: What's that?

PSYCHIATRIST: You asked me to find out whose work this trial
was. I did.

GOERING: Churchill, Roosevelt, Stalin?

PSYCHIATRIST: It came out of Roosevelt's cabinet. The man
who gave it its form was a Colonel Murray C. Bernays.

GOERING: Bernays?

PSYCHIATRIST: That was the maiden name of a great man's
wife. Freud's.

Pause.

GOERING: The man who created the Tribunal was related to
Freud?

PSYCHIATRIST: By marriage, yes.

GOERING: Hung by a Jew?

Goering laughs. The Psychiatrist smiles.

(*Laughing*) So! Now you smile! Doctor, how much do you
hate me?

PSYCHIATRIST (*Smiling*): Beyond description.

GOERING: Then how would you like to kill me?

*Light change. Echoing sounds of GIs playing basketball.
Exit Psychiatrist. Enter Counsel.*

GOERING: Well.

COUNSEL: Well.

GOERING: Did you find out?

COUNSEL: It will be at night. You'll be awakened, quickly, and rushed to a gymnasium, where the playing of basketball games masks the building of the gallows. They will hang you then.

GOERING: You can save me from that.

*Lights change. Sounds of basketball, dim. Exit Counsel and
with him, Captain and Sergeant. Goering is alone on stage.
He walks slowly to the washbasin, quietly washes his hands
and face and dries them with a towel, then moves to the
center of the stage. The basketball game stops. Sound mon-
tage, with echoes and vibrations.*

VOICES: They get to sleep!
    They don't expect anything!
    We get them out fast!
    Colonel!
    Goering first, then the others!
    Colonel, get the colonel!
    We hang them before they know what's happening!
    Colonel! Colonel!

VOICE OF COMMANDANT: What?

VOICES: Goering!
    He's on the floor in his cell!

He's in convulsions!

He's bitten something!

My God, he's turning green!

He's dead!

VOICE OF COMMANDANT: He can't be! Oh, my God! He can't be!!

VOICES: What'll we do!

How did he do it?

This will wreck the trial!

Who did it?

Who got that stuff to him?

VOICE OF COMMANDANT: Somebody *helped* that bastard! WHO??

VOICES: Who did it? Why???

The voices echo and vibrate into silence. Goering stands at center. A greenish, ghastly light falls on him. Muffled drumroll.

GOERING: Dear Swagger Stick. You will find a letter telling you I had the pill with me all the time. You know that's not possible. Somebody gave it to me. The Army can quote my letter, clear itself, and then, I hope, court-martial you.

Drumroll ends. Goering, smiling, speaks to the audience.

I am at peace with what I have done. I know you all very well. You always liked me, and saw yourselves in me. You will find other Hitlers, and other ways to go to war. When you do, he will need me, and he will call me back. I will bind myself to him again, laughing, a good number two. (*His smile vanishes. He stares out coldly*) After all, what do you think men are?

The green light fades on him.

213

April Snow

For the Ensemble Studio Theatre

Scene One: Morning.

Gordon, Grady. Gordon is stirring soup in the electric crock pot on the bar.

GORDON: So why are you giving only six readings next year?

Pause.

GRADY: Mona's come back to me.
GORDON: Again?
GRADY: For good.
GORDON: When?
GRADY: A month ago. Mona's twenty-eight now. Little Fred is nine. This week, there had to be a visit. So, there was. Doorbell rang. There was Fred, coat and tie, hair slicked down, looking angelic. Behind him stood Richard, the injured father, looking innocent. The little boy and I faced each other. "Hi, Grady," he said. "Hi, Fred." "Mama here?" "Yep." "Bye, Dad." Richard left. Mona came out of my kitchen. "Hi, Mama," said Fred. "Am I in the maid's room again?" (*Pause*) In the morning, I got up first. How

to work? Think clearly about Madame de Staël, Madame Récamier and Madame Krudener? Read Sainte-Beuve, oh, please! I studied a paragraph. Madame Krudener dying, floating down the Volga on a houseboat with her coffin by her side. She was ridiculous. All my work confronted me like a coffin. My home felt like a tomb. I felt like a corpse, and I was afraid of Mona's child. (*Pause*) They got up, made breakfast. I worked, pretending diligence. They tiptoed past my study, shushing each other. Utter silence. I hollered. "Oh, come in!" They did. Both, staring. Fred and I smiled. Like this. God. Two hypocrites. I wondered why he didn't leap over the desk, grab my throat, and throttle me. It's what I wanted to do to him. But the little boy whose mother left his father for me, *again*, he didn't do that. He tried to talk, coughed, blew his nose, as wretched as I was. Then he said, "Can I watch TV in the bedroom?" I said, "Sure." He kissed me, and he went into the room where his mother and I sleep, and watched his cartoons. He's with us every other weekend now. He says he loves me. I believe him. I want to believe him. I must. Madame de Stael, Madame Recamier, Madame Krudener, all talk happily at once. I just take it down. I love Mona. I love Fred. I stay home now. I will give only six readings next year. Do you see?

GORDON: I do. Potato soup in the crock pot. Want some?

GRADY: Oh God no. I'm never hungry now. I'm in love!

Scene Two: Noon.

Gordon, Milly. Milly sits in Gordon's lap, arms around his neck.

GORDON: The American pig, we are told, loves to hide. But not thinking he is very big, he will peer at you from behind a stick, sure he can't be seen. Like this. Hello.

He peers at Milly, like a pig behind a stick. Milly laughs and kisses him. They kiss for some time. Pause.

MILLY: Do you *have* to have lunch with that man?

GORDON: I'll be back. Four o'clock. Not a moment later.

MILLY: Why did you tell me that story?

GORDON: Thought it was funny.

MILLY: About a pig.

GORDON: Yes.

MILLY: You aren't a pig.

GORDON: It was a story.

MILLY: Nothing is just a story. I'd like some wine. May I?

GORDON: Sure. There's soup in the pot.

MILLY: Just wine. I don't eat much. You want some?

GORDON: No.

Milly pours some wine for herself at Gordon's bar.

MILLY: Always the same, this room. Your desk, Don Quixote. You had two cots, for Jimmy and me.

GORDON: I remember.

MILLY: We slept out here, watching The Late Show. Down from Riverdale, with Alice and John, to SoHo, where nobody lived then but you. With your beautiful young wife and Ruby. Who would be what, Ruby, sixteen now?

GORDON: Eighteen. Living in California.

MILLY: I know. When do you see her?

GORDON: Twice a year.

MILLY: You worry about her?

GORDON: Some.

MILLY: You worry about me?

GORDON: Some.

MILLY: I'm stronger now. Being crazy can do that for you. It taught me things.

GORDON: What?

MILLY: Things. How to live without eating. I do now but not much. When people tell stories for hidden reasons. (*Pause*) I was eighteen when I went in the hospital. In Minnesota, the treatment was—conservative. They gave me insulin shock and wrapped me in bedsheets, I was there ten long months. You sent me that book. *Grimm's Fairy Tales*. An ugly Scottish Edition with scary illustrations. Just right for a girl in a madhouse. I read and read. Giants, and monsters. Wicked stepmothers, heartless kings, and little runaways. Stand-ins, I knew. Momma, Daddy, Brother, me. You. There was one good book in the hospital library. The plays of Strindberg. Strindberg, Grimm, and me. (*Pause*) Maybe I can be crazy in a book some day. (*She laughs*) About a sane brother and a crazy sister and the crazy sister survives and the sane brother might not. I'd write it now but it wouldn't be believable. (*Pause*) When we were all together, and we came here, the family, do you remember the day I kidnapped you? Toothbrush, paste, my sweater in a bag. Off to the river, pulling you along, swinging my little bottom and batting my eyes. I was running away with you.

GORDON: I remember.

MILLY: Who packs a bag now, to run away with you?

GORDON: I go nowhere now, with anyone. I sleep here, with a nice friend once in a while, not often. To tell you the truth, recently at depressing intervals ominously increasing in length.

MILLY: Did I make you happy last night?

Gordon shrugs, then smiles.

GORDON: My God, darling, yes. But when it's time to go, you go.
MILLY: Just like that. Not one word. You'll be proud of me.
GORDON: Right. You will find your young man. I will go back to my Medocs and Marsallas and haute cuisine, which I hardly taste anyway, since I never seem to be hungry anymore. My sex life will once again be a kind of after-brandy afterthought. I'm too old to change that. (*Pause. He grins*) You have a beady look in your eye. Found him already? Time to go? I'm philosophical. Go.
MILLY: I love you. (*Pause*) I adore you. (*Pause*) I have since I was a child. I always will, as long as I live. There can never be anyone for me but you.
GORDON: You take my breath away. (*Pause*) Do you want another drink?
MILLY: If you do. Another drink, I mean.
GORDON (*Simultaneous*): I don't.

Pause.

MILLY: What do you want, Gordon?
GORDON: I want you to come to Spain with me.
MILLY: With you?
GORDON: For the summer. I've got to work on this movie. It's called A Day in the Life of Nero.
MILLY: Won't you like that?
GORDON: It pays. Blood and sex and everything like that. Come with me. Please.
MILLY: To Spain with you?

221

GORDON: Leave May 15th. Well?

MILLY: May 15! Blood and sex and everything like that! Spain?

Scene Three: Afternoon.

*Milly, Grady. Outside the window, snow begins to fall.
Milly is curled in a chair, reading a book. Pot of tea beside
her. A fire burns in the fireplace. A radio is playing a
Christmas carol: "Christmas Bells." Enter Grady, covered
with snow.*

GRADY: Oh.

MILLY: Hello. You have keys, too.

GRADY: Yes. So do you, evidently.

MILLY: Yes.

GRADY: Snow in April. Not since the 1880s, I hear.

MILLY: Yes. They're playing Christmas carols on the radio.
(*She turns the radio off*) I'm Millicent Beck. Gordon lets
me study here sometimes.

GRADY: Grady Gunn.

MILLY: Oh! Sorry. I study you in school. Gordon has all your
books here. He talks about you.

GRADY: Really.

MILLY: Want some tea? There's potato soup, too, in this pot.
Not very fancy. Here's a teacup, just waiting.

GRADY: For Gordon.

MILLY: I don't mind. Please.

GRADY: No soup. I couldn't eat anything.

MILLY: Gordon said he'd be back around four.

GRADY: All right. A cup of tea. I won't stay long.

MILLY: You can if you want to. Gordon will be glad to see you.
He likes you.

GRADY: Oh *does* he?

MILLY: That was patronizing. I'm sorry again. Here. (*She gives Grady some tea*) It's just that Gordon talks about you all the time.

Grady takes a flask from her purse, pours whiskey into her tea.

GRADY: I'll need a little of this, hope you don't mind. What does Gordon say about me all the time? I can just imagine.

MILLY: Maybe not. He says you've worked hard all your life, and deserve your success.

GRADY: Did he tell you I was married to him once?

Pause.

MILLY: No, he didn't.

GRADY: Well, I was.

MILLY: When?

GRADY: In the summer of 1954.

Pause.

MILLY: Eight years before I was born. For how long?

GRADY: Six months.

MILLY: All right, then.

GRADY: It was long enough.

MILLY: I knew his other wife. I just didn't know you'd been one, too.

GRADY: One of four.

MILLY: Four? I thought there was only one.

GRADY: Four. Estelle, me, Betty Jean, and Lucy. Four. Which of us did you know?

223

MILLY: Lucy.

GRADY: Health, home and children. Lasted four years. I was the fellow artist—six months. Estelle the buxom mother —one year, and Betty Jean the socialite—two. This man is sixty-one years old. He has been married four times, for a sum total of seven-and-one-half years. For fifty-four years of his life, he has lived alone, with crushed ice in empty rooms, and his throbbing heart. What do you think that means?

MILLY: I don't care.

GRADY: You'd better. He might marry you someday.

MILLY: Estelle for her bosom, you for your talent, Betty Ann—

GRADY: Betty Jean—

MILLY: —for her money, Lucy for home and children and me—for my youth. Is that it?

GRADY: I'm glad you were listening.

MILLY: Well, you're wrong. He isn't like that now.

GRADY: What is he like now?

MILLY: He's my contemporary. By magic.

GRADY: Really? (*She takes a large gulp of tea, chokes*)

MILLY: Are you all right?

GRADY: Yes. Snow. Fire. Whiskey and tea. Christmas carols on the radio. All in the springtime. It's confusing.

MILLY: You're in real trouble.

GRADY: You can see.

MILLY: I know what that is. I'm sorry.

GRADY: How nice.

MILLY: Gordon said you were living with a young woman who was very important to you. Who had a little boy.

GRADY: What do you think about that?

MILLY: I was crazy once. I learned not to judge other people.

GRADY: Oh, just this once. Do it.

MILLY: Maybe you feel she came to you out of prison. With her little boy.

GRADY: You aren't crazy now. You're quite right, she did. (*With bitterness*) She was sitting under a fir tree. In a white summer dress, on a white iron bench, reading my book about Colette. The weather, it was summer, was dazzling. Teal blue skies, air like spring water. She was pregnant. Separated from her husband, torturing him, beautiful, and we became lovers. She had her baby with me. I took her to that little hospital, waited. I thought I was the father! Well, I saw it first! Before he did! I named him. Frederick. That was that. They came to live with me, for a year. Then left. Came back. Left again. This was the third time.

MILLY: She's left you again. When?

GRADY: An hour ago.

MILLY: You came here to talk to Gordon. I'll get out.

GRADY: Thank you.

MILLY: Gordon will understand. He always does.

GRADY: Yes, he *will*!

MILLY: I'm sorry!

GRADY: No, I am.

MILLY: What can I say? You have your career?

GRADY: That will do.

Milly gets her coat.

MILLY: So talk to Gordon. He listens. He can help. I heard you once, on the radio. Everybody cheered. It was heaven!

GRADY: I was at my best, no doubt.

MILLY: Don't be so bitter. I don't know how you feel, but really, what do you want, love *and* literature?

GRADY: Well, yes. Once you've had it, you see, you keep trying to keep it. You don't understand that yet.

MILLY: Because I haven't been to heaven! I've been to Fifth Floor, Ward Six! I'm trying *not* to have any more of *that*!
GRADY: Really? Well, if anybody can put you back in Ward Six, it's Gordon.
MILLY: You're bitter and you're wrong.
GRADY: Find out for yourself.
MILLY: Gordon Tate is my teacher and my lover and my friend! I'm sorry you're upset, but leave us alone!
GRADY: With pleasure! (*Pause*) I beg your pardon.
MILLY: I beg yours.
GRADY: About Gordon, I do hope you're right.
MILLY: No, you don't. You know you are.
GRADY: Maybe!
MILLY: I was in an asylum. I know that look!

Exit Milly.

Scene Four: Afternoon.

Grady, Gordon.

GORDON: You think I'm behaving badly. Right?
GRADY: Right.
GORDON: The spectacle of an aging egotist consorting with an orphan out of a mental institution *revolts* you. Say it.
GRADY: She tells me you are contemporaries by magic. Really?
GORDON: You didn't see her when Alice died. John first, then Alice. She was in pieces. She could hardly talk.
GRADY: She can talk now.
GORDON: Yes!
GRADY: Fine! She's twenty-one—
GORDON: Twenty!

GRADY: Twenty, and she can take care of herself. Bless you both.

Pause.

GORDON: Then what is the matter with you?
GRADY: Fred is the matter with me!
GORDON: Mona?
GRADY: Yes.
GORDON: She left you? *Again?*
GRADY: Of course.

Pause.

GORDON: Really?
GRADY: Really.
GORDON: Why?
GRADY: Figure it out!
GORDON: Fred?
GRADY: Little Fred. The little bastard.
GORDON: What?
GRADY: My darling Fred! He was lying! He was telling me he loved me, wanted to come see me *every* weekend, and telling her, "Mommy, we want you back. Leave this old witch and come home." I mean, the nine-year-old little *bastard.*
GORDON: How can you know he said that?
GRADY: Mona told me. On the floor, hugging my knees, crying, saying goodbye! He said exactly that!!
GORDON: Oh.
GRADY: Yes.
GORDON: I'm sorry.
GRADY: Not really. But you will be.

227

GORDON: Sorry about Fred?

GRADY: About Milly.

GORDON: Maybe not.

GRADY: The trouble with you is, you won't face what's happening.

GORDON: What is?

GRADY: You want that child to live with you.

GORDON: Watch out, Grady!

GRADY: I've just been *left!* You watch out! GORDON, LOOK AT US! Our dazzling lives! Our brilliant work! Our ferocious dedication! These scrupulous, loveless lives!! We were blooming in childhood, thrilling in youth, underwhelming in development, lost in maturity and competent in age. It is almost over. So what do we do? We hunger and thirst and turn to the young, as once we turned to the sun.

GORDON: I did ask Milly to go to Spain with me.

GRADY: Will she?

GORDON: Yes, I think she will,

GRADY: If you take her, you're a son of a bitch.

GORDON: You'd have taken Mona to Spain.

GRADY: No, Gordon, I wouldn't have taken Mona to Spain. That's the difference between us. I love Mona.

GORDON: And I love Milly! Decently!

GRADY: In bed, decently, a child?

GORDON: Yes, in bed, decently, God damn you, and she's not a child! And last night the first time, after years and—

GRADY: After what, Gordon?

GORDON: I loved Milly the first day I saw her. When Alice and John brought her here, on a visit, to this loft. She was three years old, I think. Her brother a lumpy little sorehead. I even liked him, but Milly was just enchantment. The minute we saw each other, we delighted each other.

She'd jump on me, hug me, I'd melt. She'd laugh. We'd play. She grew up. She was sick, very sick for a while. She doesn't and won't ever know how I kept up with that, what it did to me. John died. Alice died. She was hanging on by a thread, and she came to me. Christ! And now, when she looks at me, and when she says she—oh, loves me, and I know, I know, she'll grow out of that—but— you're right, it's the sun! Happiness!

GRADY: But you don't love her.

GORDON: Grady!

GRADY: Not if you take her to Spain, you don't! As your baggage. An old man's *thing?* You don't!

Scene Five: Evening.

Milly, Gordon. Embers glow in the fireplace. The snow has stopped. Gordon sits on a pillow by the fire. Milly is looking out the window, a book in her hand.

MILLY: A few people, moving through snow. Too many. They could all come up here. (*Pause*) Know what Faust did when he first made his pact with the Devil?

GORDON: He corrupted an innocent child.

MILLY: That came later. Anyway, she wasn't a child. She was a buxom lass who went to bed with a good-looking man. It usually happens without supernatural assistance. No, in the old German books, the first thing Faust did was go to a tavern and order a big dinner. Then, when it came, because the place was so crowded, people jammed in back to back, eating shoulder to shoulder—well, by God, Faust for the first time invoked the powers of hell. He waved his arms and every single person in that whole nasty medi-

229

eval diner turned to stone. And he ate his supper in peace.
Would you do that?

GORDON: Of course.

MILLY: So would I. I'm Faust. You're the Devil. I've signed in
blood. (*She waves her arms*) There. I just did it. Now
nobody else can move. Just you, just me. In that snow
down there, they've all turned to stone, and no one will be
coming up here until I say so. No doorbells. The telephone
can't ring. Life waits on us, and my soul is yours. (*Pause*)
Where will you be, next Christmas?

GORDON: Right here, no doubt. And you?

MILLY: Somewhere else. Learning useful things.

GORDON: How to write?

MILLY: How to live, without you. It won't be hard. I'll find
other teachers. Get another degree. Teach, myself. Marry
a professor. Have a baby. Get divorced. Love a woman.
Drink. Be mean. Write a book about it. The full life.

GORDON: I don't like to think of you like that.

MILLY: You'll just have to. My life is my life. I'm a grubby little
intellectual moth, climbing up out of old books. I'll be a
moth forever. My little bag of hopes will stand empty. I
will blame my husband for it, and yell at my children.
Then I'll tie my hair in knots.

*Pause. Gordon doesn't look at her. She goes to him, kneels
behind him.*

Tell me about yourself. When you were a moth. (*She puts
her hands over his eyes*) No, close your eyes. Tell me. Who
was he?

*Gordon leans back against her, eyes closed. She rubs his
temples.*

230

GORDON: He was a Knoxville paperboy, wanting to be a writer. Learned worshiping Tarzan, The Shadow. Holes in his socks. Gets through his paper route by six in the morning, has time to smoke Lucky Strikes, from a green pack, read Tarzan, The Shadow. That what you mean?

MILLY: Yes. More, what you see.

Gordon leans back in her arms.

GORDON: No. Your thoughts are so much more vivid than mine. Compared to you, I'm shopworn.

Milly holds him against her, smiles.

MILLY: I love you. I love you. I can't *stop* saying it now. I won't bother you with it. But do you hear me? I love you. When I've vanished—no, keep your eyes shut—vanished into my life, all gone, don't forget me. You've made me so happy. To come into this room. To see you walk into it, where I wait for you. You make me forget what I am.

Suddenly, Gordon gets up, pulling himself out of her arms. He goes to the window.

GORDON: I'm not taking you to Spain.

MILLY: Oh. You're not?

GORDON: I thought I could but I can't.

MILLY: Oh.

GORDON: I don't want you like baggage, living off me.

MILLY: I don't care about that.

GORDON: You would. People staring at you. Bad enough at lunch and dinner. At breakfast we'd look like something out of a Bunuel movie together. You would get tired of me. I might get tired of you.

231

MILLY: Tired?

GORDON: That's the best thing that could happen.

MILLY: What's the worst?

GORDON: I couldn't come back without you. You'd marry me. You'd turn into a nurse. Oh, all right for a while. Fun. But I'm sixty-one years old. You'd be a Princess for a year. Then a friend. Then a secretary. Then a nurse. And then a slave.

MILLY: Stop.

GORDON: At the end, you'd put me in a nursing home and wait to collect.

MILLY: Oh.

GORDON: It's the truth.

A long pause.

MILLY: Oh, I believe it. I wouldn't want us looking like a Bunuel movie together. Okay. (*She smiles. She looks at her book*) "Poor Old Henry."

GORDON: What?

MILLY: A book, look, a book. Not Spanish. German. *Der Arme Heinrich.* Poor Old Henry. Not read much anymore, but I think it would make a terrific movie. Maybe you can sell it to somebody. (*Pause. She smiles*) It's about a medieval knight. Very honest, decent and brave. Not because Henry worships God or anything, he just likes being wonderful. Smooth and elegant, and in shape and witty and smart, and vain. So God punishes Henry. With leprosy. Instant old age. His eyeballs fall into his highballs, plop, like that.

GORDON: Milly.

MILLY: His supermanhood rots right away on his bones. His nose? God! A hole in his face! His fingers? Horrors! All

calcified into claws! His feet? Well, Henry can't feel his
feet at all, so he stumps around bending over, like an old
man climbing the stairs.

GORDON: Now please. Calm down.

MILLY: I'm not going to calm down! I'm going to tell you this
story! (*Pause*) Henry consults specialists. Doctors, wizards,
magicians. They all say there's only one cure. The leper's
body must be washed in the blood of a virgin. Enter a little
girl.

GORDON: I'm not surprised.

MILLY: You will be. Her name was Sigrid. She was as sick as
Henry. She wanted to be a saint. So when she realized she
could have her veins cut open and her blood donated to
famous Knight-Leper Henry, she was happy. They were
both proud. Two of a kind.

GORDON: The Leper and the Virgin.

MILLY: The title already! Knew you'd catch on! Well, no fool
Heinrich. If a crazy virgin wants to give him a bath in her
blood, can't hurt, can it? Doctors strip the girl naked!
Hang her upside down over pots and pans! Slit her veins!
Drain her blood! Ah! He sees her! All innocence and
purity! All sexy and bloody! The end!

GORDON: She dies?

MILLY: What do you think? Once the toothpaste is out of the
tube, it's a little hard to get it back in again.

GORDON: Milly!

MILLY: No, she doesn't die. Henry stops the doctors. He'll stay a
leper before he'll bathe in her blood. She did that to him.
She made out of this selfish rotten old leper a real man. He
didn't want her to die. He didn't want to hurt her. Or
maybe he couldn't take the sight of all that blood. Anyway, miracle! He gets better. His nose grows back. His

fingers move. All those rotten scales fall from his skin and his soul. God gives him back his life, and he enjoys a long and honorable old age.

GORDON: And the virgin?

MILLY: She doesn't stay that way because he marries her, you see. (*She runs to him, sits in his lap*) Just a minute! Let me sit here just a minute, like a little girl! (*She jumps up, pushes him away*) No! Just never mind!

GORDON: Milly, listen to me!

MILLY: Not one word! You didn't have to worry about me! I would have left Spain anytime. I would have said good-bye, made you proud of me. I would have married you, too, *been* your wife and your nurse. You could have had my blood, and dipped your pen in it.

She kisses him. He leans forward, embracing her. She backs away, so that Gordon falls to his knees.

MILLY: Old man. (*She runs out*)

GORDON: For Christ's sake!

Scene Six: Four A.M.

Gordon, Grady, Lucien, Bill, Thomas. They are all very drunk, fighting to be sober, alert and lucid. Lucien, Bill and Thomas are in dressy evening clothes.

LUCIEN: It's four A.M. My goodness.

BILL: Everybody's asleep. Shhh.

THOMAS: Right.

LUCIEN: Everybody.

GRADY: Me. Gordon. Milly and Mona.

All groan.

LUCIEN: Grady, not again! Spare us the scene!

THOMAS: We've been through it eighteen times with both of you! Oh, Mona! You don't know what you're doing to me, Mona!

LUCIEN: Milly! Little Milly! The pain! The anguish! Write it! "He knew she could be his daughter, and she knew he could be her father, but it didn't seem to matter at all then." Lyrical see, not too much. Dignity, calm. "It was snowing when they met, and it covered, oh, both their heads in white, so that they looked neither young nor old but alike. Very much alike." There. Just beautiful.

GRADY: You are unfeeling, Lucien. What I mean is, you don't feel. You stopped doing that. Wish I could. (*She laughs*)

THOMAS: Gordon. Grady. Lucien's here, isn't he? So am I?

GRADY: And so is Bill. Bill who?

BILL: Never mind, Grady.

GRADY: Okay. (*Pause*) Mona needs me. She does.

LUCIEN: Oh, what the hell! The woman went back to her kid. What do you want us to do about it, say she shouldn't? We know how sensitive you are, darling, and oh God the suffering, but the woman went back to her kid. Gordon's nymphet went back to her schoolbooks. What a tragedy!

THOMAS: Make the best of it, Gordon, and find another Lolita. Make the best of it, Grady, and meet Mona for lunch at the Plaza.

GRADY: You don't care what's happening inside me!

THOMAS: Of course, I care! I'm your lawyer, I care! I'm Gordon's, I care! I'm Lucien's, I care!

BILL: You're not mine.

THOMAS: Maybe I will be. And I'll care!

LUCIEN: And if Mona cares, she'll come back. She'll have to come back. I mean, she got the royal treatment, didn't she? After years 'n years of squalid marriage, dumb husband—

THOMAS: What does the dumb husband do by the way?

GRADY: He's a lawyer.

THOMAS: Oh, he is not!

GRADY: Is too! For the sanitation department. I don't know just exactly how.

LUCIEN: All right! After years of squalid marriage with a sanitation-department lawyer, cooking food and washing socks, then oh! Grady steps in, dripping Bach and mink? Two precious modern hearts, skipping beats like one? She'll come back.

THOMAS: Lesbians are intimacy junkies.

GRADY: What?

THOMAS: I said, lesbians are intimacy junkies. They get hooked on intimacy. If you really got intimate, she'll be back. Otherwise, forget it, she'll get intimate with somebody else.

GRADY: This evening has degenerated. I'm going home.

Grady lurches to her feet. Outside, snow begins to fall again.

THOMAS: Whoa! Steady standing up!

GRADY: I'm perfectly all right. Good night, gentlemen. Lucien, Thomas, Bill. Which one of these killer fruits are you going home with, Bill?

LUCIEN: I didn't hear that and neither did Thomas.

THOMAS: Yes, I did. Which one of us killer fruits are you going home with, Bill?

BILL: Gotta know?

LUCIEN: Gotta know.

GRADY: The suspense is killing us.

BILL: A killer fruit, by definition in New York, is an elegant, rich, successful, powerful gentleman, or I suppose now, lady, of high, same-sex inclinations, who will wage ferocious war over youthful flesh. You cannot attack them verbally, they are too self-assured. You cannot hope to deflate them egotistically, they are protected by their achievements. You cannot even get mad at them. They are so profoundly infantile, they only smile at you, who cannot possibly understand them. Goo. Like that. Goo.

LUCIEN: All right, goo. What's the point?

BILL: Point is I am going home to my trundle bed, to pass out in isolation and freedom. The great gurus of India and I understand the superior virtues of semen retention. It is the path to God and Co-ops. My best friend is my telephone. I trust dead writers, sometimes my agent, and the paychecks I get acting on soaps. My life and real love are incompatible, and I have the sense to see that and go to bed ONLY WHEN I PLEASE! Of course, you are all charming, and useful maybe someday, so I hope you will keep on asking me out. And that, in youthful candor, is what I think about New York!

GRADY: What a terrifying poverty-level of experience. And who drinks a whole bottle of vodka tonight? Babyface does. What you and the great gurus of India really retain, Babyface, isn't frankly all that interesting. What is interesting is what will happen to YOU in thirty years! Why ARE YOU HERE anyway, batting your eyes at three weary SoHo bohemians and this old lesbian? You give me the willies! Good night, Gordon. At least *I* know how you feel!

THOMAS: Bravo!

LUCIEN: Sold!

THOMAS: What style!

LUCIEN: What class!

Bill gets up.

BILL: I am *going* now. This has been real.

LUCIEN: Real what?

BILL: Oh, Jesus. Good night.

THOMAS: Last words.

LUCIEN: Famous.

GORDON: Get out.

LUCIEN: What?

GORDON: All of you, get out of here.

THOMAS: Oh, dear.

BILL: I knew I should have left ten minutes ago. Bye. (*He goes to door, opens it*)

LUCIEN: Gordon, really!

THOMAS: *You* want to fuck Bill, too?

Gordon slaps Thomas. Thomas slugs Gordon.

GORDON: Ow!

LUCIEN (*Simultaneous*): Hold it!

GRADY (*Simultaneous*): Gordon? You leave Gordon alone! (*She gets an elbow in the eye*) Ow! My eye!

GORDON: My nose!

GRADY: Gordon, help. I can't see!

LUCIEN: Oh, boy!

Bill runs back in, jumps on them, pushing them apart.

BILL: The door's open! Now let's GO! Break it UP!!!

LUCIEN: Bill, lay off!

GORDON: Bill?

BILL: Gordon!

Gordon swings at Bill. Bill slugs Gordon.

GORDON: Ow! My NOSE!

GRADY (*Pushing Bill*): You GET OUT of here!

LUCIEN: Stop it, Grady!

BILL: Grady, let GO!

Bill swings around, hitting Grady.

GRADY: Ow! My eye! Again!! Damn you, I can't SEE!!!

THOMAS: EVERYBODY! STOP IT!

LUCIEN: RIGHT NOW!!!

Lucien jumps on them. There is a terrific wild sprawling and a pileup on the floor by the front door. Enter Milly. She has a large white bandage taped over her head and across her left ear. She stares at them.

GRADY: I can see! It's all right. I thought I was blind. Ow, it *hurts!*

LUCIEN: What happened?

THOMAS: Gordon had something to say, and couldn't say it.

LUCIEN: About that ridiculous girl?

BILL: Whatever it was, it's dumb to hit your lawyer. *I* wouldn't do that!

He has a terrific coughing fit. They start getting off of the floor.

THOMAS: Gordon, really, sober up, can't you?

239

He slips and falls, taking others with him. They are all on the floor.

GORDON: Milly!

They stare at her. Gordon tries to get up, slips, falls. Everybody lies in a pile on the floor, with Milly staring at them.

MILLY: I didn't know you were having a party.

She turns to go. Gordon gets to his knees.

GORDON: Milly! What's happened to you?
LUCIEN (*Whisper*): That's Milly.
THOMAS: I bet.
GRADY: Milly? What?
MILLY: I didn't know how to do it. I went to a bar and got picked up by one man and I wouldn't go anywhere, then got picked up by another man and I wouldn't go anywhere, I then flirted with a married couple who got excited until I said I'm teasing, I'd never in my life do that with you, and they were furious. After that I started home.

She gets the statue of Don Quixote, sits down and looks at it. Everybody else is still on the floor.

The first man followed me, swore at me, hit me in the ear with his umbrella, yelling, "You little bitch," and ran off. It worked out the way I wanted it to. I got hurt and humiliated, went to a hospital to get my wounds treated, and saw the light still on here and came back, to make you feel as bad as I can.

GORDON: Do you *have* to play with Don Quixote right now?

GRADY: Madame de Staël, the only woman Napoleon was afraid of, spent her life passionate about a *wimp*. The elegant Madame Krudener's fashionable lover tipped his hat to her, had a heart attack, *died* on the spot, which converted her into a lifelong, utterly *ridiculous* evangelist! Madame Récamier, greatest beauty in all the history of France, stayed *virgin* until she was forty, then died horribly in love with a pompous immortal named Chateaubriand, remembered today for a *steak!* Which I am going to need for this *eye!* My God, it'll turn yellow *and* purple! Sex makes fools of everybody.

MILLY: "In last year's nests, there are no birds this year. I once was mad but now am sane." That's what Don Quixote said, when he died.

GORDON: Just give him here, will you? (*He gets up, puts Don Quixote down with his back turned*) There! Ow. My nose won't stop bleeding.

He sits again, bloody handkerchief to his nose. Bill, Thomas and Lucien observe Grady's eye, Milly's bandage and Gordon's nose. Bill gets up off the floor.

BILL: Of course it was a marvelous party, and I was enchanted by the literary conversation, but you are all really just blockheads, you know, I mean, honestly, look at you. Black eye, busted ear, and bloody nose. Really. *I'm* going home alone!

Exit Bill. Lucien and Thomas pick themselves off the floor.

THOMAS: Well, Lucien, that young man—

LUCIEN: Sad.

THOMAS: You can have him.

LUCIEN: He's all yours. When do you leave for Spain, Gordon?

MILLY: On May 15th. To write about Nero. And sex and blood and everything like that.

LUCIEN: Well, good. (*Pause*) Home alone. (*He starts out, comes back*) I wish I was famous. That would be something, anyway. Grady, did Madame de Stael say something profound about fame? And sunlight, the sun?

GRADY: She said it was the sun of the dead.

LUCIEN: "Fame is the sun of the dead." Good night.

Exit Lucien.

THOMAS: Obviously, I must top that. Let's see. French maxim. "If loving is judged by what it looks like, it looks more like hating than anything else." That's what you all look like. Me too. Home alone. Good night.

Exit Thomas. Pause.

GRADY:

"There once was a Pirate named Bates,
Who attempted to rhumba on skates.
He slipped on his cutlass,
Which rendered him nutless,
And practically useless on dates."

Now who wrote *that*, I wonder? And *why* is it running through my head?

GORDON: Old man and woman sat in a bar out West. "Want to?" said the old man. "Your place or mine?" said the old woman. "Well," said the old man, "if you're going to argue about it, let's just forget it."

242

He shrugs. They look at Milly.

MILLY: "In last year's nests, there are no birds this year. I once was mad, but now am sane."

They all nod. Grady gets up, examines her eye in a compact mirror. Outside, snow begins to fall.

Gordon, why are you staring at us?
GORDON: "In last year's nests, there are no birds this year."
MILLY: So?
GORDON: Spain.
GRADY: What?
GORDON: Spain. Let's all go to Spain!
GRADY: What a ridiculous idea.
GORDON: No, it isn't.
GRADY: Milly can't stand me.
MILLY: That's not true.
GRADY: I wasn't nice. I was mean. I told Gordon—if he really cared a thing about you—to take you nowhere.
MILLY (*To Gordon*): Did she?
GORDON: Yes.
MILLY: Oh. (*Smiles*) I think I want something to eat.
GRADY: Where would we sleep?
GORDON: We'd vote.
GRADY: Is that possible?
GORDON: I don't know. Maybe.
MILLY: What happened to the potato soup? (*She goes to the bar, opens the crock pot*)
GRADY: Potato soup?
MILLY: It's still hot.
GRADY: Is it?
GORDON: I don't want to go to Spain by myself.

GRADY: One, two, three.

MILLY: We can look like a Bunuel movie together.

GRADY: No, we'd look like a family.

MILLY: You want soup?

GRADY: Yes, I think I do.

GORDON: There's bread and wine. (*He goes to help Milly*)

GRADY: Who pays for what?

GORDON: I'd pay for Milly. And the rent.

GRADY: I might do part of that.

GORDON: Okay.

MILLY: I have three hundred dollars in the bank, and I can type.

GRADY: Oh, you can?

MILLY: Sixty words a minute.

GRADY: Then I pay half.

GORDON: Okay.

Milly and Gordon bring soup, bread and wine.

Maybe another log.

GRADY: I'm ravenously hungry.

MILLY: So am I.

Gordon puts a log on the fire. They eat the soup. The fire blazes up. The snow falls heavily.

GRADY: God, this is good.

GORDON: Hot.

MILLY: Yum.

GRADY: Old Spanish house?

GORDON: Sure.

GRADY: Bedrooms?

GORDON: Three.

MILLY: Three.

GORDON: My nose has stopped bleeding.

Grady turns Don Quixote around again.

GRADY: He's still crazy.

MILLY: The radio.

She turns on the radio. It plays "Hark! How the Bells." They look at each other, tentatively, listen to the Christmas carol, and look out the window. Gordon sets Don Quixote on the window ledge, where he stands against the falling snow. They look at each other again. They eat the bread and potato soup and drink the wine. The firelight glows.

More potato soup?

GRADY AND GORDON: Yes!

MILLY: Here.

Grady and Gordon hold out their soup bowls and Milly reaches for them. Tableau. Lights fade on the three of them, then on the April snow.

Heathen Valley

For my mother, Maitland Clabaugh,
for Samuel Clabaugh,
and for my father,
Dr. R. Z. Linney,
who loved the mountains

From the novel
Heathen Valley by Romulus Linney
Atheneum 1962

Characters

BILLY, a man of any age.

BISHOP, the Episcopal Bishop of North Carolina. Fifty years old.

STARNS, a plain, homely, awkward drifter, in his thirties.

HARLAN, a haunted, savage mountaineer, in his twenties.

CORA, a fierce mountain woman, in her twenties.

JUBA, midwife to Heathen Valley, in her fifties.

Place

The Appalachian Mountains of North Carolina.

Time

1840s.

Scene

A ramped wooden platform of the starkest simplicity. It represents an upland valley in the Appalachian Mountains of North Carolina.

On the platform sits one wooden crate. There is no other scenery. The actors are costumed but properties and actions are all mimed.

At times, to shift and focus the action of the play, characters will come to rest while narration is spoken, then come to life again. This device is used throughout the play.

Different sounds and levels of wind are used throughout.

ACT ONE

Wind. Light on Billy, sitting on the crate.

BILLY: The mist is on the slopes. Mary's Peak has vanished in the night, and only the tops of our hickories are moonlit now. From here, I can see the broken stones where the Mission was. I can hear, in the wind, the singing from the churchyard. And I can see you.

Enter Cora, Harlan, Juba, Bishop and Starns. They gather around him.

Cora? (*He turns to her. She looks at him, silent*) Harlan? (*Same*) Juba? (*Same*) Bishop? (*Same*) Starns? (*Same. They stand mute, staring at him*) If I had my house, I would never leave it. I would keep it with me always. That's what I said to you, in those days. (*He turns around, looking at them*) Now you stand under halos of mist, gray rain in your eyes. Starns, in worn-out lindseys. The black frock coat the Bishop wore. The flour-sack skirts Juba made. Cora, with her shawl and britches, and Harlan, in filth and tatters. My life as an orphan boy, with you my family, comes back to me, and I must find you again, from the beginning.

The wind stops. Starns walks into a large church, coughing slightly. The Bishop approaches him. Exit Cora, Harlan and Juba. Billy watches.

BISHOP: William Starns?

STARNS: Yessir. (*He straightens up*)

BISHOP: Are you sick?

STARNS: Jest some misery in my stomach. I'm all right.

BISHOP: You understand the position?

STARNS: Be janitor of this here church.

BISHOP: Can you do that?

STARNS: Reckon I can keep it clean, yessir. Now, I never worked for no church afore. Be honest with ye, I can't hold with it. Virgins don't have no babies. But the singing's pleasant, and people praying. Preachers talk good, some of them. You know I kilt a man?

BISHOP: I know that. In self-defense.

STARNS: Yessir.

BISHOP: Where are you from, Mr. Starns?

STARNS: Up one side the Carolinas, down the other.

BISHOP: Where were you born?

STARNS: In the mountains. 'Round Boone, the Blowing Rock.

BISHOP: Are you violent now?

STARNS: No, sir. I am not. I will not never kill no man again.

BISHOP: Women?

STARNS: I give up wimmen when I give up likker. Ain't ruint me. And I like hard work.

BISHOP: You're hired.

STARNS: Thanks.

BISHOP: That man you killed. Do you still think about him?

STARNS: All the time. Hurtful dreams and such. I see him by my bed, a-pointing at me. I kilt the man.

BISHOP: Look at me. In the name of the Father, and of the Son, and of the Holy Ghost, you need never see him again. Repent, and sleep in peace.

STARNS: Thanks.

BISHOP: Do you read and write?

STARNS: Nossir, just some figuring. I would like to learn.

BISHOP: Billy!

BILLY: Yes, sir! (*He moves to them, quickly. He seems younger now*)

BISHOP: Billy comes to us from the State Orphanage. He attends our School for Boys. Billy, Mr. Starns will be the janitor at St. Stephens.

STARNS: Hidy.

BILLY: Hello.

BISHOP: Tell Billy what you want, Starns.

STARNS: I want to read and write and study the government.

BISHOP: Teach him, Billy.

The Bishop turns away.

BILLY (*To Starns*): I'll try.

STARNS: Thanks.

Starns turns away. Billy looks at him.

BILLY: An hour every morning, three on Saturdays, for two solid years. I never saw a man work so hard.

STARNS (*Memorizing*): The powers—of the govermints of the United States—is divided in three parts. The ex-ec-ec-cu-tive, the leg-is-la-tive and the ju-di-cial.

BILLY: You really killed a man?

STARNS: Yes, I did. Watauga County blacksmith. He cut me, I cut him, with barlow knives. That's how I got my misery

in my stomach. Awful. In prison ten year account of it.
Don't you never kill no men, Billy, you hear?

BILLY: I hear. (*He turns to the Bishop*) Well, he can read now,
Bishop. He can write, and he's studied the government.

Change of light.

BISHOP: Starns! Billy!

They move to him, quickly.

A man was here yesterday, to talk to me. The botanist Asa
Gray. He's been in the Smoky Mountains, collecting
plants. There he came upon a valley, closed in by ridges,
where the few people he saw have forgotten their religion. Evidently they live dreadful, primitive lives, debased into savagery. They are violent, carnal and heathen.
At Christmas, Gray said, they celebrate the Nativity in
drunken riots, feuds, and sexual orgies. He called the
place Heathen Valley. I am going to climb those mountains, find those people and take to them the Word of God.

STARNS: Yessir. Well, good luck.

BISHOP: You think me foolish?

STARNS: Something like that, yessir.

BISHOP: I need a guide. You were born in those mountains,
Starns, and you've done well at this church.

STARNS: As a janitor, yessir, not as no mountain scout.

BISHOP: I need you.

STARNS: Bishop, you will come across things in them mountains benasty a man's mind! Why you got to go there?

BISHOP: To save souls! That is what I do! In the slave quarters,
in the prisons, in the asylums! It is never enough! I am not
an armchair Bishop! When the poor of this earth need me,
I go! Now they need you! Well?

STARNS: When?

BISHOP: In June. We'll need a boy for the horses. Billy?

BILLY: June?

They turn away, backs to him.

June! When summer, and my life with you, began. What a sight! A schoolboy, a janitor and a Bishop, climbing the Great Smoky Mountains!

Billy throws himself into their arms, laughing, and joins them on their trip. Wind.

STARNS: Yonder's Grandfather Mountain. See his face?

BISHOP: Doesn't look like a face to me.

STARNS: Shore hit does, you not looking right. Slant your head a smidjin to the right. Now squint. Jest do it, Bishop.

BISHOP (*Smiling*): All right.

STARNS: 'At great long rock ain't the jaw, hit is jest the nose. All that rest of him's the mouth and chin. See?

BISHOP: Oh. Yes! But according to our map, it shouldn't be there.

STARNS: 'At's according to a map. Rock sight is something else. That there is Mary's Peak, what overhangs the valley. We been through Dagman Gorge, Tarface and Stand Around Gap, crossed the Watauga River, yonder stands the Grandfather. Heathen Valley's up that west ridge. We commence now a climbing powerful steep. Bishop?

BISHOP: Ready.

STARNS: Billy?

BILLY: Yo.

STARNS: Up we go.

*Starns, Billy and the Bishop walk, climbing to Heathen
Valley. Enter Harlan, a ragged, wild-eyed man, carrying a
rifle, mimed. He aims it at them, follows them with it. Light
on Harlan, and on Billy, who breaks off from Starns and the
Bishop to watch him. Exeunt Starns and Bishop.*

BILLY: And while we climbed, you were watching us. Harlan!

HARLAN: Go on! Toil up them slopes. Till ye look like ants. (*He
lowers his rifle*) Ants. And worms. Creatures of the dirt,
pass me by.

BILLY: Madman? Animal? Harlan?

HARLAN: I see ants and worms.

BILLY: When your father died, Harlan. What did your mother
say?

HARLAN: She said, "Hep me now! Lift this, Harlan! Come on,
do it!" Me lifting the bed with Paw on it, getting it moved
with our ma moaning and yelling and hissing and whistling, "Begone, Harlan! Git me the blood-axe, boy!"

BILLY: The spell, the charm: the axe and the blood.

HARLAN: And me running to the woodpile, bringing the axe
and her howling, slamming it down in the floor where the
bed was, an axe with blood on it from the goat we'd killed,
and her saying, "Quick now, 'fore the power goes out of
it!" And me and Margaret lifting the bed again, on top of
that axe biting the floor. And her saying, "Now git me his
razor, boy!"

BILLY: Axe, blood, razor—

HARLAN: And I went and got my paw's old razor out of the
chest. I give it to her and Maw throwed back one of his
arms, a-whistling through her teeth. She shaved off some
hair, making it into a spitball, giving it to me, saying, "To
the white birch, by the clearing!"

HARLAN: Run, run, crazy, crazy, run! Me with my maw yelling, crazy, a-running to cut a hole in the birch tree, stuff
in my pore daddy's armhair, and seal it up with mud and
bark.

BILLY: Axe, blood, razor, hair, a white birch tree, the hole and
the seal and the spell.

HARLAN: Doing it fast and hard as I could, Maw watching me
all glittery-eyed and whistling, and that night, when our
daddy died, beating us, saying we'd faulted the spell a-
purpose so's hit would kill him!

BILLY: What did your sister say?

HARLAN: Margaret she said she'd be strong if'n I wasn't, teach
us never never again trust in no kind of spells or charms
like our maw, but to live together quiet and when time
come, die that way.

BILLY: When did you marry your sister?

HARLAN: The night after Maw died and we buried her. Margaret was a fury in the cabin, changing things thisaway
and that, cussing me for being worthless. She cooked, give
me supper. We sat quiet for a while and then, oh—(*He
moves away, falls to his knees*)

BILLY: Harlan, animal, heathen.

HARLAN: I would have slept outside, in the shed, and left you
alone, Margaret, but you say no, no, get in here, Harlan,
with me now. There we be, you pulling away from me in
the one bed you'd left standing, teasing me about my
great youthfulness, calling me gazer eyes, and baby
brother, and such. You hit me, right on the nose, laughing
under the quilt, pulling my hair and kicking me in the
back and hitting me again, until I take hold of you and
you say, "Harlan, do this now," and have me stay on you.
(*Pause*) And we was married then, me and my sister, one
to the other. (*He stands up*)

BILLY: And now she lies before you, your mountain sister and your mountain wife. She's gone, Harlan.

HARLAN: Shot dead! And me to shoot the man what done it! My baby Jean, in her crib, Daniel Larman didn't see. So I will load them on my sled, and take them to my field, and put them in the dirt forever.

BILLY: What do you think when you bury them?

HARLAN: I think no spells or charms. I throw down the last clod, lean on my shovel. It sinks into the dirt. It hits one of them down there. (*Pause*) I dread to pull it up. (*Pause*) I can't touch it again. (*Pause*) I leave it there.

Exit Harlan.

BILLY: And you went in your cabin then, with the baby left alive in it. And while you were there, running down the slopes, came—Cora!

Enter Cora, running.

CORA: Harlan! Harlan! I want my baby! Harlan, you hear??

Enter Harlan, to face her.

HARLAN: Cora, git out of here!

CORA: Jean's mine!

HARLAN: Git on home!

CORA: I give Jean back, didn't I? I never faulted you or your wife! But Margaret's dead and gone now, and you'll be in that cabin playing with my Jean like I was dead and gone too, Harlan!

HARLAN: You stay away from Jean!

CORA: She's my baby, too!

HARLAN (*Simultaneous*): I'll break ye damn neck!

Harlan seizes Cora by the shoulders. Cora claws his eyes and face. Harlan cries out. Cora seizes Harlan, knees him in the groin. Harlan falls to his knees. Cora pulls Harlan's head back by the hair, stands above him. Then suddenly and savagely, she kisses him. Then she pushes him away and turns.

CORA: I'm going in the cabin, Harlan. Shoot me.

Cora exits, then reenters, finding the cabin, going in, seeing a small wooden crib on the floor. She moves to it, takes her shawl from her shoulders and sets it down: it becomes her baby. She looks at her baby, in its crib, with love and fear. She touches it. Around her the room is bathed in warm firelight. Harlan follows her, stands watching her.

Jean? It's your momma. Oh. Sleeping in the nicest crib. Under this little quilt, all beautified with thready birds, and tiny apple trees. (*She looks around*) It is decent here.

HARLAN: Margaret kept it that way.

CORA: I see she did. Walls clean. Rug on the floor. Many chairs. A loom.

HARLAN: She carded her wool here, made our clothes.

CORA: Wood floor smooth. Walls chinked. Chimney drawing. Fire.

HARLAN: Whiskey, too.

BILLY: You got warm, Cora, from a fire and applejack whiskey. You wiggled your fingers and Jean come awake.

CORA: She's got my finger. (*She laughs*). She knows her momma.

BILLY: You played with your baby then, in the cabin where
    Harlan lived with his sister-wife, whilst you was running
    on Sand Mountain, wild as a man.
HARLAN: Git up, Cora. Move.
CORA: If I choose where.
HARLAN: Choose then.

Cora takes Jean to the other side of the stage.

CORA: I choose here, Harlan.
BILLY: You laid down on their bed.

Cora lies down. Harlan kneels beside her.

HARLAN: You ever go up Sand Mountain again?
CORA: Not never again.
HARLAN: You tell me why not?
CORA: I have Jean in my arms. I am in this bed.

Harlan lies down with her.

BILLY: So you slept, in that bed, with the baby in the daytime,
    glad Cora left her family on Sand Mountain.

*Billy stamps his foot by their heads. Harlan and Cora wake.
Change of light: harsh, threatening.*

CORA: Oh!
HARLAN: Oh!

They both jump up. Cora holds the baby.

ROMULUS LINNEY

BILLY: The Larman family! With Grandpa Jacob Larman, carried on a sled pulled by his sons. Shad, Cardell, Earl, dimwit Cief, Coleman Larman, his brothers Tate, Spenser, and Nolan. With guns!

Cora steps forward, from behind Harlan.

CORA: Daniel's dead, Grandpa Jacob! He brooded on Harlan's taking his field, and he went off and kilt Harlan's wife, and his chillun!
HARLAN: Then I kilt him! I allow that to yore face!
CORA: Warn't Harlan's fault, Grandpa Jacob. Don't you let Earl or Cardell do nothing now!
HARLAN: If you want to know where I left yore boy, I will take you there.
CORA: Harlan, you'll never come back!
HARLAN: Hush, woman.
CORA: Hit warn't Harlan's fault! He don't know it, but—but—
HARLAN: Whut? Spit it out!
CORA: Grandpa Jacob, it was me made Daniel mad about that field! I wanted my baby back so bad, I called Daniel coward, sent him off hateful to get Harlan.
HARLAN: God damn.
CORA: I got to tell them. They'll kill ye if I don't. I'm a-doing it for you Harlan!
HARLAN: You bitch. Give me Jean.
CORA: Harlan, no!
HARLAN: Give me the baby, Cora.

Harlan takes the baby from her.

CORA: Harlan!

HARLAN: Go on!

CORA: I never thought Daniel would do what he did!

HARLAN: Git! (*To the Larmans*) I will take you men where I shot Daniel. You can take him and lay him out. Shoot me, do what you damn well please, jest never let this woman have this child.

Cora and Harlan go off. Enter Bishop and Starns. Billy joins them, climbing. They come to the valley, out of breath. Billy falls on his back, laughing. They look about.

BISHOP: Familiar, Starns?

STARNS: Some of it is.

BILLY: About two hundred acres. Bottomland. Rich, it looks like.

STARNS: That's Mary's Peak. Yonder is Sand Mountain.

BILLY: The valley was cleared once. Look at the stumps. But only one cabin, maybe a store of some kind. Deserted, otherwise. Starns, I never heard of good land left like this.

STARNS: Valley is empty 'cause men dassent live there.

BISHOP: Why not?

STARNS: A body's in plain sight there. It was cleared, all right, but then, it was like a war. There was—Larmans, there was Tates, there was—Newells—yessir— (*Pause*) I ought to remember how they kilt each other. I don't.

BISHOP: Look at the mist. (*Pause*) Heathen Valley.

They stare at the valley.

BILLY: And in that valley, in that store—Juba!

Enter Juba, followed by Harlan and Cora.

JUBA: Them Larmans had me lay out their Daniel. Wash him off, get him decent in clean woolsey-lindseys and a black coat.

BILLY: We came into that shack of a store, Juba, and there you were, dressing a corpse with a hole in its head. Around you stood the meanest men ever I saw.

Starns and the Bishop pull Billy behind them. The Bishop steps forward, facing Juba.

BISHOP: Good afternoon.

JUBA: Shad, don't. Cardell, hold on to Cief. Earl. (*To Bishop*) You men will speak to me. Who be ye?

BISHOP: This is Mr. Starns. This is Mr. Cobb. My name is Ames.

JUBA: What be ye business?

BISHOP: I want to talk to you.

JUBA: Whut about?

BISHOP: How you live here.

JUBA: Shad, put it down. Cardell. Earl. (*Pause*) Grandpa Jacob? (*She listens. She nods. To Bishop*) That old man yonder can't talk but he can decide, and I'll tell ye what he decides. So. How do we live here?

BISHOP: In sin. This valley, by the few who have been here, is called Heathen Valley. The Valley that Forgot God. I came to see if that is true and if it is, what can be done about it.

JUBA: What are you, a God damned sheriff?

BISHOP: I am the Episcopal Bishop of North Carolina.

JUBA: That's a little bigger than a circuit rider, is it, with the same skin?

BISHOP: I want to help you.

JUBA: Why?

BISHOP: That's a dead man. With a bullet in his head.

JUBA: I reckon.

BISHOP: What are you going to do about it?

JUBA: Grandpa Jacob? (*Pause*) All right. I'll tell ye how we live here.

Juba shoves Harlan and Cora out before them.

That dead man is Daniel Larman and yes, he got hisself shot. (*She points to Harlan*) By that man there. Because Daniel Larman shot that man's wife and two chillun. Now he did that because that man's wife, who was both a sister and a wife, was also Daniel Larman's cousin, and she nattered her husband, that man there, into taking a field from Daniel Larman, who come shot her. (*She points to Cora*) The woman standing yonder was Daniel Larman's sister. She has a baby by that man there, give it up and now wants it back. To git the child back, she wormed and wormed Daniel Larman about being robbed of that field until by God Daniel Larman went off a-shooting, and got shot hisself, got found just now and laid out by me. That's the way we live here, Bishop. What are you going to do about it?

BISHOP: Ask you one question.

JUBA: Ask.

BISHOP: Do you remember Jesus Christ?

JUBA: Of a sartin. He passed through here about a month ago.

BISHOP: You pretend you don't know what I mean?

JUBA: Oh, I know what you mean! And I know you're a damn fool to holler sin over a dead man! You ain't got manners a body needs serving guts to a bear!

STARNS: Bishop. (*He steps in front of the Bishop. Gently*) I'm William Starns. My daddy's name was Theadore. My mother's name was Hester. I left home when I was about twelve. We lived up the north slopes from this valley.

Juba stares at him.

JUBA: I thought I'd seen them bones in yore face afore. I knowed both your momma and your daddy.

STARNS: Hear what happened to them?

JUBA: Your momma's dead, I know that. Milk-sick, fifteen year ago. Place where they lived burned down, two, three year later. Nobody knows what happened to your daddy. You had a brother.

STARNS: Run off, afore me.

JUBA: I was there for him. Then for you.

STARNS: Me?

JUBA: When you was borned, Mister Starns, hit was into these hands.

STARNS: You're Juba, the midwife.

JUBA: 'At's it, Mister.

STARNS: I swear.

JUBA: Welcome home.

STARNS: Bishop. It is true we are way up the mountain. It is true hard things happen here. But that is not because nobody is heathen savages or no kind of foolishness like that. They are just poor. Poor folks have poor ways. (*To Juba*) It's pleasant to be here again.

JUBA: That man a real Bishop?

STARNS: Yes, he is.

JUBA: What does a real Bishop do?

STARNS: Runs churches. Means well. Talk to him.

Juba confronts the Bishop again.

JUBA: Bishop, nobody here has forgot the church. We just wish
we could. Once upon a time, we know we come here to git
away from churches. I can't tell you when or just why, but
we did. The worst of them was called the King's Church,
and people here hated it. There may be a Bible or two
around, and a body or so, like me, thank ye, who kin read
if'n they take a mind to it, but no schools, no sheriffs, no
Bishops, no Kings, and thank God, no churches. You best
go back down the mountain afore you find yoreself some
harm.

BISHOP: And leave you in sin? A human soul has been murdered. By that man there, and you stand around him with
blood in your eyes. You going to kill him? (*He points to
Harlan*) Murder again? That right? Let him go? That
right? Who keeps that woman's baby? Who decides these
things, and by what measure? With all your hard talk, and
your stiff-necked mountain pride, you don't know, do you?

JUBA: Damn this man. Shoot him, Cardell.

STARNS: Uh, hold on. We don't mean to low-rate a body.
Bishop means to help. Hear him out. Bishop, what you
aim to do? I mean, *do*, you know, as well as say?

JUBA: What do you want here, anyhow?

BISHOP: Civilization. (*Pause*) Order. Decency. (*Pause*) The
eternal goodness of the Christian Church.

STARNS: Bishop, them are fine words. Bodies here appreciate
every one. And the Church, you know, can do things.

JUBA: Like what?

STARNS: I don't know, exactly. Something. Bishop?

BISHOP: Buy the field. Pay both families an equal price.

STARNS: And them what perished over it can be buried in it,
put to rest there or something. Bishop?

BISHOP: In a valley that forgot God, I can see a Mission and a
Church. On that field, by those graves, I can see a Chapel,
and a schoolhouse. I see civilization, and peace.

STARNS: I said he'd know.

JUBA: And what'll a church do, besides talk us to death?

BISHOP: It will show you how to praise the God who made you.
Sing the Doxology, Billy.

BILLY (*Singing*):
Praise God from whom all blessings flow,
Praise Him all creatures here below—

BISHOP (*As Billy sings*): The Church of Jesus Christ will bless
the babies born in your hands. It will teach them how to
live, how to grow, how to treat their children.

BILLY (*Singing*):
Praise Him above ye heavenly hosts,
Praise Father, Son and Holy Ghost.

BISHOP: When it is time, it will show them how to die, and lay
them to rest, in eternal peace.

HARLAN: Spells and charms!

BISHOP: Spells? Charms?

HARLAN: I'll not have none of it!

BISHOP: But, man, when you buried your wife and children,
what did you do? Just put them in the ground and walk
off?

HARLAN: Hit's all Margaret wanted. Me, either.

BISHOP: You left nothing to mark their graves?

HARLAN: Left the shovel. Don't know why.

BISHOP: The *shovel*?

STARNS: Bishop. Poor folks have poor ways. So this here Mission
can have a backyard, then? For these here graves? Right?

BISHOP: I can give this poor man a Christian burial today. (*To
Harlan*) I can bless your wife and children, at the same
time.

STARNS: And bury, with them, this eternal meanness and killing. (*To Harlan*) Is that a charm? A spell?

HARLAN: I don't know.

JUBA: Grandpa Jacob? (*Pause*) We'll hear more.

Wind. They turn out, make a line.

BILLY: If I had my house, I would never leave it.

BISHOP: A Mission, in Heathen Valley.

BILLY: I would keep it with me always.

BISHOP: To run it I propose William Starns.

STARNS: Yes, I will do that.

JUBA: Grandpa Jacob?

HARLAN: Charms and spells.

CORA: A baby, Harlan, a baby.

BISHOP: One. By oral catechism, teach to the children of Heathen Valley the fundamentals of our Christian Faith.

STARNS: I'll need first to get up a barn, sheds and a spring-house.

BISHOP: Two. Teach them the fundamentals of grammar and simple calculation.

BILLY: Heathen Valley will be my mother.

STARNS: I can plant this spring and see to orchards and some livestock.

BISHOP: Three. Conduct one service daily.

BILLY: Heathen Valley will be my father.

CORA: I want my baby. I want my own.

JUBA: It will depend on Grandpa Jacob. Unless he says go to school, no boy will.

HARLAN: Charms and spells. They still scare me!

CORA: My baby, Harlan! She's mine!

BILLY: Home.

STARNS: My own!

BISHOP: A Church in Heathen Valley!

Light on Starns and the Bishop.

STARNS: I still got trouble believing virgins ever have babies. But Bishop Ames, of the Christian Church, poor folks have poor ways. Mine do here. If you can give them a decent life, then I will believe what you believe. I will serve you as best I can, and ask you to take a sinful man into your Church today.

BISHOP: Kneel.

Starns kneels before the Bishop.

The name is from the Greek, di-a-ko-nos. It means servant, minister. William Starns, I find you morally, spiritually and intellectually fit to be Deacon in the Episcopal Church of North Carolina. With the gift of this Christian book, *The Confessions of Saint Augustine*, I appoint you today first Missionary to Heathen Valley. God bless you.

STARNS: Thanks.

BILLY: Deacon Starns! Converting savages!

Starns rises.

STARNS: I am partial to goats and vegetable gardens as well as cows and corn.

BILLY: Bishop Ames! Raising money!

BISHOP: I will tell all the world about these lost children of God!

STARNS: We'll likely farm wheat and barley, too.

BISHOP: Their souls will be my soul! I will be one with them!

STARNS: And it seems to me this ground might be good for cabbages, somehow.

269

BISHOP: I will say that I see around them not their brutal mountains but the Towers of a True City! Goodbye, Billy! Goodbye, Starns! Goodbye, my friends! Never doubt my devotion to you and to this valley! I will speak in the counties and in the towns, in the states and in the cities, in the pulpits and at the conventions! I will let no church alone until they understand what must be done! Farewell!

Exit Bishop. They stare after him.

STARNS: So long. (*Pause*) We'll be right here.
BILLY: And we were. Clearing and planting. Building the Missionhouse. Raising the chapel and the schoolhouse. Trying to get people to come to church and they wouldn't.

Exeunt Cora and Harlan.

And what Starns did about it. And how it got told over and over again. Like Starns and Grandpa Jacob!
JUBA: Starns, Grandpa Jacob is haunted by a razorback hog.
STARNS: What?
JUBA: He's sartin hit's a-coming to git him, has nightmares of it a-dragging him off to hellfire. A damn monster hog commenced coming around Grandpa Jacob's ever day, after chickens, cats, puppies, little babies even, any kind of slop. Nary a Larman rifle gun has stopped him yet. Grandpa Jacob knows when the razorback comes in the cabin, he'll die.
STARNS: Believes that, does he?
JUBA: He positively does.
STARNS: Tell him I do, too.

Exit Juba. Enter Cora. Billy steps back and watches.

CORA: Mr. Starns?

Starns doubles over, coughing.

What's wrong with you?

STARNS: A misery in my stomach. Pay it no mind.

CORA: You a preacher now?

STARNS: Half a one.

CORA: How can a body be half a preacher?

STARNS: I'm a missionary. That's half preacher, half hired help. What can I do for you?

CORA: It's Harlan. He's got such trouble. He rides his horse all night. Says witches are a-riding him. He showed me tangles in his horse's mane he swears are the witches' stirrups. Says they pull him off his horse and get him down and ride him, too. He's cut and bruised. He thinks them witches are sometimes his dead sister-wife and their chillun. And Jean, our baby, he won't let me see. I know he leaves her alone all the time. Hit's dangerous!

STARNS: I reckon.

CORA: Well?

STARNS: You got a brother named Cief?

CORA: Yes but Cief's witless. He's always been pitiful in his mind. Nothing you can do for him.

STARNS: Hit's what you do for him's the question.

CORA: And what's that?

STARNS: You keep him pitiful, what I hear. He runs to you like a baby. You tend his body, and him almost a grown man. No wonder he's pitiful.

CORA: God damn preacher! Cief is a half-wit, you fool, with his miseries and wants like everbody else but worse! What woman will ease him ever, if not me? He's got to have a little comfort in his life!

STARNS: But not from you!

CORA: From who then? My God and Lord Jesus both! Yore mind is simply benastied, is it, by a woman's hands on a half-wit's body? Why? You want them on yours, Mister Son of a Bitch Missionary? That it?

STARNS: No, that ain't it. But I see why you're mad.

CORA: Oh, ye do? Man, you are downright peculiar, you know that? You ever have a woman atall?

STARNS: Yes.

CORA: Why ain't you got one now?

STARNS: Why ain't you got a man?

Cora jumps on Starns, knocks him down and straddles him.

CORA: You dolesome bastard, don't pick words with me!

STARNS: I've said it before, poor folks have poor ways. Me in particular. I have never been much with the ladies.

CORA: Why not?

STARNS: I left off women and likker. Ain't kilt me.

CORA: Went and got religion instead! Damn preacher! All talk and no comprehension! How can you blame me for Cief?

STARNS: I never said you corrupted your brother!

CORA: God corrupted him, preacher! Fried his damn brains for him when he was born! Cuss out Lord Jesus and leave me alone!

Cora beats on Starns, who suddenly grabs her wrists, throws her off, and straddles her.

STARNS: All right! I beg your pardon!

CORA: All right, yourself, then.

Starns gets off her.

STARNS: Cief is still young. A boy pitiful, living off his sister, is one thing. A grown man pitiful is something else. He's got to learn that there are more things in the world than his sister's hands. You go live with Harlan, he'll have to. No?

CORA: I will allow you that.

STARNS: He can cut wood, I've seen him. Send him down here. I will talk to Harlan about your baby.

CORA: 'At a bargain?

STARNS: 'At's a bargain.

Exit Cora. Enter Juba.

JUBA: Get you what now?

STARNS: Four buckets. When you've made your corn likker, put the mash in the buckets. Put two outside for that razorback to find, anothern on the porch, and anothern inside the cabin by his bed.

JUBA: That'll bring the razorback in the cabin!

STARNS: 'At's right.

Exit Juba. Enter Harlan.

HARLAN: I'll have nothing to do with ye, preacher! Git!

STARNS: What's wrong with building a church?

HARLAN: Devils. Witches.

STARNS: What about them?

HARLAN: They live in church corners.

STARNS: Where in the world did you hear that?

HARLAN: Everbody knows it, nobody says it.

STARNS: Witches. Them what rides you like a horse?

HARLAN: You know that about me?

STARNS: I been ridden, too, by demons and such, creatures dead and gone. Mine have come after me, too. You ain't so

273

all by yourself as you think you are. Suppose a church
don't have no corners.

HARLAN: It's a building, it has to.

STARNS: Not if I cut off the corners, it don't. Be eightsided,
instead of four.

HARLAN: Git off my land.

STARNS: After I flat tell you this. That baby of yours needs a
momma. All right. I'm going. But you think now.
Mommas and churches. Harlan.

Billy puts the crate at center. Starns gets up on it.

Young gentlemen, ladies. This is the Valle Sanctus Mis-
sion School of the Episcopal Church of North Carolina.
We will begin this morning by learning a chant. Sing
with me. Na-na-na-na-na-na-NA-NA— (*Pause*) Hush.
You're supposed to sing, not laugh. (*Pause*) Next child
hoots at me gets horsewhipped. I know I sound like a
donkey but hush. So. Sing with me. Na-na-na-na-na-na-
NA-NA— (*He grins*) You're right, it's awful. (*He laughs*)
Everybody fancies laughing. I do, too. So do it like that.
Ha-ha-ha-HA-HA-ha-HA-HA!

*The chant is taken up, like that. It sounds calm and easy and
good.*

Agin, like that!

Plainchant.

So. Laugh first, then sing. All right. Agin.

*Plainchant. Starns gets off his crate, sets it aside. Enter
Cora.*

CORA: Starns, what are you a-doing with Cief?

STARNS: I'm sending him out with John Barco and them boys going off to girdle trees. Cief! You do what they tell you! You get an axe of your own and you get to snap a chalk line! Go on, now!

CORA: He won't be able.

STARNS: If you keep a-telling him so! Let *them* say that.

CORA: What about Harlan?

STARNS: That'll take time.

CORA: Did you see Jean?

STARNS: She was in the cabin when I was there.

CORA: She'll perish. He'll neglect her to death.

STARNS: Maybe not. I understand you're scornful about woman's work. Come work with me. I'm driving pilings.

Enter Juba. Exit Cora.

JUBA: Starns! The damn hog's right behind the cabin! Grandpa Jacob seen him!

STARNS: Tell Grandpa Jacob hush. What the hog-a-doing now!

JUBA: Eating on that first bucket of mash.

STARNS: Let him. Close yore eyes and hold out yore hand.

JUBA: What fer?

STARNS: To please a man afore he dies.

Warily, she does. Starns puts something in her hand.

Open up.

JUBA: What's this here?

STARNS: I never thanked you proper fer gitting me born.

JUBA: My stars, a comb. You make this?

STARNS: Cora's brother Cief made that. When cows die, cut off their horns, boil them four hours, spread them flat in a

275

clamp all night, file in the teeth, and set it in a cold spring. I showed Cief how and he made that and we're giving it to you.

JUBA: I thank you, sir.

STARNS: Don't say nothing about it.

JUBA (*To herself*): I'd had me a comb like that onct, when I was a girl pleasant as flowers, but it got lost. Now I had it again, and it was just the softest, creamiest thing. I put it to my head that night, and just scratched and scratched, it felt so good. (*To Starns*) You tell Cief Larman I am much obliged.

STARNS: I will.

Exit Juba. Billy calls out to Starns.

BILLY: Starns! Word from the Bishop! There's lots of notice taken, Starns! The Bishop has got people talking about this place everywhere! Baltimore, Washington, even New York City!

STARNS: Well, good.

BILLY: He says we'll do great work here. With a school and a farm and a clinic bringing folks to church. We will cleanse these people of their filth and squalor. We will bathe them all in the light of Jesus Christ!

Enter Juba.

JUBA: Jesus Christ! There that thing is!

Together, Starns and Juba face front.

STARNS: I see him!

JUBA: He does look like a Demon, Starns. Got a body might near big as a horse.

STARNS: Go on, Demon, eat that mash.

JUBA: Razorback curved up powerful spiny! Glittery black eyes, poked back in his puffed-up, hairy head! Mean thing!

STARNS: Eat, hog. Go on, eat.

JUBA: He's at the door!

Starns holds on to Juba, she to him.

STARNS: Let him in.

JUBA: Here he comes! He's a Demon!

They jump back.

STARNS: He's a hog! Stuffed full on three buckets of mash, wanting more!

JUBA: Here he comes!

They jump back. Pause.

He's fell over.

STARNS: He leaned over slantwise and a leg give out. Whup, here he comes again!

They jump back again. Pause.

JUBA: Both legs give out.

STARNS: Down belly whumpus.

They crouch forward together, looking.

JUBA: Look at them little red eyes. He can't move.

STARNS: He's a-wondering why he's on the ground.

They stand up.

JUBA: This pig is drunk.

STARNS: As corned as any man. Let Grandpa Jacob see that, then put a barrel to the silly thing's head and smoke all that ham.

BILLY: Starns and the Demon Hog. Starns and the Idiot's Comb. Starns and—

Enter Cora, running.

CORA: Starns! Starns!! (*She runs to him*) God Almighty, he's kilt her! He's got her down there dead!

STARNS: Got who, Cora?

CORA: Jean! Harlan's got her down by them graves! In a winding sheet!

Everybody moves quickly about the stage. Onto the platform steps Harlan, holding Cora's shawl as the baby, with a shovel under one arm. Cora, Juba and Starns confront Harlan.

STARNS: Harlan, put down the shovel. Give us the baby.

HARLAN: She's dead. Margaret done it. I tried to take Jean away. I hid her in a foxcave I know. But Margaret came when I slept. I woke up and seen Margaret had Jean by the neck, choking her to death. Orlean and Joseph was there, too. They said, "We want Jean with us."

CORA: Harlan, give Jean here. You never seen nobody.

HARLAN: Yes, I did! Talking to me plain as you are!

CORA: Give Jean here.

HARLAN: She ain't yours!

STARNS: Best let us have her.

HARLAN: Margaret said bury her here. Without no charms or spells, and I will.

CORA: Starns—

STARNS: Hush. (*To Harlan*) All right. I'll hold her while you dig.

HARLAN: I'll not trust you.

STARNS: What can I do if the child's dead? Just let me see, man. Then dig the grave.

Cora moves toward Harlan.

HARLAN: Cora!

He holds the baby out to Starns. Starns walks away slowly inspecting the baby.

STARNS: God damn it, she's still alive!

CORA: Jean!

JUBA AND BILLY: Oh!

Starns kneels, back to us. They crowd around him.

STARNS: Give me room!

Starns mimes holding the baby, and reaching into her throat. Juba, Cora and Billy lean forward.

It's something in her throat!

Starns pulls something out of the baby's throat.

JUBA, CORA, BILLY: Ah!

Starns hands it to Juba, who looks at it.

STARNS: She's breathing. No more blood in her mouth. Cora. (*He gives the baby to Cora*) What was that thing?

Juba rubs the blood off something, holds it up.

JUBA: Hit looks like a knuckle bone of some kind.

STARNS: Knuckle? Foxcave! (*He turns to Harlan*) Bones in that cave? You leave the baby with foxbones?

HARLAN: I tell you, Margaret—

STARNS (*Mad*): Never mind no dead woman! What do you feed this child, rocks and dirt? Man, if you won't take care of her, Cora will!

HARLAN: Don't do that!

STARNS: We got to!

CORA: No, you don't! Not like this!

STARNS: Ain't that what you want?

CORA: No it ain't. Me and Harlan's grateful for what you just done. We are. But you don't know what he suffers. I do. Nobody will be Jean's pa but Harlan. Thank you and hush.

STARNS: She's your child too, Cora.

CORA: Not unless her daddy says so. Never!

They all look at Harlan.

HARLAN: I say so.

CORA: You're wrong about Margaret. You told me yourself she never stinted on our Jean, even if she wasn't none of hers. She'd a never kilt this baby, Harlan. What you seen wasn't really there. Hit warn't Margaret.

HARLAN: I am a crazy man, and a sorry father. I know it.

CORA: You're her daddy. She's all right, Harlan. Here. I will never keep her from you.

Cora gives Harlan the baby, moves away.

HARLAN: You come with her.

CORA: Only if'n you want me.
HARLAN: Well I do.

Cora joins Harlan. Pause. She looks at Starns.

CORA: You kept your bargain with me, Starns. (*Pause*) I'll always be true to Harlan, but if'n I wasn't, and if'n you ever took up likker and women again, I'd hope you'd fancy me.
STARNS: You know I would. Whenever you need me, you come on.
CORA: I thank you, sir.
STARNS: Don't say nothing about it.
BILLY: Starns and the Babythroat Foxbone.
JUBA: Starns and the Whistling Corncrib.

Billy gets the crate again, puts it at center.

CORA: Starns and the Haunted Log Kitchen.
BILLY: Starns and the Day the Cabbages Walked.

Starns stands on the crate. Juba, Cora and Billy sit before him. Harlan stands away from them.

And Starns, a-preaching!
STARNS: This here is from the Book of Saint Aw—gust—tyne. "What Do We Love when We Love Our God." (*He reads painfully*) "What do—we love—when we love our God? We love—no—shining lights of earth. We love—no—sweet music or singing." Well, we do, sometimes, but not too much. "We love no fragrance of flowers, perfumes, soaps and spices, no milk and honey, no sweet—ah—flesh—the body desires to embrace." I don't reckon he

means a body can't love a flower or good strong soap, but Jesus Christ is just more important. "No, it is not—these things we love—when we love our God."

BILLY: The worst preacher in the history of religion.

JUBA: Starns and How Everybody Loves God.

CORA: Including Harlan.

Starns steps down from the crate.

STARNS (*To Harlan*): It's built with a four-foot flush—east, west, north and south. Not one corner to it, Harlan. No witch can hide in there. When you can't sleep at night, when evil things ride your back, you come and sleep here. This church is built for you.

Harlan joins them quickly, sits by Cora.

BILLY: Starns and the Cornerless Church. Where he read sermons copied by hand from *The Confessions of Saint Augustine.*

JUBA: Short ones.

CORA: But it wasn't all sermons.

BILLY: Starns and the Letters of Fire!

ALL: STARNS AND THE LETTERS OF FIRE!

JUBA: That's when John Barco, laziest man in the mountains, jumped right up in the middle of a sermon!

BILLY: "Praise God! I just seen three letters of fire, a-burning in the sky. G! P! C! They mean Go! Preach! Christ! That's what God wants me to do! Get down, Starns, and let me up there!"

STARNS: John Barco. I ain't saying warn't no GPC. You seen it, in the sky, and Lord Jesus put it there. But it don't mean Go Preach Christ. It means Go Plow Corn! You do that and then come to church.

JUBA: Harlan!

CORA: Harlan. Go on. You now.

HARLAN: One day a fine Moses-eyed preacher with charms and spells and a black beard and Bible come here. He was a big bug in the mountains, so Starns had to let him preach and he got up in the pulpit. (*He stands on the crate*)

CORA: And he said:

HARLAN: Will all the women in this church, sitting here before me, on this Sunday morning, when I say "Now," cross yore legs. "Now!"

Cora and Juba cross their legs.

CORA AND JUBA: And all the women crossed their legs.

HARLAN: Now that the gates to hell are shut tight, I'll preach the Word of God! (*He gets down from the crate*) But he didn't, hee hee, because Starns, hee hee, had him by the neck and beard dragged out of the pulpit and throwed him down the steps and out the door!

BILLY: And went back himself to speak, apologizing to the ladies, reading that same sermon as always, from Saint Augustine.

Starns sits on the crate, speaks intimately to them.

STARNS: "And yet—when we love our God—we do love a kind of richness and beauty—a kind of—shining light—a kind of sweet melody—flowers—soap and spices and milk and honey. We love—on earth—the weather and the flesh of the children of Heaven." Amen.

ALL: Amen.

STARNS: Praise God.

ALL: Praise God.

BILLY: Starns and the Children of Heaven.

ALL: Starns and the Children of Heaven.

Enter Bishop. Everybody jumps up. The Bishop looks at them, sternly. He turns about, looks sharply.

BISHOP: Starns.

STARNS: Yessir.

BISHOP: Where are the corners of this church?

STARNS: It's a theological situation, Bishop. I done the best with it I knowed how.

Pause. The Bishop frowns.

If I done wrong, tell me. I'll fix it. I can fix these simple things, because you showed me the way. There wouldn't be nothing here without you. If you don't like what you see, you tell us!

He points to the crate. The Bishop mounts it, stares at them sternly, then smiles.

BISHOP: Well, it's a church. God bless you! (*He steps down and shakes hands with them*)

ALL: Thank you, Bishop! Welcome back, Bishop!

BILLY: Starns and the Children of Heaven.

JUBA: When we buried Grandpa Jacob Larman, Starns had me speak over him, something no woman hereabouts ever been allowed to do. After the funeral, a marriage: Cora and Harlan, finally. Then, five minutes after that, a baptism, and not one word said agin it by nobody. The Bishop had Starns christen their baby. Jean Margaret, her name was.

A mimed wedding and christening. Harlan shakes hands with Starns.

HARLAN: I do feel better for these charms and spells. I thank ye.

STARNS: Don't say nothing about it.

JUBA: And that night, a wedding dance, with mountain beer Starns knowed how to brew, jest water poured over bumblebee combs and left to ferment, but it give a body enough of a drunk to dance right, and we did.

Billy, Juba, Cora and Harlan look with wonder at a great crowd coming to a barn dance. Starns and the Bishop stand aside.

BILLY: John Barco was there—

JUBA: All the Larmans—

CORA: My kinfolks Earl and Shad and Cardell—

HARLAN: And their wives and chilluns—

BILLY: All kinds of slope folks—

CORA: From the east and the west—

JUBA: And the north and the south—

BILLY: Over one hundred souls—

HARLAN: Bringing their fiddles and mouth harps—

CORA: Dulcimers and banjos!

BILLY: Songs so old, nobody knew where they came from. "Prince Charlie," and "The Chimney Sweep." "The Downfall of Paris," nobody knowing a Prince, or what a chimney sweep was, or what about Paris made it fall down.

JUBA (*Pointing*): Earl Larman paraded in here with this god-awful woman, I mean no teeth, scars on her face and dirt an inch thick, and danced her around us like she was the Queen of Egypt.

CORA (*Pointing*): Griswold Plankman and his wife he never took nowhere and never let say a word when he did, they come and danced, too, amazing the world.

HARLAN: John Barco said, "Is that Harlan dancing?" and I said, "Yes! It is Harlan! Dancing!"

Mountain music.

BILLY: We paraded in here, to the great country tunes of fine arrivals into grand estates, the old Infare songs of homecoming and feasts and days of joy. Entrance, and arrival, where we would live forever!

Music swells.

Juba!

Juba steps forward, bows.

Cora!

Same.

Harlan, with baby Jean!

Same.

Starns!

Starns shakes his head.

Starns!

Starns won't.

Well, me then!

Billy moves to center, holds out his arms.

If I have my house, I will never leave it! I will keep it with me always!

Cora and Juba step forward, and lead Billy by the hand into his house.

ALL: Come in, Billy! You're home, Billy! Come in!!
BILLY: And then plain old hoedown reels and quadrilles and boxes!
ALL: Hooo—eeee!!!!

Billy, Cora, Harlan and Juba run to four corners. Music fast, furious and loud. They clap and stomp.

One-two-three-four!

Billy does a swift do-si-do with Juba.

Swing around and a swap you've made! Your pretty girl for my old maid!

Cora and Harlan.

There goes a girl and I'll go with her! Way off down the mountain!

All four dance forward, bow, and dance back.

I'll be true t'my true love, 'fmy love'll be true to me!

They stomp and clap.

CORA: Hey, Starns! Come on and dance!

BILLY: Give him some more beer!

HARLAN: Dance, Starns! I did!

JUBA: I know he wants to!

They look at each other, hoot, and run together to Starns, surrounding him, pulling him out on the dance floor, breaking away and leaving him there. They clap, urge him on. Starns steps once, twice, hops, the music faster and faster, then with a whoop, he dances before them, face, hands and body stiff but his feet flying.

STARNS: Hooo-EEEE!!!!

Then Starns staggers away, wiping his face, and grinning. Cora, Harlan and Juba turn their backs, and, to softer music, dance again, in place.

BILLY: When his lungs give out, Starns went outside, and so did I and so did the Bishop.

The Bishop stands behind Starns. Billy watches them. A sound of wind. Music.

We looked out at the mountain night, over the graves and the Missionhouse Valley. Faint were the fiddles, hardly heard the dancing feet, because the night wind blew loud and cold down the great steeps and ridges, but we heard them, and we knew the Missionhouse was alive, like a heart in a strong body.

Starns breathes deeply. The music is very soft. Cora, Juba and Harlan sway slowly to the music.

ROMULUS LINNEY

STARNS: My own.

BILLY: A kind of richness and a kind of beauty.

BISHOP: There will be more than this.

STARNS: I have found my own.

BILLY: A kind of shining light.

STARNS: Lord God Almighty, I never thought about You there before, but I do now.

BISHOP: This is only a beginning.

BILLY: Flowers and spice and milk and honey.

STARNS: I give You thanks.

BISHOP: Dancing will become worship.

BILLY: The weather and the flesh.

STARNS: For my own, on this earth.

BISHOP: Earth will lead us to heaven.

BILLY: Three years of it! Of happiness beyond description, in Heathen Valley!

Cold, fierce mountain wind.

Starns, you have your own! Bishop, you have your ring! Billy, you have your home!

||||||||||||||||||||||||||||||||||||||||||||||||||||||||||||||||||||||||||||||||||||||||||

Act Two

*As before. Starns sits on the crate, reading from a ledger.
The Bishop listens to him, but paces back and forth, both-
ered. He carries a black garment, rolled up, under his arm.
Billy watches.*

STARNS: Baptisms, sixteen. Confirmations, ten. Marriages, six.
Burials, eight. Offerings, four dollar and eight cent. Divine services have been held at places following, that is,
not counting those here at the Mission. On September the
tenth, at the store of James Rode above Carson's Fall—
(*His voice becomes lower as he continues reading, and Billy
speaks over him*) —and there was one soul received. On
September twenty-second, in front of a cabin owned by a
Mr. Hartfoot, I don't know just where but it's marked on
the map. There was no one received, but many stood and
listened and received the gospel in a kindly way.

BILLY (*Over Starns*): It became a ritual, every year, on your
spring visit, Bishop. Starns tallying every sacrament,
every service, every lesson, every penny, every nail, and
you would listen.

STARNS: Forty-seven children now in the school, thirty boarding through winter. Preaching circuit a circumference of

sixty-five mile. Two cots have been added to the clinic and a pine table on which a man can be laid for treatment.

The Bishop turns away, paces. Billy watches.

BISHOP (*Over Starns*): But why? What purpose? Have we done our work for crops, dances, and a dispensary? It is for the glory of God, not for a settlement of farmers, that we are here.

STARNS: Shipment of cattle stock from Pennsylvania received, and duly pastured. Orchards now expanded to include peach and cherry, in one hundred twenty-three acre.

BISHOP: Starns.

STARNS: Yessir?

BISHOP: Is that Cora? There? Harlan?

STARNS: Yessir, and a new baby. A boy. They named him Jacob. See Jean, riding on Harlan's shoulders?

BISHOP: They look very happy.

STARNS: Reckon so.

BISHOP: You've been quite the matchmaker here.

STARNS: Harlan and Cora got their family together, when time come. I didn't do much.

BISHOP: I envy you. On this mountain, all the time. I visit, and that's all. (*Pause*) It is simpler up here. I can see— eternity.

Starns laughs, points.

STARNS: They're together all the time. Harlan and Cora. Won't leave each other one minute. She even plows with him. Jean rides his shoulders, see, like a horsey, like that.

BISHOP: They make a handsome family.

STARNS: I swear they do.

BISHOP: It is good to be happy, when we are young.

STARNS: Hit is of a sartin!

BISHOP (*Pacing*): And it is dangerous. We can love the earth too much.

STARNS: Huh? Sorry, I was watching Cora.

BISHOP: We came here to change a people who forgot God. They did it then in riots and orgies. They can do it again, in dances, farming, schooling. The danger is the same.

STARNS: Yessir, 'at's so. Now, there's three hundred fifty-five acre of wheat and buckwheat, barley, potatoes—

BILLY: Was it here it happened? Over three years? WHEN???

Change of light. Spot on Billy and Bishop.

Bishop?

BISHOP: Yes, Billy?

BILLY: Where? Was it here?

BISHOP: No, no.

BILLY: I keep trying to find it. Put my finger on it. Know just where it was everything in my life got changed forever. If it wasn't here, where was it?

BISHOP: Are you blaming yourself?

BILLY: Like a child, yes. I think and I think, I did something wrong. Here, there! It wouldn't have happened but for me!

BISHOP: It was not your fault.

BILLY: Then whose fault was it? You'd say Starns!

BISHOP: No, I wouldn't.

BILLY: He'd say you.

BISHOP: Yes, he would.

BILLY: Would he be right?

BISHOP: No.

BILLY: Why not? It has to be somebody!

BISHOP: You are an orphan, my boy, and you think that a home on earth is the answer to everything. It isn't.

BILLY: Then what is?

BISHOP: The answer to everything is God, alone. What that means. Where that is. When I was a boy—

BILLY: I don't want a sermon from you!

BISHOP: This isn't one. You loved me too, didn't you?

BILLY: Yes.

BISHOP: As your friend?

BILLY: Yes.

BISHOP: Then do not judge me. When I was a boy, I was alone, too. Both my mother and my father were atheists. And I knew that they were wrong, and that I would spend all my life, every hour of every day, finding God. Not some idea of God. Not some pale abstract Divinity with a lukewarm sun for a face. Not some stupid thundering Father, with a fist for a reason. God. Think, Billy. The power that moves the stars. The answer to every yearning. To the riddles we cannot even imagine exist, much less solve. The God of Job and the God of every tiny insect. I knew I would find God while I lived, and for that day, for that moment, all my life on earth was only a preparation. All my studies in school, nothing else. All my advancement in the churches, nothing else. All my good works, nothing else.

BILLY: And all that happened here, nothing else? Only a preparation for you to find God?

BISHOP: Exactly! Look no further, Billy, This is why everything had to be as it was.

BILLY: Is that what happened to you then?

BISHOP: Yes.

BILLY: In Heathen Valley?

BISHOP: In Heathen Valley, I found God. At last.

BILLY: Then what happened, had to.

BISHOP: Of course.

Light fades from them, back to what it was.

(*To Starns*) Didn't you hear what I said?

STARNS: Yessir. You said don't forget God. I won't.

BISHOP: That is not what I said.

Enter Juba.

JUBA: Old Bertha done it good. The whole Tate family, that pregnant Morris girl, and them mean Harrell sisters, all swore they'd baptize their babies soon as they have 'em.

BISHOP: Old Bertha?

JUBA: Bishop.

BISHOP: Who's Old Bertha, Starns?

STARNS: She helps baptize bastard chilluns. Tell him.

JUBA: I misdoubt he'd interest hisself.

STARNS: Tell him.

JUBA: Old Bertha is a dirty hag what collects bastard baby souls, and flies through the air with them on the back of a dirty calico skirt, all tattered out behind her.

BISHOP: Flies through the air?

JUBA: Over the mountains, at midnight. And on her filthy skirt, the dead babies lie, scared and crying in the black night, a-moaning and a-wailing—oh, hit is powerful spooky! (*She chuckles*) Scared them Tates witless, and that no good Morris girl, too.

BISHOP: May I ask the point of this unpleasant fairy tale?

JUBA: So long, Starns.

STARNS: Hold on, Juba. Bishop don't understand. Be patient with him.

JUBA: The point of the fairy tale, Bishop, is I git wore out midwifing a bastard baby I know will get murdered by its momma, or its head smashed in by its daddy, or left in the pigpen to git stomped into slop and et by the sow. If'n Old Bertha kin help that condition, then she will, whether you like it or not.

Exit Juba. Enter Harlan.

HARLAN: See, it's like a baby. I made this charm out of birch bark, Jean's hair, and goat's blood. It's a charm for me and my chillun. I want it spoken over.

STARNS: Ask the Bishop.

HARLAN: I have come to accept spells and charms. For the protection of my family, I made this here. I want you to say something to it and give it some power.

BISHOP: I can't do that.

HARLAN: Why not?

BISHOP: Such charms don't exist.

HARLAN: You won't speak to it?

BISHOP: No.

HARLAN: Starns, will you?

STARNS: Give it here. (*He takes it from Harlan*) Whatever power I got in me, I hope goes right into whatever this is, to help Harlan and protect Jean. That good enough?

HARLAN: Of a sartin. (*He takes it back*) I reckon Bishops hold with some charms but not with others. Hit's confusing.

Exit Harlan. Enter Cora.

CORA: Starns, I left you some corn and hickory nuts, from Cief.

STARNS: Bishop, we raised her brother Cief a little cabin, and he gets by alone now, just fine.

CORA: Except for my two nights a week. Remember that!

Exit Cora. Starns moves quickly to the Bishop.

STARNS: Cora is touchy about Cief. She don't like to talk about him afore just anybody.

BISHOP: She spends two nights with her brother?

STARNS: Yessir. Can't say why myself.

BISHOP: Yes, you can! This is the woman we married? Changed her from her primitive ways? Living adulterously with her brother?

STARNS: Only twict a week!

BISHOP: Starns!

STARNS: I don't know it fer sartin.

BISHOP: Well, find out. And if she is, stop it!

STARNS: You reckon that's so easy!

BISHOP: I don't care if it's *easy* or not! Stop it!

STARNS: I heared you.

BISHOP: Old Bertha, flying through the air? A grisly totem, made out of goat's blood? Organized incest? These practices must not continue. A Christian cannot live in barbaric illusions.

STARNS: Well, I can't tell them that.

BISHOP: Why not?

STARNS: I can't say here's Almighty God with a daddy-white beard, sitting on a golden throne divided in three parts of some Trinity while a Virgin never touched goes and has His divine baby, and then turn around and tell them they are a-living in some barbaric illusion. You want to, go ahead.

BISHOP: I will.

Starns goes back to the crate.

STARNS: I got to get on with my accounts now.

BISHOP: By all means.

STARNS (*Reading again*): Beans, clover and hay, and best of all them cabbages that do so well. Now since January 1st, 1859, we've had—

The Bishop resumes his pacing. Billy follows, watching.

BILLY (*Over Starns*): Bishop, listen to him. It's a farm that prospers, a school that teaches, a hospital that heals and a church that doesn't presume. Isn't that enough? Can't that be enough?

STARNS: Marriages, three. Burials, four. Six births and one christening. Juba reckons we'll get tother five come summer. Church offering, total two dollar and thirty-nine cent. (*He closes his ledger*) That's it, Bishop.

BISHOP: Perfect as always.

STARNS: Bishop? Is something wrong?

BISHOP: Yes.

STARNS: Well, what? I'll fix it.

BISHOP: Oh, will you?

BILLY: Just leave it alone!

STARNS: Shorely. You tell me what, and I will.

BISHOP: Can you "fix" the hunger of man for God?

STARNS: Huh?

BISHOP: That is not so simple.

STARNS: Nossir.

BISHOP: First, you must know what it is.

STARNS: Huh?

BISHOP: You don't understand what I'm talking about.

STARNS: Yes, I do. Wanting God. I reckon we do.

BISHOP: Are we hungry for God here? Or do we farm and sweat and eat cabbages, do what we please, think what we

please, trade one superstition for another, and call that our
Mission?

STARNS: Well, no. We go to church, too.

BISHOP: Like a party, or a house-raising or a meeting hall?
Another merry scene?

STARNS: Oh, I see what you mean. Yeah, too much laughing in
church, you're right.

BISHOP: That's not what I mean.

STARNS: Well, what do you mean?

BILLY: You don't come to it all at once. But over the years, with
the Bishop's visits, we hear it, words getting sharper, hard
looks colder, and longer.

BISHOP: We need more than cabbages.

STARNS: What's wrong with my cabbages?

BISHOP: We must rise above them, somehow.

STARNS: How? We're down here, ain't we?

BISHOP: Where your happiness will not last!

STARNS: Hit shore won't if the crops ain't in. Bishop, you mean
we ain't being good-enough Christians somehow? That it?

BISHOP: That is not it.

STARNS: What is?

BISHOP: We must hunger! And thirst! For God! No matter how
I prosper—here or anywhere else—I am still far away
from Him!

STARNS: Yessir. What do you want me to do about that?

BILLY: Bishop, be careful!

BISHOP: Try to understand me.

BILLY: Starns, watch out!

STARNS: I understand, all right, you're picking us to pieces.

BISHOP: How will we worship our God? With cabbages and
corn, and bucolic pride, like a country fool?

STARNS: Don't reckon I fancy being called a country fool.

BILLY: He didn't call you a fool.

STARNS: Yes, he did. Mountain people ain't religious like you are. They feel it! They worship. But they don't bend no knees! It ain't in their nature!

BISHOP: If we forget our Lord Jesus Christ, then we have not done the work of the Lord here, we have done the work of the Devil, and I will have none of it! Starns!

BILLY: Not like this. Don't.

BISHOP: I will. (*To Starns*) Sunday belongs to the Lord, not the land. There will be no manual labor performed at this Mission on Sundays, sunup to sundown.

STARNS: Chilluns *have* to work on Sundays, some!

BISHOP: This is your Bishop's decision! Excuse me, please.

Pause.

BILLY: Don't talk to him like that.

BISHOP: I will. Excuse me, please!

Starns, quickly, moves away.

Billy.

BILLY: Sir!

The Bishop holds out the folded black garment. Billy takes it.

But why?

BISHOP: To bring us all closer to God.

BILLY: Aren't we close enough as it is?

BISHOP: I think not.

The Bishop takes off his frock coat. Billy holds up the folded garment, lets it fall open. It is a black cassock. Billy helps the Bishop put it on. the Bishop hands Billy the frock coat.

In the ancient world, there were many Heathen Valleys. Each with its own Jesus. There was a great deal of dancing, and rejoicing. It was all delusion. Only the rock of the Church endured. Why? Because it was put there not by man but by God.

Billy takes a cross from the frock coat. He hands it to the Bishop, who puts it around his neck.

Human happiness is a temptation. It does not really exist. Human life, by itself, is nothing.

BILLY: Nothing?

BISHOP: Worse than nothing. It is dirt. Where you will lie, when your soul stands at judgment.

Billy moves away. The Bishop walks about.

Starns.

STARNS: Yes, Bishop?

BISHOP: Do you know what this is?

STARNS: Uh. Black wool dress of some kind.

BISHOP: It is a cassock.

STARNS: What's a cass-sock?

BISHOP: It was the dress of the clergy in the Middle Ages.

STARNS: Men wore these?

BISHOP: I would like them worn here.

STARNS: By who?

BISHOP: Everyone.

STARNS: Me?

BISHOP: Everyone.

STARNS: I never wore no dress before.

BISHOP: It is not a dress. It is the ancient garment of the Church of Christ.

They stand facing each other.

STARNS: Nossir.

BISHOP: I beg your pardon?

STARNS: I said I can't wear no dress.

BISHOP: It is not a dress!

STARNS: You want me gone?

BISHOP: I do not want you gone. I want you to obey me!

STARNS: Well, I won't wear no dress! Get somebody else!

BISHOP: We are not talking about a dress!

STARNS: About what then?

BISHOP: The way to salvation! This cassock teaches us humility. It makes us look the same before God. The way to salvation is to become no one, for God.

Pause.

STARNS: Horseshit. The way to salvation is to be somebody, *for* somebody!

They stare at each other, shocked. Then they fight.

BISHOP: You will not understand! Centuries of the Church—

STARNS: I don't *care* about no centuries of no church!! I care about this place right here and right now!

BISHOP: Which will disappear! Which will vanish! Taking the heathen with it! Only the Church—

STARNS: Aw, God damn this!! Get yourself somebody else!

BISHOP: I will!

STARNS: Fine!!

BISHOP: Starns!!

STARNS: Bishop?

BISHOP: This Mission depends on you. You can't desert it!

STARNS: Getting fired ain't deserting!

BISHOP: All right. I will compromise. If the schoolchildren wear the cassocks, I will, for now, be satisfied. Will you?

STARNS: It's your Mission.

BISHOP: Under God, whose Bishop you will from now on obey.

STARNS: Fine.

BISHOP: Thank you.

Starns turns away. Harsh spotlight on the Bishop at center. Billy brings the crate to the Bishop. The Bishop kneels before it, and begins to chant in Latin, the Dies Irae. Church bell, tolling a harsh double ring.

(*Chanting*) Dies irae, dies illa, solvet saeculum in favilla, teste David cum Sibylla.

BILLY: Prayers in Latin. Against the Day of Wrath. To the Dead. To the Virgin. In the ancient language of God.

The Bishop continues to chant the Dies Irae. Enter Harlan, Cora and Juba.

HARLAN: Boys wear that thing?

STARNS: Called a cass-sock.

HARLAN: Hit's a spell, and a bad one.

CORA: I don't like them things. Ain't natural.

JUBA: Starns, the boys wearing cass-socks look like crows walking around. What's it fer?

STARNS: Bishop knows. I don't.

BILLY: They look like little monks. In a monastery.

CORA: What's a mon-es-tery?

STARNS: Bishop says cassock's the garment of the true old Church. I don't like this, but you'll not fault him. Without the Bishop, none of us'd be nowhere. I'd be in jail again maybe, or dead, and the rest of this valley'd be up them slopes eating dirt. We got a good thing here, and we got it because of him!

Starns points to the Bishop. The Bishop holds out his arms.

BISHOP: Let us pray. (*Pause*) Let us pray!

Billy and Starns kneel with him.

What will it profit a man if he gain the whole world and lose his own soul?
CORA: Starns! Starns!

Starns starts to rise.

BISHOP: Starns!
CORA: I know it's Sunday Service, but Cief's in trouble, Starns! Laid open his leg plowing might near the bone. I tied it up, but you got to come now!

Starns starts to go to Cora.

BISHOP: Starns!
CORA: Starns!
BISHOP: Forgive us our childish sins, and *rebellions!*

Starns kneels again. Cora moves away from him.

HARLAN: I lowrate praying, when a body is cut and bleeding. Margaret would, too.
JUBA: This Bishop is moving on.

The bell continues to toll. The Bishop rises and stands on the box.

BISHOP: It is not enough! It is not enough to feed my body with cabbage! It is not enough to feed my soul with communal prayers! (*He steps down from the box and falls to his knees*) I must hunger! And in that hunger, I must bend and I must break, for the love of Jesus Christ, who was broken on the cross, for me!!

He prostrates himself, arms outspread, on the ground. Bell, louder. Cora steps onto the box above the Bishop.

CORA: I know it would be good to live forever in the Lord, if not me, then my children. But when I see children in black dresses, when I hear singing I can't noway comprehend, and listen to do-this, do-that, I want to say, the devil take it, give my babies a sugar stick, and go to bed with my husband. Judge me for that!

Exit Cora. Harlan gets up on the box.

HARLAN: Hit is all coming about, like Margaret said hit would. The witches and the demons have come again, the specters and the haints. They are almighty and always.

Exit Harlan. Juba gets on the box.

JUBA: This man is acting like the fool I said he was first day I laid eyes on him. Oh, he is on the ground all right, in a slather of words, dizzy with praying! But what he really wants is me on my knees boo-hooing how bad this life really is. I know this life. I seen too many babies, in and out of it, born and die, with no reason why. Leave it that way!

Exit Juba. The bell very loud, suddenly ceases. Silence. Change of light. The Bishop rises. He is at peace with himself. Starns sits at center, thumping on the wooden crate. The Bishop moves to him. Starns stares at the Bishop.

STARNS: What the hell you mean, you are leaving?

BISHOP: Every man must save his own soul. I must save mine.

STARNS: It ain't that easy. What about us? You give us wonderful things to do here. Now you'll just walk away?

BISHOP: Yes, I will walk away.

STARMS: Why?

BISHOP: Because I love God.

STARNS: Maybe you love God, all right, but you shore don't love us.

BISHOP: It is God I serve.

STARNS: You serve yourself is who you serve! When poor folks with poor ways don't serve *you* no more, it's goodbye, down the road and so long!

BISHOP: You can put man before God. I cannot!

STARNS: I will put Cora and Harlan before God, you damn right! They need me! God don't!

BISHOP: You think you are Jesus Christ in this valley, and you are not!

STARNS: A course not! *You* are!!

Pause.

BISHOP: I see. (*He turns away from Starns*) In the conventions, in the congregations, and everywhere else. You are no different from all the others. No one really worships here. Christ is an excuse. For the rabbit warren. The Sunday social. It is all fellowship!

STARNS: And why not?

305

BISHOP: God is not fellowship! God, Starns, is love!!

STARNS: Oh, no, He ain't! Whatever God is, that He ain't! Because I know what that is! That is my square, scored-off beams, set so flush an ant can't get between. That is these pegs what won't never rust. That is Cora's hand on my shoulder, and Harlan decent for the first time in his life. You can't fool me about God and His love. That is up there in the thunder and the rain somewheres. It ain't my brother's hand. It ain't my sister's song. I know what love is. You shut your mouth!

Pause.

BISHOP: Goodbye.

BILLY: And it was over.

The Bishop moves away. Starns moves away. Billy moves to the Bishop.

BISHOP: My father and mother were atheists. I was first a Baptist, then a Methodist, then a Presbyterian, then an Episcopalian. None of it was enough.

BILLY: What is enough?

BISHOP: I am going to Rome. Where I will give to the Pope my Episcopal Bishop's ring. I am sorry if you do not understand. I have found my way. God bless you.

The Bishop holds out his hand. Billy backs away from him, not taking it.

BILLY: And you went there. On a Christmas Day, you gave the Pope your Bishop's ring. And on that same day, in New York, you were formally deposed.

The Bishop moves away. Billy stops him.

Bishop.

The Bishop turns. Billy throws his frock coat to him. Exit Bishop. Enter, looking after him as he goes, Juba, Cora, and Harlan. A long pause.

HARLAN: Dee—posed?
CORA: He ain't a Bishop no more?
BILLY: No.
JUBA: What is he, then? Got to be something.
BILLY: The word is Apostate.
JUBA: What does that mean?
HARLAN: Left one set of spells, joined anothern?
CORA: 'Nother Church?
BILLY: Yes.
CORA: What does he do?
BILLY: He prays.
CORA: In that foreign language?
BILLY: Yes.
JUBA: In that cass-sock?
BILLY: Yes.

Pause.

JUBA: Reckon that's what he wanted then.
CORA: Not us.
BILLY: No.
HARLAN: Fancied one thing one day, something else the next. Religion.
STARNS: HUSH UP!!

They look at him, astonished.

BILLY: It can't be the same, Starns!

STARNS: Yes, it can!

BILLY: Everything will change!

STARNS: I won't let it!! Now go on about your business! Git!!

Juba, Cora and Harlan turn away and exit. Starns walks past Billy, calling out to mountain people

Hey! Now, looky here! Hey! Looky here!

BILLY: And off you went, with Bibles and roots and herbs and lotions. To tend poor folks with poor ways.

Starns speaks to mountain people.

STARNS: You keep on coming to church! Keep on a-planting crops with me! Everything's going to be jest the same! I promise it!

BILLY: The Church says no more farm. No more school. No more church!

STARNS: What?

BILLY: Black cassocks? Prayers in Latin? And now its Bishop in *Rome*? It wants this place forgotten!

STARNS: I'll farm anyhow!

BILLY: With what? On whose land? Yours?

STARNS: I'll preach then!

BILLY: How? These people support a church? Money's cut off. No more supplies. No more seed. Church owns this land, Starns. You'll do what it tells you.

STARNS: Oh.

BILLY: There does have to be a tenant. So you can stay on, for thirty dollars a year. Like a janitor.

STARNS: Oh. I can?

BILLY: And everything will be what it was, in Heathen Valley.

Enter Harlan, running.

HARLAN: Margaret? That you? (*He stops, looks about*) Where are you? (*He sees no one*) I know you're here. Where? (*He turns about, looking for her*) Ah. You standing there now. (*He backs away*) With my babies. Blood on their faces. Oh, God, my dead babies.

Enter Cora.

CORA: Harlan. It's Cora. What you doing standing in the yard?
HARLAN: I thought I saw Margaret here.
CORA: Oh, Harlan.
HARLAN: Where are the children?
CORA: In the cabin.
HARLAN: Get 'em out here.
CORA: Why?
HARLAN: Their daddy wants to talk to them, that's why. I been neglectful of my offspring.
CORA: What you fixing to say to them?
HARLAN: Things they need to know. About the living, and the dead.
CORA: No, Harlan.
HARLAN: What Margaret always told me, and I know is true.
CORA: No.
HARLAN: Margaret was a wise woman, Cora. I'm good for nothing. You just a bitch. The children need her.
CORA: You're not a-going to do it, Harlan!
HARLAN: Get out of my way.

He pushes her aside. They exit. Enter Juba.

JUBA: Starns, if'n a midwife is needed, I will always come. But for that reason only. You're deserted, man. I feels benastied down here now.

Exit Juba.

BILLY: What's here for you now?
STARNS: Poor folks with poor ways!
BILLY: Well, you fool.

Exit Billy. Starns is alone on the stage. He speaks to his mountain people.

STARNS: I know you're tired a-listening to me and I don't have the right words, but don't go away. We done built this up now, don't leave it. Hit's good. Don't—leave. Don't. (*He looks around. He sees he is alone*) All right. Come back when you can.

Starns sits on his crate. Enter Cora, holding her new baby. Billy enters, watches.

CORA: Starns? Yoo-hoo Starns? (*She kicks at something with her foot*) Lizard. Hateful thing, git. Starns? You in there?

Starns coughs, holds his stomach.

STARNS: Cora. (*Coughs*)
CORA: Your stomach still hurt you?
STARNS: Something in it won't go away. Come in.
CORA: I hate this. You living in the gristmill now.
STARNS: It'll do.
CORA: Nobody comes down here no more at all?

STARNS: Billy does, sometimes. Juba.

CORA: What do you do here now?

STARNS: I tend the place. Sit here, Cora. Rest yeself.

Cora sits on the upturned box.

CORA: We're taking you at your word, me and my little boy. We come to live with you.

STARNS: What?

CORA: We got to.

STARNS: Where's Jean?

CORA: She's with Harlan. She won't leave him. I brung little Jacob but she wouldn't come.

STARNS: What's happened now?

CORA: This morning Harlan told me Jean wasn't mine. He commenced telling her I'm not her momma, Margaret was. He's scary again. I can't live with him no more.

STARNS: He's your husband now. You have to.

CORA: I'm scared. Not for me, for my chillun!

STARNS: Don't matter.

CORA: The man's crazy, Starns. He can't help it, but he is, and it's worse.

STARNS: Tell him to come down here and talk to me.

CORA: He won't. Harlan says you don't got no powers no more, now that the Bishop's gone. I got to stay with you!

STARNS: I can't tell you, leave your husband!

CORA: Why not?

STARNS: It ain't decent! If the Bishop was here, he'd know what to say. I don't!

CORA: But he ain't here. Harlan's right. You ain't the same man. (*Pause*) You won't take me in?

STARNS: No.

CORA: You said you would. If I ever needed you. (*Pause*) Go away?

STARNS: Go away.

CORA: All right. I will. (*She moves past Starns, stops with her back to him*) Goodbye.

Exit Cora. Enter Juba. She sets the box down and sits on it. Starns, holding his stomach, lies down with his back leaning against hers.

BILLY: Abandoned, sick, with your stomach misery deadly now, with a midwife tending your death as she had your birth, Starns we knew you were dreaming of your God who left you, of your Judas Bishop you loved so much.

STARNS (*Asleep*): Ah. Ah. How come? How come?

JUBA: Starns?

STARNS: Where you been? Everything's ruint.

BILLY: We could hear you talking to him, as you may have seen him, your maker, stepping across mountains like magic, with the mist curling around his arms like smoke.

STARNS: Bishop! Come back! Come back!!

He reaches out for the Bishop, crawls on his knees, collapses, coughing. Juba holds out her arms to him.

JUBA: Starns!

He crawls back to her. He vomits into her hands.

This here looks like red coffee grounds. So. (*She rests his head against her*) I'll make ye some boneset tea. You sleep some more.

Pause. Enter Harlan, very slowly.

HARLAN: Wrong, wrong, wrong, oh wrong. I have done wrong. But I fancied it so much for a while. Home, children, wife and church. And for every evil thing there'd be a spell against it Starns would know, a charm for it the Bishop could use. Fool, fool, Harlan, ever to conceive it!! Because Margaret was right. There ain't no such things. There ain't no heaven where everthing will be all right again, and the charms and spells what makes us think so are terrible things. They are lies! Best have done with everthing! (*He looks about*) Jean? My girl? (*He sees her*) Jean, you are in the yard, frightened of yore miserable daddy. But if I call, you will come to me, taking my mean hands in yours, like you always have. Jean, come along. Come along, honey, to me.

Exit Harlan. Light on Billy, holding up one hand.

BILLY: To cut roots you need a barlow knife razor sharp. I have mine when I stop to see Starns. I am hoping to cut ginseng with it.

Light on Cora, running on, breathless.

CORA: No, Jacob. It is not for me I am running now. It is for you. I would not run from my husband, my son, if not for you. I will not let him get you, I will see to that. I will see that you are safe!

Light changes. Cora holds out the shawl that is the baby, and lets it fall open. She puts the shawl about her shoulders.

But if it was only me, I would turn and let him find me. And I would tell him what is in me. I would hold out my arms and say I am still the same woman, I do not care, do what you want, for what does it matter, let me be told, where the body goes when the heart is cold!

Harlan appears behind her, grabs her.

Harlan!

He cuts her throat. Wind, at gale force. Harsh light. Billy rushes to Starns.

BILLY: He's got Cora in that foxcave, Starns! He's already killed his little Jean!
STARNS: Harlan!
JUBA: Starns, you can't go out there!

Starns staggers to his feet.

STARNS: Harlan!

Harlan turns, holding Cora.

HARLAN: You damn scoundrel!
STARNS: Let her go.
HARLAN: You want what's left of her? Here!!

He releases Cora, who falls at his feet.

STARNS: WHY DID YOU DO THAT?

Harlan waves a knife at Starns.

JUBA: Starns, watch out!
HARLAN: You lying son of a bitch!
STARNS: Damn you!

Harlan swings his knife at Starns, who jumps back.

HARLAN: Hex this! Conjure this!
BILLY: Starns!

Billy holds up his knife. Starns turns, grabs his hand, taking the knife, turns back as Harlan attacks him. Starns meets Harlan, stabs him in the stomach, bending him double. They struggle, locked together. Then Starns throws Harlan to the ground, where he falls on Cora. Starns stands above them, stricken.

JUBA: Starns! Warn't yore fault, man!
STARNS: Ah!!! Ahhhhhhh!

Juba gets Starns to the crate again, sits on it. Starns, groaning, holding his stomach, lies between her legs. She holds him. Cora and Harlan exit. Wind dies out. Firelight. Billy comes to look at them.

JUBA: Go on. Holler, Starns. Whatever you've a mind to.

Starns grips Juba's hand again, arches his back in spasm.

STARNS: Ahh! Ahhhh!

Juba grips his hands, puts her head against his.

JUBA: Yell, Starns. Like a baby. Be just like a baby, all over agin!

Starns lies back exhausted.

STARNS: I am sorry to cause you so much trouble.
JUBA: Don't say nothing about it. You want to pray, Starns, or read the Bible?
STARNS: No. Virgins don't have no babies.

Pause. Starns holds Juba's hands. They wait, Starns thinking, Juba tending him with iron objectivity.

You was midwife, to me.
JUBA: I was.
STARNS: Into your hands I got born.
JUBA: Plot, jest like that.
STARNS: Tell me about it—being born.
JUBA: One body coming out of anothern.
STARNS: How was that for me?
JUBA: Well, I kept the lanterns low, the fire hot, and the husband quiet. I set you to warm water in a wood basin and got you quick to yore momma's flesh agin. One body, out of anothern, and back.

Starns sees something, points.

STARNS: We used to have clay, in the walls.
JUBA: Chinked up the logs. Hit melted when a fire was hot.
STARNS: I used to dig it out, and eat it.
JUBA: Children do.

Starns arches his back again, in spasm. Juba grips his hands.

STARNS: AHHHHH!!!

JUBA: Go, Starns. Go, baby, to God.

Starns dies. Juba holds him. Wind.

BILLY: If I had my house, I would never leave it. I would keep it with me always.

Juba and Starns get up. Enter Bishop, Cora and Harlan. They all stand around Billy and look at him. Wind.

So tell me now. Will I see you again? Do we live again, with God in Heaven? Bishop?

BISHOP: In the name of the Father and of the Son and of the Holy Ghost, yes! We will live forever. (*He kneels*)

BILLY: Harlan?

HARLAN: No charms, I thank ye. No spells fer me. (*He sits*)

BILLY: Cora?

CORA: Life is as pleasant as the flowers are made. But when it is over, it is over. (*She sits*)

BILLY: Juba?

JUBA: The babies come, the babies go, that's all of God I had to know. (*She steps back*)

BILLY: Starns?

STARNS: Poor folks has poor ways. (*He hunkers down*)

Wind.

BILLY: So where will I go, when I've lived my life, and it is my turn to follow you? Will I dance with you in Heaven, some angel playing on an ivory fiddle, or lie down dead with you forever in some blackdirt valley like this one? Either

317

way, for it is you I will seek. In your smiles was my hope, from your pain came my understanding, and either way, I will never come loose from you again, my mountain family, ghosts, my own.

Light fades.